IRAN

PROFILES · NATIONS OF THE CONTEMPORARY MIDDLE EAST
Bernard Reich and David E. Long, Series Editors

ABOUT THE BOOK AND AUTHOR

Iran is the only Middle Eastern state to have preserved its national identity through the upheavals of the Arab, Turkish, and Mongol invasions. It is heir to the richest culture in the Middle East—a culture that extends far beyond the state's political boundaries.

This introduction to Iran traces elements of continuity in Iranian society from pre-Islamic times to the turmoil of the Islamic Republic. John Limbert discusses the persistence of religion as a dominant force in Iran's politics and society; the attraction of unorthodox doctrines such as Mazdakism, Baha'ism, and revolutionary Shi'ism; the tradition of strong, charismatic leadership; and the constant problem of ruling peoples of diverse tribal, religious, and linguistic affiliations.

He finds explanations for recent political changes in conditions peculiarly Iranian and examines the emerging postrevolutionary society along with some of its new institutions, including the revolutionary guards, the assembly, the neighborhood committees, and the Friday prayer leaders. Pointing out the continuing tension between pragmatism and revolutionary ideology, Professor Limbert looks at the probable course of events as Iran begins rebuilding its economy and establishing stable political institutions.

John W. Limbert is with the U.S. Foreign Service, currently serving as political officer at the U.S. Embassy in Algiers.

IRAN

At War with History

John W. Limbert

Westview Press • Boulder, Colorado

Croom Helm • London and Sydney

Profiles/Nations of the Contemporary Middle East

The views expressed in this book are those of the author and not those of the Department of State or the United States government.

Copyright © 1987 by Westview Press, Inc.

Published in 1987 in the United States of America by Westview Press, Inc.; Frederick A. Praeger, Publisher; 5500 Central Avenue, Boulder, Colorado 80301

Published in 1987 in Great Britain by Croom Helm Ltd., Provident House, Burrell Row, Beckenham, Kent, BR3 1AT

Library of Congress Cataloging in Publication Data
Limbert, John W.
 Iran, at war with history.
 (Profiles. Nations of the contemporary Middle East)
 Bibliography: p.
 Includes index.
 1. Iran. I. Title. II. Series
DS254.5.L56 1987   955   86-15803
ISBN 0-86531-448-9 (alk. paper)

British Library Cataloguing in Publication Data
Limbert, John W.
 Iran: at war with history.—(Profiles: nations of the
 contemporary Middle East)
 1. Iran—Social conditions
 I. Title II. Series
 955'.054   HN670.2.A8
 ISBN 0-7099-4107-2

Printed and bound in the United States of America

The paper used in this publication meets the requirements of the American National Standard for Permanence of Paper for Printed Library Materials Z39.48-1984.

10 9 8 7 6 5 4 3 2 1

To Dr. A. T. (d. 1978), who served humanity for fifty years and whose rich legacy was the nobility of his children—and whom a merciful creator spared the sight of the collapse of his world and the dispersion of his family.

Contents

Tables and Illustrations

Preface and Acknowledgments

My good friend and colleague David Long first asked me in late 1981 about doing a book on Iran for the Westview profile series. Having spent almost half of my life involved with Iran in some way—as a teacher, a student, and, most recently as a prisoner—I accepted the task with pleasure.

In a book of this size, it is not possible to deal adequately with such rich subjects as Iranian literature, music, art, folklore, religion, and philosophy. Each of these subjects deserves its own chapter, if not its own book, and I hope that the reader who seeks more detail on these topics will refer to the Bibliography for further reading and profit. For the sake of simplicity, I have limited the items listed there mostly to works in English; needless to say, there is a vast literature about Iran of great interest to the dedicated scholar in other languages such as French, German, Russian, Arabic, and Persian.

I also acknowledge to my Iranian friends that no outsider can understand, much less communicate, many of the subtle realities of their culture and history. Much of that culture remains a closed book to non-Iranians. I can only ask my friends to display a generous amount of *gozasht* ("tolerance"), that most Iranian of human characteristics, for the inevitable misreadings of their nation they find in this book.

Why still another book on Iran? The revolution and its chaotic aftermath have produced excellent studies and memoirs by diplomats, political figures, academics, journalists, ex-hostages, wives of ex-ambassadors, and others, and each of these works provides valuable insights into recent events. But Iran did not come into existence in 1979 with the inauguration of ABC's "America Held Hostage." At that time, Iran had had over 2,000 years of recorded history as a distinct nation. That history may not explain or have justified a national temper tantrum, but it can tell us more than the nightly headlines and often disjointed portrayals offered the viewing public in 1979 and 1980.

I have subtitled this work "At War with History" because present-day Iran is exactly that: A nation's brutal and intolerant present has declared war on its own past. Granted, there is much of Iranian tradition within the revolutionary movement, especially the attempt to restore national dignity and independence after centuries of humiliation and weakness. But ancient Iranian traditions of creativity, intellectual curiosity, and tolerance of human diversity have little to do with the current obscurantism: the mindless chanting of slogans, the goon squads of so-called God's partisans (*hezbollahis*), and the obstinate triviality of authorities obsessed with minutiae of personal (especially female) conduct.

This work is long in history with ethnology a distant second. I have tried as much as possible to deal with what is known and not to try explaining history by group psychoanalysis or by statements about the "Iranian character," the "Islamic mentality," and that favorite of *Newsweek*, the "Shi'ite martyr complex."

It is not that all such statements are false. The point is that they conceal more than they explain. Exactly what, after all, is a Shi'ite martyr complex? How does it differ from a Sunni, Christian, or Jewish martyr complex? The problem is that such analysis implies that certain fundamental character defects of Muslims in general and Iranian Shi'ites in particular have caused Iran's current political turmoil. The same analysis implies that these defects have led Iranians to choose to live under a fanatical and brutal regime. In fact, few Iranians have ever chosen any regime at all, much less the present one. The reality is that Iranians are, like all of us, victims, not of their national character, but of their special history. In Iran's case, that history is a very long and usually tragic one.

In this book, I make no attempt to conceal my admiration for Iran and Iranians—for their warmth, loyalty, creativity, wit, courage, tolerance, and ability to endure hardship and adversity. Nor do I attempt to conceal my distress at their present ordeal or my distaste for brutality, misrule, and exploitation, whether by kings or ayatollahs.

Any work that deals with Iran must deal with the inevitable confusion between the words "Iranian" and "Persian." Most simply, Iran is the country in which Iranians live; Persian is (1) the mother language of about half of all Iranians, (2) the only official language of Iran, and (3) one of the two official languages of Afghanistan. In the nineteenth century, the names Persia and Persian came to replace Iran and Iranian in European sources. In the 1930s, the Iranian monarch, Reza Shah, officially asked foreign countries to use "Iran"—

the name by which Iranians had always known their land. Of course the matter is not so simple. As adjectives, Persian has one meaning and Iranian another. Thus, Persian literature is literature composed in the Persian language; Iranian literature could be literature in any Iranian language (Kurdish, Persian, Gilaki, Baluchi, etc.) or literature associated with Iran in another language (Arabic or Turkish, for example). In that sense, the adjective "Persian" refers to one variety of Iranian literature, language, culture, carpet, etc.

An obligatory word about transcription and dates. I have transcribed Iranian words as an educated Persian speaker now pronounces them. Thus, I have made no distinction between varieties of z, s, and t. Nor have I distinguished between the *hamzeh* and the *ein*, which Iranians, to the dismay of Arabic speakers, pronounce identically. The specialist will already know the original spelling of the words used, and to the nonspecialist, the variety of z in the original Persian can hardly matter. In proper nouns I have followed the most common English usage: Isfahan, not Esfahan, for example. I have avoided diacritics except in a few cases and have used q to represent both the Persian *qaf* and *ghein*, except in cases where the distinction is necessary. For simplicity, I have written dates in the Christian era; the interested reader can easily convert these dates into the Iranian-Islamic solar calendar or (not so easily) into the Islamic lunar calendar.

With respect to acknowledgments I scarcely know where to begin. Many Iranian friends who shared their knowledge with me must of necessity remain anonymous. I thank them for their patience with my misunderstandings of their country and for the lessons in humanity and courage they have taught.

I must thank my good friend Terrance O'Donnell who helped open my eyes to the depth of the beauty that lies hidden in so much of Iran. My friend Michael Jerald provided many of the photographs. In the academic world, I owe thanks to the scholars Richard Frye, Firuz Kazemzadeh, the late Manuchehr Mohandessi, Farhad Kazemi, Sha'oul Bakhash, Leon Carl Brown, Jerry Clinton, Mansour Farhang, and Roy Mottahedeh who have guided me through the riches of Iranian history, religion, and literature. I am honored to have friends with so much scholarship and understanding. I owe special thanks to Professor James Bill of Texas University who consistently uses his brilliant powers of political analysis while others turn to wishful thinking. Also I must thank Dr. William Olson of the U.S. Army War College who patiently read most of this manuscript and made many generous suggestions. Those parts of Chapter 5 dealing with the Iranian elements in the revolution originally appeared in an article

"Indigenous Revolution" in the October 1983 issue of the *Foreign Service Journal*.

I must also thank my colleagues in the Department of State for their advice and help. Michelle Picard and Bill Hezlep of the Geographer's Office drew the maps in Chapters 1 and 2. The American University allowed me to reproduce the map in Chapter 5 from *Iran: A Country Study*, ed. Richard F. Nyrop. Michael Jerald of the School for International Training in Brattleboro, Vermont, and the archives of the Agency for International Development generously provided photographs. Stephen Grummon, David Long, Ralph Lindstrom, Larry Semakis, and Bruce Laingen all provided constant encouragement and advice. Of course the opinions in this work are entirely my own and in no way reflect the policy or views of the U.S. government.

At the U.S. Naval Academy I must thank Ms. Samantha Erb who patiently taught me to use the word-processing computer. I must also thank my Annapolis colleagues Pope Atkins, Bob Rau, Michael Halbig, Joe Jockel, and many others for providing support and such a congenial environment for the writing of this book.

Most important, I owe the deepest gratitude to my beloved wife and companion, Parvaneh, and to our dear children, Mani and Shervin. Their love and understanding sustained me through the entire work. My children found the key to composition when they compared my writing the book to a trip by car from Annapolis to Vermont. During one particularly difficult stretch of work (Chapter 3, I believe), they kept asking, "Daddy, are you *still* in New Jersey?"

                                                                    John W. Limbert
                                                    Djibouti, Republic of Djibouti

1

Iran-zamin

Iran-zamin, "the land of Iran," means more than a place of habitation and extends beyond the present political entity. For Iranians, Iran-zamin is that area where Iranian peoples have maintained their special way of life through centuries of invasion, social change, and political and religious trumoil. Iran-zamin is the birthplace and home of a unique Iranian culture—the product of an ancient relationship between diverse peoples and their homeland.

THE PHYSICAL ENVIRONMENT

Map 1.1 shows the approximate frontiers of Iran-zamin, which includes peoples of many languages, religions, and customs and extends beyond the political boundaries of Iran into areas where non-Iranian peoples traditionally lived under Iranian political and cultural influence. On the west, the area identified as "Greater Iran" begins in the foothills of the highlands east of the Tigris-Euphrates Valley. In the northwest, the transition occurs in the Armenian and Kurdish highlands of eastern Anatolia. In the north, the frontier of Iran-zamin lies in the southern and eastern Caucasus and in the steppes and mountains of central Asia. The regions of Yerevan, Baku, and Shirvan (west of the Caspian Sea) and of Bukhara and Samarkand (east of the Caspian) are within this frontier. The eastern boundary lies in present-day Afghanistan and Pakistan. The frontier is well-defined only in the south, where the northern shore of the Persian Gulf marks the beginning of Iran-zamin. (It could even be considered to include some of the gulf islands and coastal settlements on the Arabian Peninsula, where Iranian influences are strong.) In the southwest, Iran-zamin includes Khuzestan, that part of the Mesopotamian low-lands historically under Iranian rule.

1

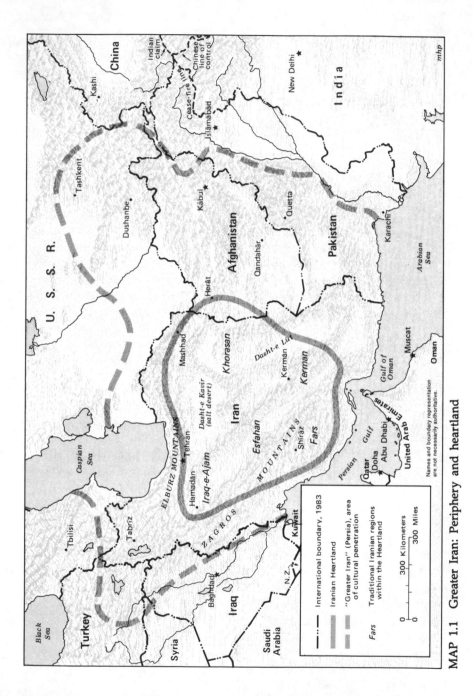

MAP 1.1   Greater Iran: Periphery and heartland

Legend:

— · · — International boundary, 1983

▬▬▬ Iranian Heartland

▬ ▬ ▬ "Greater Iran" (Persia), area of cultural penetration

Fars Traditional Iranian regions within the Heartland

0 — 300 Kilometers
0 — 300 Miles

Names and boundary representation are not necessarily authoritative.

THE HEARTLAND

As shown in Map 1.1, modern Iran includes almost all of the traditional heartland and parts of the periphery of Iran-zamin. Those artistic and cultural features historically considered "Persian" belong to the Iranian heartland, stronghold of the nation's culture—the home of the Persian language, Iranian Shi'ism (with its great shrines at Mashhad, Qom, and Shiraz), the ornate *shahr-baf* ("city-woven") Persian carpet, Persian painting and architecture, and traditional Persian town planning, gardens, and classical music. Within this area, too, are the monuments of the great Iranian empires of the past and most of the ancient Iranian cities, the setting for the nation's cultural life.

The Iranian heartland is a plateau, a region of mountains, deserts, and irrigated agricultural land. On the north, the Alborz (Elburz) Mountains divide the plateau from the coastal lowlands of the Caspian Sea and from the Turkoman steppe. On the south, southwest, and west, parallel ranges of the Zagros Mountains separate the heartland from the lowlands of the Persian Gulf coast and Khuzestan and from the mountainous tribal areas of Lorestan (Lurestan) and Kurdestan. To the east and southeast, the plateau region gradually merges into the highlands of Afghanistan and the deserts of Baluchestan.

The major physical features of this heartland plateau are its rim of mountain ranges and its interior basin of two great deserts, the Dasht-e-Lut and the Dasht-e-Kavir. Water from the surrounding mountains drains into the interior basins; what is not used for agriculture and settlements is lost in the deserts. The Dasht-e-Kavir, located in the north of the interior basin, is mostly saline mud covered with a hardened salt crust. The Kavir, which lies at an altitude above 3,000 feet, separates Isfahan (Esfahan) and the central province from Khorasan. The Dasht-e-Lut is an immense depression in the southern part of the interior basin. Ringed by mountains, its lowest part lies less than 1,000 feet above sea level. The Lut, a region of saltwater, sand dunes, and high winds, forms a difficult barrier between Kerman and the neighboring regions of Khorasan and Baluchestan.[1]

Two factors—terrain and water—have controlled the distribution of population in the Iranian heartland. Most settlement has been on communication routes and in agricultural areas between the mountains and deserts. Rainfall is generally insufficient for dry farming, so most farmers must rely on irrigation water; only the Isfahan region benefits from the water supply of a major perennial river, the Zayandeh-Rud. Other towns are located where the inhabitants could construct underground canals (*qanats*), using the existing slope of the land to bring water from higher elevations. This topography and irrigation method has confined permanent settlement to a relatively narrow band of territory between mountain and desert. Settlements too high on the mountain would be located above the qanat exit, and towns located too far from the mountains would be beyond the range of qanat water and exposed to encroachment of nearby deserts.[2]

Where water is available, settlement has occurred in a variety of climates, each having a characteristic agriculture and economic life. The *sardsir* ("cold lands") lie above 6,000 feet in northwest Fars, the western parts of Isfahan and Iraq-e-Ajam, and the mountainous regions of Khorasan. Typical sardsir agriculture consists of cereals, apples, plums, pears, melons, and walnuts. In the southern half of the country, usually below an elevation of 3,000 feet, lie the *garmsir* ("warm lands"). This climate is subtropical, and production of cereals gives way to citrus and dates in the lower valleys of Fars (Kazerun, Jahrom, and Darab), in the Tabas depression of Khorasan, and at Bam at the eastern edge of Kerman Province. Since climatic extremes in the sardsir and garmsir limit permanent agriculture, both regions are important areas of pastoralism and home to most of Iran's nomadic population.

Most of the major urban centers and agricultural areas of the Iranian heartland are located in the *mo'tadel* ("temperate") zone, at elevations generally between 3,000 and 6,000 feet above sea level. Teheran (Tehran), Isfahan, and Shiraz are all within this zone. Mashhad, in the northeast, is on the border of the temperate zone and the sardsir. Mo'tadel region agriculture includes cultivation of cereals, vegetables, and a wide variety of fruits including grapes and pomegranates. Since the climate is better suited to permanent, settled agriculture, pastoralism is relatively rare in this zone.

Map 1.2 shows the traditional provinces of Iran within the country's modern boundaries. On the great plateau, settlement and communication are delicately balanced between desert and mountain. Since communication routes had to avoid both extremes of terrain, the main roads linking the centers of major agricultural areas pass through transition zones between mountain and desert. The settlements north of the great salt desert, on the east-west highroad between Mashhad and Teheran, lie in one of these transition zones at elevations most suitable for bringing water by qanat from the neighboring Alborz Mountains. Towns such as Shahrud (now Emamshahr) and Nishapur lie in cultivated areas settled since early Islamic times, if not earlier. Although these modern cities do not always occupy the exact sites of the earlier towns, traces of older settlements are usually found within a few miles of the modern urban centers. The ancient "desert

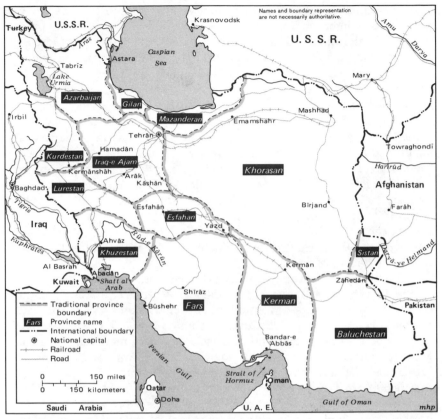

MAP 1.2 Iran: Traditional provinces

towns" of central Iran, such as Kashan, Na'in, and Yazd, are also balanced between mountain and desert. They are located on the northeastern side of the Zagros Mountains, where the combination of water and elevation allows permanent agriculture. The terrain permits easy northwest-to-southeast communication on a route between the central deserts and the mountains.

Settlement follows a different pattern in Fars, where parallel ranges of the Zagros Mountains divide the region into numerous narrow valleys. Elevation, not latitude, makes the climate of these valleys sardsir, garmsir, or mo'tadel. The broken, mountainous terrain and the absence of vast deserts and plains mean that wells, springs, and streams often replace qanats as the major source of water. Although there are perennial rivers in Fars (the Mand and the Kur), the major urban centers of the province have historically been located away from the rivers. The variety of climate and the mountainous terrain make Fars nomad country par excellence. The migratory tribes move from their winter quarters near the Persian Gulf to the summer pastures in the highland districts of Ardakan and Semirom. Most of these migrations take the nomads through or near Shiraz, the major city of the province. Although founded in early Islamic times as a military camp, Shiraz is now a transit point and market town for the nomads of Fars.

The mountainous topography of Fars has isolated its various settled regions and, with the exception of Shiraz, has kept the towns small. Settlement in Fars is not firmly welded to the pattern of desert, mountain, and qanat as towns grew as the political centers of regions important for their agriculture, their military position, or their location on a strategic trade route. Lar and Jahrom, for example, two relatively "recent" towns, grew in response to trade-route changes within the last six centuries. The recently (1971) completed Shiraz-Bushehr road has bypassed the ancient town of Kazerun, which may suffer because of this rerouting of traffic.

Iraq-e-Ajam, the region northwest of Isfahan, is another exception to the pattern of settlement determined by desert, mountain, and qanat. Mountain ranges surround high, spacious plains that are broken by low, irregular ridges. Relatively abundant rainfall permits dry farming on the open plains and in areas watered by mountain streams. Much of this area is sardsir; the major cities of Arak and Hamadan are famous for their cold winters and mild summers. The towns in this region are mostly centers of agriculture and transporation. Hamadan, one of the oldest continually inhabited sites in Iran, is located on the historic highroad from the Iranian plateau to the Mesopotamian lowlands.

THE PERIPHERY

Regions on the periphery of Iran-zamin, such as Azarbaijan, Mazanderan, and Sistan, have ancient historical links to the heartland, but the influence of Persian culture is weaker in these areas. The most obvious sign of this culture—the Persian language—disappears as a spoken idiom and is replaced by dialects of Turkish, Arabic, Kurdish, Baluchi, Lori, and Gilaki. The hold of Shi'a Islam also weakens in some areas of the periphery as there are numerous followers of Sunnism among the inhabitants of Kurdestan, the Persian Gulf coast, Baluchestan, and the Turkoman steppe.

Azarbaijan

Azarbaijan, with its rich agriculture, dense population, strategic location, and active trade and industry, is the most important of Iran's frontier regions. Historically, it has borne the brunt of foreign incursions into Iran by expansionist neighbors to the north and west—Romans, Byzantines, Turks, Caucasians, and Russians. The area has been a defense bastion, a guardian of Iranian tradition, a center of political activity, an economic center, and a stronghold of Shi'a Islam.

Azarbaijan is one of the most heavily urbanized regions of Iran, and the combination of its cold and temperate climates and its relatively heavy rainfall make it a productive area for cereals, dairy products, meat, fruits, and vegetables. It contains three major towns—Tabriz, Urumiyeh (Urmia, formerly Reza'iyeh), and Ardabil—and numerous small towns, such as Marand and Maragheh, which lie in prosperous agricultural areas. Azarbaijan is dominated by two mountain systems. In the east, about twenty miles west of Ardabil, the peak of Sabalan rises to 14,000 feet. Sahand, south of Tabriz, rises to 12,000 feet and provides water to settlements both north and south of the mountain.

The history of Azarbaijan has always been closely linked to the history of Iran. By tradition, it was the homeland of the prophet Zoroaster and the location of the holy fires that are so important in his religion. Alexander the Great never conquered the region (which was known to the Greeks as Media Atropatane), so it was less influenced by Hellenism than other Iranian regions. In the ninth century A.D., Azarbaijan was the center of a violent, anti-Arab and anti-Islamic movement called the Khorram-din, but Ardabil was the ancestral home of the Safavid dynasty, which made Shi'a Islam the Iranian state religion in the sixteenth century, and today Azarbaijan remains a stronghold of Iranian Shi'ism.

Although strongly Iranian in culture, present-day Azarbaijan is not Persian in speech. Following migrations of Turks into Azarbaijan in the eleventh century, almost all the inhabitants of the region, by a process still obscure to historians, became speakers of a Turkish dialect called Azari or Azarbaijani. The Azarbaijani language is spoken beyond the official boundaries of the provinces, in the town of Qazvin, which is about 75 miles west of Teheran, in villages around Hamadan and Saveh (about 80 miles southwest of the capital), and in some regions along the Caspian coast. The original Iranian language of Azarbaijan survives as the Tati language, which is spoken in isolated villages and in the Talesh hills near the southwestern corner of the Caspian Sea.[3]

Gilan and Mazanderan

Gilan and Mazanderan are the two provinces of the Caspian coastal region. This region, known in medieval times as Tabarestan, includes the coastal plain, which varies in width from two to thirty miles; the foothills on the north side of the Alborz Mountains; and the eastern slopes of the Talesh hills. Abundant rainfall and a temperate climate make this region unique in Iran for its greenery and forests. It produces all of Iran's tea, most of its rice, and is an important center of citrus, silk, and cotton production.

Although isolated from the Iranian plateau by the steep slopes of the Alborz, the Caspian region has always been important in Iranian history. Its unique climate, forests, and wildlife have earned it a special place in national folklore, and its productivity makes it a vital part of the Iranian economy. Because of its isolation, the Caspian region was less affected by the Arab invasions of the seventh century than the rest of Iran. The coastal lowlands were not conquered by the Muslims until the middle of the eighth century, and the highlands resisted the invaders for another 100 years.[4] The mountains and forests of the Caspian region have provided its people with a refuge against outside invasions and cultural influences and have allowed the region's inhabitants to preserve their unique folk culture of languages, music, costumes, and cuisine found nowhere else in Iran.

The Turkoman Steppe

To the east of Mazanderan, the Caspian coastal plain gradually merges into the Turkoman steppe, a fertile region straddling the frontier of Iran and the USSR. This area, including the towns of Gonbad-e-Kavus, Bojnurd, and Shirvan, is inhabited by farmers and Turkoman horse nomads. The western part of this region is an open plain less than 500 feet above sea level, lying between the Alborz Mountains and the Atrak River. Farther east, the steppe is enclosed between two mountain ranges and reaches elevations of between 3,000 and 4,000 feet. In addition to its Turkoman inhabitants, Kurdish tribes, brought to the region in the seventeenth century, live in the east around Bojnurd.

Sistan and Baluchestan

Sistan and Baluchestan lie to the southeast of the heartland, separated from Kerman by the southern reaches of the Dasht-e-Lut. This area is characterized by low rainfall, high temperatures, scattered settlements, and poor communications. In Baluchestan the parallel ranges of the Zagros Mountains become irregular ridges in a desert terrain. The few small towns of this area are either on the coast— e.g., Minab, Jask, and Chahbahar—or, like Zahedan, at road junctions. The Sistan basin and its center Zabol lie less than 2,000 feet above sea level in an area that was once very productive but has recently suffered from severe drought. This region now supports only a limited amount of oasis agriculture, and much of the population has emigrated to more prosperous areas of Iran or to the Persian Gulf emirates in search of better economic opportunities.

The Persian Gulf Coast

The people living on the coastal plain of the Persian Gulf and on the southern slopes of the Zagros Mountains have traditionally remained very distant from the life of the heartland. Misrule, neglect, poverty, religious differences, and isolation have made these people culturally and economically closer to the Indian subcontinent and the Arabian Peninsula than to the Iranian plateau. Many Iranians consider coastal towns such as Bushehr and Bandar Abbas (Bandar-e-Abbas) to be places of exile. The gulf coastal plain and mountains are another of Iran's areas of refuge, in this case for Sunni Muslims living in the coastal towns and in the remote inland regions of Khonj, Evaz, and Khormoj. Although some of the enterprising inhabitants of this region have joined the mainstream of Iranian life in Shiraz and Teheran, many others have migrated across the Persian Gulf to become prosperous merchants in the oil and trading centers of Dubai, Bahrain, and the other emirates. A hot, humid climate and a lack of fresh water have limited agriculture in the gulf region, and isolation from the major population centers of the plateau have limited port activity. The Iran-Iraq war, however, revived the port of Bandar Abbas by interrupting traffic at the railheads of Khorramshahr and Bandar Khomeini (formerly Bandar Shahpur), located about 1,000 miles to the northwest within easy range of Iraqi air attack.

Khuzestan

Although geographically distinct from the Iranian plateau, the Khuzestan region, with its sea-level plains and foothills of the Zagros Mountains, has traditionally been ruled from the heartland. Politically and economically, this region has always been very important for Iran. In pre-Islamic times, it was the center of the Elamite civilization, the location of the administrative capital of the Achaemenian empire, and a center of prosperous agriculture. In the early centuries of Islam, Khuzestan remained a rich province but later suffered severely from periods of anarchy and the breakdown of central government control. After long neglect, the area has revived in the last fifty years thanks to the oil industry, the trans-Iranian railroad, agricultural development, industrialization, and port expansion. Although its towns and industries have recently suffered severe war damage and many Khuzestanis have become refugees, the region still has the potential to recover its prosperity after the war ends.

Despite its inhospitable summer climate, Khuzestan's economic development has attracted numerous immigrants from other sections of Iran. The inhabitants of the coastal and western regions of Khuzestan are mostly Arabic speakers, sharing the language and the religion— Shi'a Islam—of the southern Iraqis. The inhabitants of Dezful and Shushtar, ancient towns in the foothills of the Zagros Mountains, speak Iranian dialects. Where water and soil are suitable, winter agriculture in this subtropical region can be profitable, supplying fresh fruits and vegetables for export and for the markets of the plateau.

Kurdestan and Lorestan (Lurestan)

The mountainous frontier regions of Kurdestan and Lorestan occupy the area between the Mesopotamian lowlands and the western edge of the Iranian heartland. East of this region, water drains into the interior basins of the plateau or into the Caspian Sea. To the west, the rivers flow into either lowland marshes or the Tigris-Euphrates system. The area is bisected by the great highroad from Hamadan in the heartland to Baghdad via Kermanshah, Shahabad (now Islamabad), and Qasr-e-Shirin, and the climate is usually either temperate or cold. Subtropical conditions exist only in the southwestern part, along the Iraqi border near the towns of Qasr-e-Shirin and Ilam.

Although most of this western region receives enough rainfall for dry farming, there are few towns and poor communications. Kermanshah (1976 population, 290,000) is the only major city in the region, and it owes its prosperity to its location on a major communication route. The rugged terrain has limited both large-scale agriculture and easy communication within the region or with the Iranian heartland. Isolation has made this region a refuge for tribal peoples speaking Lori and Kurdish, both Iranian languages. Shi'a Islam predominates among the Lors and the Kurds of Kermanshah and Bijar (a small town on the eastern edge of the region), and Sunnism is dominant among the Kurds living north of Kermanshah and west toward the border with Iraq.

THE ECONOMIC ENVIRONMENT

TRADITIONAL ECONOMY

It would be misleading to represent the traditional economy of Iran-zamin as constant or unchanging. That economy was never static, and the image of the Iranian farmer working his land in some timeless fashion oversimplifies and conceals a complex and dynamic reality. Civil strife, periods of stability under strong rulers, foreign wars, changes of dynasty, and invasions all brought good times and bad to the Iranian economy. But the good times never lasted very long as the Iranians were never able to sustain the prosperity they achieved during certain eras, such as the tenth and seventeenth centuries. Invasions and domestic anarchy brought about the breakdown of trade, neglect of irrigation works, and depopulation of towns and villages. Economic relations with the outside world also changed as political instability forced traders to seek new markets and new, secure trade routes.

Despite these changes, the basis of Iran's economy remained constant until about half a century ago. Until that time, most Iranians engaged in agriculture or the associated transport and processing industries. The backbone of the economy was the production of cereals (chiefly wheat and barley) to feed farmers and the urban population. Because of the high cost of transporting grain by land (mostly by pack animal), each city depended on its hinterland for basic foodstuffs. The city of Shiraz, for example, received its grain, beans, onions, and other vegetables from the farms of the Shiraz plain and the nearby regions of Sarvestan, Kavar, and Marvdasht. The nomadic population, living on land unsuited for permanent agriculture, supplied much of the country's meat and dairy products. Without navigable rivers or convenient outlets to the inhospitable Persian Gulf coast, most of Iran's trade followed well-defined, historic land routes, which mountains and deserts had determined. In times of prosperity and security, farmers devoted time to more specialized crops, such as grapes, which they could cultivate in the temperate regions of Urumiyeh, Shiraz, and the plains west of Teheran. Processors converted this perishable fruit into valuable trade items such as wine, vinegar, molasses, raisins, and the sour fruit called *qureh*. Prosperity and security also permitted farmers in the subtropical regions of Fars (the *garmsirat*) to produce the costly essences of rose, violet, jasmine, almond, and other flowers that were the bases of perfumes, medicines, and food flavorings.

Iranian cities remained basically centers for trading and processing agricultural production, and their fortunes depended on the state of agriculture in the surrounding countryside. Although there was some manufacturing for export, notably of textiles and carpets, most urban trading—such as the selling, processing, and transporting of food—depended directly or indirectly on agriculture. The wealth produced in the rural areas supported the rich urban culture and the administration, and the urban-dwelling artists and scholars also ultimately depended on agriculture for support. Although poets and historians probably did not eat very much, the mosques, public fountains, schools, hospitals, and public baths of the towns required substantial revenues for their building and maintenance. Fourteenth-century Shiraz, for example, had more than 500 mosques, sufi retreats (*khaneqah*), schools, and other pious foundations. Although some of these were humble structures, many were large enough to require endowments from many small villages and rich agricultural regions.

Iranian cities shriveled and many died when man-made or natural catastrophes disrupted agriculture and trade. Urban life could not survive without income from the villages, and teachers, students, and preachers abandoned their mosques and schools when economic ruin in the countryside cut off the endowments that paid their stipends and maintained their buildings. Without income for repair, some of the finest urban water systems and public buildings in Iran fell into ruin. When cereal production declined and the price of bread rose, much of the urban population, already facing unemployment because of the general collapse of trade, found themselves forced either to migrate or to starve. When rulers demanded higher taxes from farmers to support courts and armies, the results were more abandoned farmland and greater hardship in the cities. Buildings were ruined by neglect, and entire urban quarters were abandoned when their inhabitants' livelihoods disppeared.

MODERN ECONOMY

Agricultural land remained the basis of Iran's wealth until the middle of the twentieth century. Although the British concessionaire William Knox D'Arcy discovered oil in Khuzestan in 1908, the resulting income had little effect on the Iranian economy until the 1920s, and the oil industry remained on the country's economic periphery for several reasons.[5] First, the Iranian government had little political authority over the remote, oil-producing areas of Khuzestan, especially during the chaotic first two decades of the twentieth century. Power in that region remained in the hands of local Arab and Bakhtiyari (Bakhtiari) chiefs, and they negotiated independent agreements with the British oil company as though the Iranian central government did not exist. Second, the Iranian government's revenues from oil remained small. Until the original D'Arcy concession was renegotiated in 1932, the government received only 16 percent of the net profits of the Anglo-Persian (later Anglo-Iranian) oil company.

Third, the management, ownership, and operation of the oil company were entirely British. In 1914, the British government purchased a controlling interest in the original concession, and the Iranians found themselves in an unequal commercial relationship with a powerful foreign state. The British set the prices, the amount of output, and the destinations to which the oil was sent, and they used their own formulas to determine profits and the amount of revenue accruing to the Iranian government. During oil negotiations between the company and the Iranians in 1920, the latter were represented by a British treasury official sent to Iran by the British government.[6] Fourth, in relation to its Arab neighbors, Iran was a large, populous country with important resources besides oil. Until the 1920s, the most important sources of state revenues were, as they always had been, the income from customs duties, state lands, and internal taxes.[7]

In the late 1920s and 1930s, oil income and internal taxes financed the economic modernization program of the monarch, Reza Shah Pahlavi. The government built electric power plants, roads, telecommunication facilities, government office buildings, and textile, cement, and food-processing factories. State monopolies and taxes on sugar, tea, and other consumer goods kept prices high and gave Reza Shah the money to finance his costly projects, such as the monumental trans-Iranian railway. The chief motives of his economic policies were tightening internal security, extending the power of the central government, and imitating Ataturk's modernization program in neighboring Turkey. Whatever their economic purpose, the new roads and railroads restored central government control to remote areas that for decades had given only nominal allegiance to Teheran. In the towns, the twentieth-century monarchs, the ruling Pahlavis, tore down ancient walls and gates and forced straight, wide avenues through traditional quarters. These changes were supposed to give towns a modern look, allow easy access for security forces, and weaken traditional networks of neighborhood organization.

Reza Shah's modernization programs increased government spending tenfold between 1923-1924 and 1941-1942. Much of this spending paid for the building of factories, schools, government offices, roads, railroads, and power plants; for salaries of the new military and civilian managers of the centralized state; and for imported military and civilian goods. Reza Shah, remembering how Iran had lost its sovereignty to Western creditors during the late nineteenth and early twentieth centuries, was determined to avoid foreign debt. He paid for part of his modernization program with oil revenues, which throughout his reign remained only about 10 percent of government income, and for the rest with the income from state monopolies and indirect taxes on consumer goods. His spending squeezed the ordinary Iranian even harder when the world economic depression in the 1930s reduced the market for Iran's major exports of oil, carpets, and agricultural products.

Following the economic disruptions of World War II, Iran began to earn significant income from oil after Mohammad Reza Shah Pahlavi's 1953 coup (see Chapter 5). A 1954 agreement with the operating oil companies ("the consortium") established a fifty-fifty split of revenues, then the practice in other Middle Eastern oil-exporting countries. Once the Iranians had regained some of their crude-oil markets lost to Arab producers during the 1951–1953 oil nationalization crisis, the new income (maintained by a growing world demand for oil through the 1950s and 1960s), combined with foreign aid and loans, brought a burst of economic activity that lasted, with occasional interruptions, until the revolution of 1978–1979.

During those twenty-five years, oil revenues became the single important source of government revenue, especially following the quadrupling of OPEC crude-oil prices in 1973. Following that increase, the government undertook such an ambitious development plan that it wiped out the country's revenue surplus in two years and forced Iran to seek loans from international banks and to maintain its crude production at a high level of 5–6 million barrels per day. This growing importance of oil caused a relative decline in agriculture and other traditional parts of the economy. The oil bonanza also eliminated any need for establishing a system of direct, progressive taxation.

At the same time, an overvalued Iranian currency kept imports of food, consumer goods, and capital goods relatively cheap, and Iran's agricultural and carpet exports became uncompetitive in the world market. A combination of factors—neglect, mismanagement, population growth—forced Iran to import food for perhaps the first time in its history. As agriculture stagnated and the cities boomed, every year hundreds of thousands of farmers left their villages for the towns in search of construction, transportation, and factory jobs. Only 30 percent of Iranians were living in cities in 1952; by the time of the revolution against the monarchy in 1978, this figure had reached almost 50 percent.[8]

REVOLUTIONARY ECONOMY

From the beginning of the revolution, many of its leaders, including the current leader of Iran, Ayatollah Khomeini, and his associates, viewed economics with suspicion, as something foreign that would corrupt the pure, Islamic nature of their movement. They attacked the people who urged the revolutionary regime to concentrate on economic aims and argued that Iranians who followed traditional, European economic wisdom—whether Marxist, socialist, or capitalist—would, at best, compromise the goals of the revolution and, at worst, betray the revolution itself and its devoted supporters among Iran's *mostaz'afin* ("deprived population"). Khomeini himself, in the late summer of 1979, ridiculed those who sought to moderate revolutionary zeal in order to protect the country's economic infrastructure:

> Some persons have come to me and said that now the revolution is over, now we must preserve our economic infrastructure. But our people rose for Islam, not for economic infrastructure. What is this economic infrastructure anyway? Donkeys and camels need hay. That's economic infrastructure. But human beings need Islam.[9]

Despite the leader's hostility to any discussion of economic infrastructure, one of the stated goals of the revolution was to redress the economic and social inequalities that had prevailed under the monarchy. Although there was disagreement over details and about what constituted "Islamic" economics, almost all sides in the revolutionary coalition agreed that Iran should cancel expensive military purchases and large construction projects, such as the Teheran subway and the Bushehr nuclear power plant, while cutting oil production to a level that would both produce an adequate income and conserve Iran's most valuable (and irreplaceable) resource. In 1979, experts estimated that Iran could sustain crude production at about 3 million barrels per day without the need for sophisticated oil field technology or expensive foreign personnel. At the same time, this level of production would produce enough income to permit government investment in neglected sectors such as agriculture, education, and low-cost housing. Ending the spending bonanza would check the uncontrolled migration of villagers seeking better opportunities in the cities and relieve the resulting pressure on urban services and housing. If Iran could achieve such an economic balance, it would no longer need foreign loans, which the government had been forced to seek to maintain the high spending levels of 1973–1975.

But the war with Iraq, the failure to moderate extreme revolutionary positions, misguided oil-pricing policy, and the depressed state of the world petroleum market after 1981 all overturned this strategy before it could take effect. The first two years of revolutionary rule showed Iranians that their country's economy was still tied to the major Western industrial states and almost completely dependent on the income from crude-oil sales. From 1977 to 1981, West Germany, Japan, the United Kingdom, and Italy were still among the five leading exporters of goods to Iran. The only qualitative changes in Iran's world trade relations were a sharp drop in imports from the United States and an increase in goods purchased from the USSR. The U.S.-organized boycott of Iran during the 1980 hostage crisis had little effect. With a substantial oil income, Iran simply realigned its sources of supply to allow Japan, West Germany, France, Italy, and the United Kingdom to take the former U.S. share of the market. Despite the boycott and despite the Iranians' stated goal of self-sufficiency, the dollar value of Iran's imports from Western industrial nations grew 16 percent between 1979 and 1980 and another 6 percent between 1980 and 1981.[10]

Iran could import the food, raw materials, and manufactured goods it needed by selling enough of its crude oil at a high enough price. At the same time, such a guaranteed source of income helped the regime preserve its revolutionary purity in defiance of world opinion. But the wolf reached the door when Iran's balance of trade with the industrialized countries shifted from a $2.3-billion surplus in 1980 to a $2.0-billion deficit in 1981 because the country could not continue selling its oil at previous prices or in previous amounts. In the succeeding years, despite austerity measures, oil sales generally have not covered Iran's import bills, and the government has had to spend its reserves to make up the deficits.[11]

Instead of concentrating on correcting the excesses of the monarchy's misguided policies, the revolutionary government has had to struggle for economic survival. The regime has not had the resources, the political will, or the competence to achieve its stated goals, and instead of a balanced economy, six years of Islamic government brought Iran:

1. Continued economic austerity, including rationing and shortages of food, cloth, home appliances, automobile parts, and heating and cooking fuel. Austerity has also meant foreign exchange controls and limits on foreign travel and study.

2. Inflation in almost all economic sectors, especially housing and consumer goods. Rationing and import restrictions have created a black market, which supplies scarce goods at high prices. The Iranian currency has lost almost 90 percent of its value against the dollar, and the retail cost of imported goods has soared as a result. Population growth, especially in the large cities, has further increased the cost of housing and other urban services.

3. The war with Iraq, which has become a major burden on the Iranian economy. The 1985-1986 budget estimated that

direct and related war costs would reach about $13 billion, or about a third of the nation's $39-billion budget.[12]

4. A government budget that has been in persistent deficit. Although Iran needs to produce an estimated 1.8–2.0 million barrels of oil per day to supply its own domestic needs (about 650,000 barrels per day) and to sell abroad to buy munitions and basic foodstuffs, the country cannot depend on a reliable, stable market for its oil. Production since 1981 has varied from 400,000 to over 2 million barrels per day. Despite the budget deficits, Iran has stayed out of debt by spending from reserves and by imposing greater austerity measures when necessary.

5. Diversification of the country's foreign trading partners. Iran has made arrangements with Turkey, Pakistan, and Syria to barter crude oil for food, textiles, industrial goods, and fertilizers, and it took advantage of the rise of the dollar against European currencies to buy manufactured goods from the United Kingdom, Japan, Italy, and West Germany. Although some observers believe that Iran's willingness to trade with the West is a sign of new pragmatism in the regime, this trade is more likely a means for avoiding political suicide by keeping the Iranian population fed at a minimum level.

Many outsiders have believed (or hoped) that Iran's economic problems would bring down the revolutionary regime. But somehow it has survived while staying out of debt, keeping essential services running, paying the costs of the war with Iraq, and feeding its population. It has done so, in part, by forcing the middle class to cut its standard of living and by making visible efforts to assist the poorest of its people. The regime has benefited from the dams, power plants, roads, and other facilities it inherited from the monarchy. There was enough fat in the shah's military and civilian programs so that canceling expensive purchases brought substantial savings with little loss to the economy. The treasury also benefited from confiscations of the property of monarchist officials and from ceasing to pay pensions to an estimated several hundred thousand retired Iranians living outside the country (their pensions now revert to the government after six months' absence). Khomeini's own austere way of life has set an example of economy that many Iranians seem willing to follow. Even in fighting the Iraqi war, the government has chosen the path of austerity, concentrating its military purchases on relatively inexpensive items such as small arms, artillery, ammunition, and spare parts for existing weapons. As a result, the country's wartime military budget is still less than the peacetime budget under the monarchy.

The revolutionary authorities have publicly declared their disdain for materialist ideologies and at the same time have taken great pains to preserve a minimum standard of living for the Iranian population. The revolution, however, has not changed the reality of Iran's social and economic conditions. Daily life in Teheran, home to 15–20 percent of the country's population, still resembles that in other swollen capital cities of the third world—Cairo and Mexico City, for example—which are choking to death on traffic, air pollution, sewage, and too many people. Overcrowded schools and hospitals are nothing new in Iran, but the flight of professionals and specialists has affected the quality of medical care and education. Many of the best-educated Iranians have left, and the regime is trying to get by with those remaining behind. Housing remains a problem in all of the major cities and is aggravated by the influx of more than 1 million Afghans and as many Khuzestani refugees.

We know less about conditions in the villages, except that farmers have benefited from high food prices and from the regime's continued free-market policies. These benefits, however, and the rural development work of the *jahad-e-sazandegi* (reconstruction crusade) have not lessened the pull of the cities or stopped the continuing influx of villagers into the towns in search of employment for cash wages. Furthermore, when a villager joins the urban population, he joins a group—the urban mostaz'afin—that provides the basis of the revolutionary government's support. As such, he becomes the beneficiary of the regime's efforts to keep this group satisfied, at least at a minimum level.

By most standards, Iran's economic future is bleak. However, the regime's survival will probably continue to confound those experts who regularly predict its collapse because of inflation, shortages, deficits, and mismanagement. Iran has been able to survive economically so far by rearranging the shah's spending priorities, by keeping the revolution's mostaz'afin constituency fed, by maintaining tight austerity measures, and, when essential, by applying small doses of pragmatism. Nor has the revolutionary regime attacked the economic position of the important bazaar merchants, who originally provided vital support for Khomeini's cause. Despite talk of nationalizations, most business remains in the hands of private owners, and they have been able to maintain the minimum supply and distribution of essential goods. Unless Iran's petroleum markets disappear for a long time, the current regime should be able to keep the economy going indefinitely—albeit at a minimum level of activity.[13]

2

The Peoples of Iran

Iranian society resembles a mosaic or a Persian carpet in which varied languages, religions, and tribes, like distinct colors and textures, form an intricate yet coherent design. Within this ethnically heterogeneous society, the Islamic religion and the Persian language have been the dominant cultural strains. But Iran is home to many different peoples, who together form a nation with a unique identity and history, one of shifting balances among ethnic groups and of conflict between the central authority and the centrifugal forces of regionalism and tribalism. The patterns and colors—to return to the comparison—have not remained constant. Changes in the ethnic and regional balances of power have often brought profound social and political upheavals to Iran. Whoever attempts to rule Iran—whether in the name of dynastic glory or religious ideology—must come to terms with the same centrifugal forces and secure the allegiance of diverse peoples.

Within the country and this society, geography has created inaccessible refuges—protected by deserts, mountains, and forests—in which inhabitants have preserved unique languages, religions, or ways of life. Much of the periphery of the country has provided refuges for Sunni Muslims (in Baluchestan and Kurdestan and on the Persian Gulf coast), obscure languages (the Iranian dialects of southern Fars), and tribal federations (the Kurds of the western and northwestern frontiers). Within the heartland, the remote desert towns of Yazd and Kerman have sheltered a small Zoroastrian community, the remaining followers of Iran's pre-Islamic state religion. Other areas of Iran are home to Isma'ilis, followers of a branch of Shi'a Islam now centered in east Africa and the Indian subcontinent; to Georgians transplanted from the Caucasus to the Daran region west of Isfahan; and to Kurdish Ali-Ilahis or Abl-e-Haqq, followers of a little-known religion, in the villages around Kermanshah.

19

ETHNIC GROUPS

Ethnic identity is complex in Iran. Centuries of migrations, invasions, and forced transfers of peoples have obscured physical distinctions among Iranians and have eliminated identifiable Persian, Kurdish, or Turkish characteristics. The mixed population is best classified by some combination of easily identifiable characteristics such as language, religion, or tribal affiliation (see Table 2.1)—a Kurd, for example, is anyone whose native language is one of the Kurdish dialects.

No official ethnic census of Iran exists. Iranian governments have been sensitive to ethnic questions, and since the 1920s, official policies have emphasized homogeneity and have underestimated the numbers and importance of linguistic and religious minorities. Because of the delicacy of nationality questions, the authorities have been suspicious of ethnographic and linguistic research, whether by Iranians or foreigners. Iranian history contains many instances of the separatist aspirations on the part of Arabs, Turks, Kurds, Baluchis, and others being manipulated by foreign powers to the detriment of the central government.

With that caution in mind, the reader should remember that the numbers of the various ethnic groups shown in Table 2.1 are only estimates. Similarly, the distribution of peoples shown in Map 2.1 is approximate and based on incomplete data. Published information on this subject is scarce and usually contains wide variations— estimates of the Kurdish population, for example, vary between 1 million and 6 million. The figures do, however, give an approximate picture of the multicolored human mosaic in Iran and of the relative numbers of the ethnic groups the country contains.

IRANIAN SPEAKERS

Iranian languages are part of the Indo-European family of languages, which includes English, German, French, Greek, and Russian. Outside of Iran, Iranian speakers include Kurds in Iraq, Turkey, Syria, and the USSR; Ossetes in the Caucasus; Tajiks in Soviet central Asia and Afghanistan; Pashtuns in Afghanistan and Pakistan; and Baluchis in Pakistan, Afghanistan, Oman, and the Persian Gulf emirates. The Iranian languages spoken within present-day Iran are divided into two major groups: the southwestern, of which Persian is the most important, and the northwestern, which includes Kurdish, Baluchi, and the Caspian languages.[1]

TABLE 2.1
Major ethnic groups

Group	Estimated Number (millions)		Percentage	
Iranian	26.5		70	
Persian		19.0		50
Kurdish		2.5		6.5[a]
Gilaki and				
Mazanderani		2.5		6.5
Lori		1.0		2.5
Baluchi		0.5		1.5
Other Iranian		1.0		2.5
Turkish	10		26	
Azarbaijani		8.5		22
Qashqa'i		0.5		1.5
Turkoman		0.25		0.5
Other Turkish		0.75		2.0
Semitic	1.0+		3	
Arabic		1.0		2.5
Assyrian and				
neo-Aramaic		0.05		--
Armenian	0.25		0.5	
Other	0.25		0.5	
Total	38.0		100.0	

[a]Percentages are rounded off to the nearest 0.5 percent.
Sources: These estimates are taken from a variety of sources,
including Richard F. Nyrop, ed., Iran: A Country Study (Wash-
ington, D.C.: American University Foreign Area Studies, 1978);
W. B. Fisher, ed., The Cambridge History of Iran, vol. 1, The
Land of Iran (Cambridge: Cambridge University Press, 1968);
National UNESCO Commission, Iranshahr, 2 vols. (Teheran: Uni-
versity Press, 1963); Fredrik Barth, Nomads of South Persia:
The Basseri Tribe of the Khamseh Confederacy (Boston: Little,
Brown and Company, 1961); and Donald L. Stilo, "The Tati
Language Group in the Sociolinguistic Context of Northwestern
Iran and Transcaucasia," Iranian Studies 14: 3-4 (Summer-
Autumn 1981).

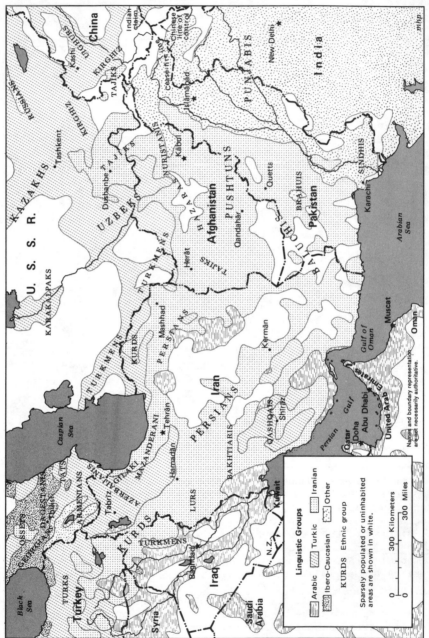

MAP 2.1   Peoples of Southwest Asia

Persians

The Persians are the largest and most important single ethnic group in Iran, and approximately half of the Iranian population speaks some dialect of Persian as a native language. Mostly townspeople and settled farmers, Persians dominate the heartland of Iran-zamin: Their language, their artistic traditions, their Shi'a Islam, and their ancient traditions of urban and village life have shaped the Iranian-Islamic civilization that is characteristic of the Iranian plateau. Isfahan, Shiraz, Mashhad, and Kerman are the main Persian-speaking towns (although Persians originally predominated in Teheran, its population now contains many non-Persian immigrants). A non-Persian hinterland surrounds some of the Persian-speaking towns; Hamadan, for example, is mostly Persian-speaking, but the villages nearby are Turkish. Farther west, the people of Kermanshah speak Persian and Kurdish, but the surrounding villagers speak only Kurdish.

Although Arabs, Turks, and other non-Persians have traditionally dominated the politics of Islamic Iran, the Persians have been culturally dominant for centuries. Their language carries the prestige of a national language and symbolizes Iranian nationality among speakers of all languages and dialects. Persian is the language of polite literature, government, and education, and except for Armenian, Persian is the only officially printed living language of Iran. Historically, the influence of the Persian language extended beyond the political boundaries of Iran into the non-Arabic parts of the Islamic world, especially Turkey and the Indian subcontinent, where Persian was studied in the schools as the language of literature and diplomacy.

The influence of radio and television has done much to spread knowledge of Persian and to standardize the spoken language. The dialects of the various towns (Teheran, Shiraz, and Isfahan) are mutually intelligible, differing only in specific words and everyday expressions. Colloquial Persian—lacking articles, gender, and case—is a relatively easy language for the outsider to learn, and one reason for its simplicity is its historical role as a lingua franca for peoples speaking widely varying native languages.

In much of the Middle East, native spoken languages were gradually replaced by Arabic following the Islamic conquests of the seventh century A.D. In Iran, however, Persian never succumbed to Arabic, although classical Arabic carries great prestige as the language of the Quran (Koran) and of Islamic scholarship and Iranian schools teach Arabic as a language of prayer and ritual. Modern Persian, although linguistically unrelated to Arabic, has derived its script, some forms of expression, and much of its vocabulary from Arabic.

Although scholars attempted to rid Persian of Arabic loanwords during the Pahlavi era (1925–1979), Arabic has remained the source of vocabulary for abstractions and the terminology of politics, law, philosophy, and religion. Although many commercial establishments display signs with a Persian name, most Iranians still call bakeries, baths, groceries, and butcher shops by their traditional Arabic names.

Modern literary Persian, in both its written and its spoken forms, is rich and complex. It has changed very little since its first appeared as a language written in Arabic script in the tenth century, and a thousand years after composition, the poetry and prose works of the medieval masters of Persian literature are still intelligible to a twentieth-century audience. Although some modern writers have reproduced colloquial usages, most written works are in an idiom that is different from the spoken language and must be learned separately. Thus, Persian composition and literature are often difficult subjects for Iranian school children, especially those from non-Persian-speaking homes. The existence of numerous literary conventions, the gap between written and spoken languages, and the presence of numerous Arabic loanwords and expressions mean that people with the ability to compose clear and correct Persian are rare. Depending on the background of the writer, much of modern Persian prose sounds like a direct translation from English, French, or Arabic.

Kurds

Other Iranian ethnic groups compose about 20 percent of the population. An estimated 2.5 million Kurds live in the west and northwest of Iran, in the provinces of Kurdestan, West Azarbaijan, and Kermanshahan (Bakhtaran). Other Kurdish communities are found in northern Khorasan, and outside Iran in Turkey, Iraq, Syria, and the USSR. The Kurds speak an Iranian language of obscure origin and claim to be descendants of the pre-Islamic Medes. Linguists divide Kurdish into two dialect groups: the northern, *Kurmanji*, spoken north of the town of Mahabad (which lies just south at Lake Urmia), and the southern, *Sorani*, spoken from Mahabad south. The majority of the Kurds are settled farmers, although some are city dwellers and others live a nomadic life. The Kurds are distinguished from other Iranians by language and by the fact that most of them are attached to Sunni Islam. In their social organization, the Kurds have traditionally followed tribal leaders and the sheikhs of the great sufi orders such as the Naqshbandiyyeh and the Qaderiyyeh.

All Iranian central governments must come to terms with the uniqueness of the Kurds. As a people with their own literary tradition, history, language, and social organization, the Kurds have not always been willing subjects of a Persian-speaking, Shi'ite central government. Harsh climate and rugged terrain add to the difficulty of controlling the Kurdish regions. Nevertheless, any Kurdish autonomy or independence movement faces serious difficulties, and central governments have exploited traditional Kurdish rivalries by supporting one tribe against another. Despite the differences between Kurd and Persian, the Kurds have historically identified themselves with Iran. Within the Iranian mosaic, one of their traditional roles has been to guard the western and northwestern edges of the Iranian heartland.

Baluchis

Approximately 500,000 Baluchis inhabit southeastern Iran—one of the poorest regions of the country—and are part of a larger community living in Pakistan and Afghanistan. Like the Kurds, the Baluchis are mostly Sunni Muslims and live as settled farmers and nomadic pastoralists. Historically, control of the Baluchis has proved difficult for Iranian central governments, although disunity and poverty have hindered the growth of movements for independence or autonomy.

Lors (Lurs)

Other Iranian-speaking tribal groups inhabit the central Zagros ranges between Kermanshah in the northwest to Shiraz in the southeast. About 1 million people, collectively known as Lors, live in the provinces of Lorestan, Bakhtiyari, and Kohkiluyeh. Although called by different names throughout this region (Lor, Bakhtiyari [Bakhtiari], Boir Ahmad), all of these tribal peoples speak dialects of Lori, an Iranian language of the southwestern group. Whereas the Iranian Kurds and Baluchis are both parts of ethnic groups that are divided among a number of countries in the Middle East, the Lors lived almost exclusively in Iran.

Traditionally, the Lor peoples guarded the approaches to the Persian heartland against invaders from the west and southwest. In the fourth century B.C., Alexander the Great's armies entered central Iran through what is today the Boir Ahmad region northwest of Shiraz, and in the seventh century A.D., the Arab armies defeated the Iranians at Nahavand, in the northern part of Lor country. Although the mountainous terrain of the Lor regions has given the inhabitants some independence from the Iranian government, the separatist or autonomist spirit is weak in the region. Unlike the Sunni Kurds and Baluchis, the Lors share an attachment to Shi'a Islam with their Persian and Turkish neighbors.

Caspian Peoples

The Gilakis and Mazanderanis inhabit the plains and foothills of the Caspian littoral, speak distinct (northwestern) Iranian languages, and preserve a unique folklore. About 2.5 million townspeople, farmers, and fishermen live in this fertile region. Except for a few Sunni communities in the isolated Talesh hills overlooking the southwestern corner of the Caspian Sea, these peoples are overwhelmingly Shi'a. They are economically, culturally, and politically among the most advanced peoples of Iran. Although physically isolated from the Persian heartland by the high ranges of the Alborz Mountains, the Gilakis and the Mazanderanis are closely integrated into the overall Iranian mosaic. Although Gilan was the location of a short-lived armed uprising (the jangali ["forest people"] movement) after World War I, in which participants demanded national reforms and regional autonomy, the inhabitants have usually identified their interests with those of the Iranian nation as a whole.

Other Iranian Groups

Other groups of Iranian speakers live in scattered areas around the country. Although some of these languages are popularly referred to as dialects (*lahjeh*), most linguists believe that these peoples speak distinct Iranian languages. There are the southwestern Iranian languages of the garmsirat in Fars, for example, Bastaki and Khonji; there are the northwestern languages of the central plateau, for example, the dialects of Kohrud and Miameh; there is the Tati language group in Azarbaijan, a northwestern Iranian language spoken in an overwhelmingly Turkish region; and there is the language of Semnan, which is famous among Persians for being hopelessly unintelligible.

TURKISH SPEAKERS

The Turkish peoples, speaking languages of the Altaic family, are tightly woven into the fabric of Iranian life. Turkish speakers are found almost everywhere in the country, and about one Iranian in four speaks some form of Turkish as a native tongue. Turkish-speaking dynasties held military and political power in Iran almost continuously from the eleventh century into the twentieth, and the modern Persian vocabulary, especially in the areas of military, politics, and administration, has borrowed heavily from Turkish. Iranian family names ending in *lu*, *chi*, or *bash* often indicate Turkish origin.

Azarbaijanis

After the Persians, the Turks of Azarbaijan are the most important ethnic group in Iran. The language of Azarbaijan, sometimes called Azari or Iorki is similar to the language of the Azarbaijan SSR, where the Baku dialect is considered the standard form. It is more distantly related to the Turkish of Istanbul and the Turkish Republic. Map 2.1 shows the location of the approximately 8.5 million Azarbaijanis who live in northwestern Iran as townspeople and settled farmers in some of the nation's most important industrial, commercial, and agricultural regions. Business-minded emigrants from this region live throughout Iran—much of the Teheran bazaar, for example, is traditionally Turkish speaking.

These energetic people have helped bring outside commercial, cultural, and political influences into Iran. The Azarbaijanis' ethnic affinities with the Turks of Istanbul and of the Caucasus have given them a window on European politics and commerce as well as a tradition of political activism. Azarbaijan was a center of the constitutional movement in the first decade of the twentieth century. In February 1978, one of the earliest major uprisings of the Islamic revolution occurred at Tabriz; and in December 1979, forces of the opposition Muslim Republican Peoples' party held the city for several days against central government forces loyal to Ayatollah Khomeini. Azarbaijanis are also in the forefront of Iranian business and have a long tradition of trading with Europe. They wield power beyond their numbers in transport, distribution, and both wholesale and retail trade.[2]

The Azarbaijanis are also strong supporters of the Shi'a tradition. Ardabil, one of the major towns of eastern Azarbaijan, was the ancestral home of the Safavid kings, who, with the support of Turkish tribesmen from Azarbaijan and eastern Anatolia, took control of Iran in the early sixteenth century and established Twelver or Imami Shi'ism as the state religion. The Azarbaijanis' deep attachment to Shi'a Islam, although dividing them from their Sunni Kurdish neighbors, has helped them forge strong ties with other Iranians, especially the Persian speakers of the heartland. These bonds have also limited the effectiveness of nationalistic appeals urging Azarbaijanis to identify with the (Sunni) Turkish peoples of Anatolia and central Asia.

Numbers and influence mean that Azarbaijanis are not so much an "ethnic minority" as "Turkish-speaking Iranians." Azarbaijanis and Persians together compose almost 75 percent of the Iranian population, and these two Shi'a ethnic groups form a ruling partnership that dominates Iranian politics, culture, and commerce. Although a separatist regime, with Soviet backing, ruled Azarbaijan for over a year following World War II, separatism does not command a wide following among the Azarbaijanis. Periodic demands for provincial autonomy and decentralization are based more on a desire for greater participation in planning and spending decisions than on feelings of ethnic exclusiveness. Although one complaint against the last shah was that he imposed the Persian language and culture on ethnic minorities, the Islamic revolution has not led to any strong movement in Azarbaijan to replace Persian with Turkish in schools and offices.

Other Turkish Peoples

There is no clear geographic boundary between Turk and non-Turk in Iran. Mixed populations of Turks, Kurds, Persians, Gilakis, and others live within the various ethnic areas shown on Map 2.1. In addition to the Azarbaijanis, there are an estimated 1.5–2.0 million ethnic Turks living mostly in Fars, Kerman, and Khorasan. In these regions, the word "Turk" was originally synonymous with nomad, and most of these Turkish-speaking groups today are organized tribally and live as nomads or as settled farmers.

The best-known Turkish tribal group is the Qashqa'i in southern Iran. Speaking a language related to Azarbaijani and organized into six major divisions (ta'ifeh), the Qashqa'i nomads migrate twice a year between the lowlands south and west of Shiraz and the higher elevations between Shiraz and Isfahan. Relations between the central government and the Qashqa'i, who traditionally follow their tribal leaders, have always been uneasy, and the advent of the Islamic Republic has not changed this pattern. The number of Qashqa'i, like the numbers of other ethnic groups, is uncertain. Published figures vary between 200,000 and 600,000.

An estimated 250,000 Turkomans live near Iran's northeastern frontier with the USSR on some of Iran's richest agricultural land. The Turkomans, best known for their carpets and horses, speak a language that is distinct from the Turkish of Azarbaijan, and most are followers of Sunni Islam. Other Turkish groups are the Afshars in western Iran and Kerman; the Shahsevens of Azarbaijan and the Qom region; and the Turkish tribes of southeastern Fars who are part of an Arabic-Persian-Turkish federation, called the Khamseh ("five tribes").

OTHER ETHNIC GROUPS

Approximately 1 million Arabs live in Khuzestan, along the Persian Gulf coast, and in isolated regions of Khorasan. The Khuzestani

Arabs share the dialect and the Shi'a creed of the inhabitants of southern Iraq; the coastal Arabs are mostly Sunni and speak a dialect resembing that of the Arab side of the gulf. In southern Fars, the Arab Sheibani and the Arab Jabbareh tribes are part of the Khamseh federation. The small groups of Arabs in Khorasan are mostly members of tribes living along the northern edge of the Dasht-e-Kavir.

Other small groups of Semitic-speaking peoples inhabit Iran. The Assyrians in the northwest and the Jews in Kurdestan and West Azarbaijan speak a collection of dialects known as neo-Aramaic. There are perhaps no more than 50,000 speakers of these dialects living in Iran, although Aramaic speakers can be found among Iranian, Iraqi, and Turkish immigrants to Israel.

The Armenian community of Iran speaks an Indo-European language unrelated to the Iranian group. Estimated at between 200,000 to 300,000, these people are concentrated in Azarbaijan, Teheran, and Isfahan—in the last, they have their own suburb, called Jolfa. The Armenians have a vital role in the Iranian economy as skilled workers, professionals, technicians, merchants, and until the revolution, manufacturers of alcoholic beverages. The Armenian community is one of the most literate in Iran and is the only non-Persian ethnic group that regularly teaches and publishes newspapers and other materials in its own language.

Iran also has some other small ethnic communities. For example, there are communities of Muslim Georgians living in the Daran region west of Isfahan, and in the far southeastern part of the country, there are communities of Brahu'i, who speak languages related to those of southern India.

RELIGIOUS GROUPS

In addition to language, religion can also determine ethnic identity in Iran, and any ethnic map of Iran that ignored religion would show only part of the complex Iranian mosaic. Table 2.2 shows the approximate numbers of the various religious groups, and Map 2.2 shows the distribution of minority religions throughout Iran.

SHI'A AND SUNNI ISLAM

Between 85 and 90 percent of the Iranian population adheres to a minority branch of Islam called the *Shi'a*, or, more precisely, the *Shi'at Ali* ("party of Ali"). About 10–15 percent of the world's Muslims belong to this branch of Islam; the rest, called *Sunnis*, are followers of the *Sunna*, or "tradition."

TABLE 2.2
Religions

Group	Estimated Number (millions)		Percentage	
Muslim	37		98	
Shi'a		33		88
Sunni		4		10
Christian	0.300		1.0	
Armenian		0.250		--[a]
Assyrian		0.050		--
Jewish	0.050		--	
Zoroastrian	0.025		--	
Other (Baha'i, Isma'ili, Ali-Ilahi)	unknown		unknown[b]	
Total	37.375		100	

[a]Very low percentages are not recorded in this table.
[b]"Other" religions make up the difference.
Sources: These estimates are taken from a variety of
sources, including Richard F. Nyrop, ed., Iran: A
Country Study (Washington, D.C.: American University
Foreign Area Studies, 1978); W. B. Fisher, ed., The
Cambridge History of Iran, vol. 1, The Land of Iran
(Cambridge: Cambridge University Press, 1968); National UNESCO Commission, Iranshahr, 2 vols. (Teheran:
University Press, 1963); Fredrik Barth, Nomads of
South Persia: The Basseri Tribe of the Khamseh Confederacy (Boston: Little, Brown and Company, 1961);
and Donald L. Stilo, "The Tati Language Group in the
Sociolinguistic Context of Northwestern Iran and
Transcaucasia," Iranian Studies 14: 3-4 (Summer-
Autumn 1981).

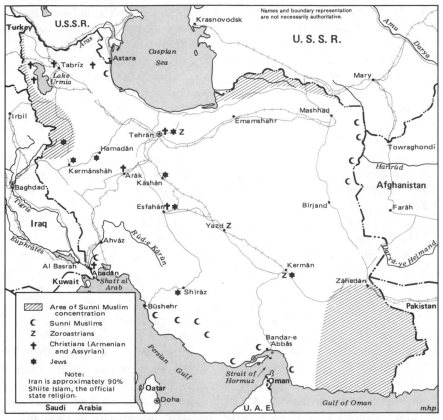

MAP 2.2   Iran: Minority religions

Chapter 4 discusses the relationship between Iran and Shi'a Islam, a movement that began as a political dispute about the succession to the leadership of the Islamic community after the death of the prophet Mohammad in 632 A.D. Although the majority of Muslims accepted the election of the prophet's friend, companion, and father-in-law Abu Bakr as caliph (successor), a minority supported the claim of Ali b. Abu Talib, the prophet's son-in-law and first cousin. The Shi'a supported the cause of the prophet's family and gradually developed the belief that Ali and his male descendants (through the prophet's daughter Fatemeh) were infallible *Imam*s (leaders) in whom all temporal power resided.

Schisms about doctrine and succession occurred within Shi'a Islam, and the dominant branch, called "Imami" or "twelver" Shi'ism, has been the state religion of Iran since the beginning of the sixteenth century. Its adherents also live in Bahrain, the eastern province of

Saudi Arabia, Iraq, Turkey, Lebanon, the USSR, Afghanistan, and Pakistan. Smaller groups of Shi'a, known as Isma'ilis ("seveners") and Zaidis ("fivers") are scattered throughout the Islamic world.

Imami Shi'ism maintains that the line of Imams continued from Ali until the twelfth Imam went into concealment in the ninth century. This "Imam of the Age" (*Imam-e-zaman*) remains alive and will reappear on the judgment day to overthrow usurpers, reassert the rights of the family of the prophet, and establish perfect justice in the world. In Shi'a doctrine, this hidden Imam, sometimes referred to as the *Mahdi* ("rightly-guided one"), still holds all legitimate authority on earth, and kings, presidents, and other temporal rulers are illegitimate unless they rule as his representatives (see Chapter 5).

Just as Persian is dominant on the linguistic map of Iran, Shi'a Islam occupies the central place among the religions. Although ethnic Persians compose no more than half of the inhabitants of Iran, Shi'ism is the creed of between 85 and 90 percent of the population. It is followed by the two major ethnic groups—Azarbaijanis and Persians— and by most Gilakis, Mazanderanis, and Arabs. As already noted, Shi'a Islam has created a bond among various ethnic groups that speak different languages and follow different social customs.

Sunni Islam is the creed of about 10 percent of the population. In general Sunnism predominates on the periphery of Iran-zamin and among the ethnic groups that are separated by history and geography from the mainstream of Iranian culture. The most cohesive Sunni Muslim groups are the Kurds, the Baluchis, and the Turkomans, all of whom inhabit areas far from the centers of Persian civilization and maintain connections with coreligionists and members of their ethnic groups outside Iran. Other Sunni communities are small and scattered. In southern Fars and on the Persian Gulf coast, poverty and religious discrimination have forced many Iranian Sunnis to migrate to the Arab sheikhdoms.

NON-MUSLIM GROUPS

Non-Muslims make up a very small segment of the Iranian population—between 1 and 2 percent. Despite their small numbers, the Iranian Christians, Jews, and Zoroastrians have added a special color and richness to Iran's life and culture. The special aptitudes of these non-Muslim communities—their talent for trades, crafts, agriculture, and music—have contributed to the distinct Iranian national identity.

Among the Christian minorities, language and religion are closely linked. For the 50,000 Assyrians, who live mostly in West Azarbaijan and Kurdestan, there is no longer a single church to provide cohesion. The nineteenth- and twentieth-century European missionaries converted many Assyrians to Protestantism and Catholicism from their traditional allegiance to the ancient Nestorian church. Their small numbers, modest economic status, and concentration in remote areas have kept the Assyrians mostly out of the main currents of Iranian life.

The Christian Armenians have the strongest sense of national identity of all of the Iranian religious minorities. A distinctly Armenian church, language, literature, and music and a long history as an independent nation have enabled the Armenian people in Iran to preserve their unique culture while living as a minority among Iranian Muslims. Although geography and economics have placed the Armenians close to the centers of Iranian life in the major towns, Armenian schools, churches, and social clubs have preserved this community's identity and ethnic cohesion.

The small Zoroastrian community, an estimated 25,000, is largely concentrated in the towns of Yazd and Kerman. The Zoroastrians speak an Iranian language known as Gabri, and they have preserved the religion of pre-Islamic Iran and the memory of Iran as a world empire before the Arab invasions of the seventh century A.D. Although Zoroaster was an Iranian prophet and Iran was the original homeland of his faith, the largest and most important Zoroastrian community is now the Parsis in Bombay. The Zoroastrians of Iran are mostly small merchants who do not have the wealth or the position of their coreligionists in India.

The Iranian Jews have a cultural importance beyond their number, which is estimated at 50,000, and Iran is rich in history for Judaism: The reputed tombs of Queen Esther at Hamadan and the prophet Habbakuk at Tuyserkan (a small town about 50 miles south of Hamadan) are still revered sites. The Jewish minority is closely tied to the Islamic mainstream of Iranian life, and unlike the Assyrians, most Iranian Jews live in Persian-speaking areas among Shi'a Muslims. In contrast to the Armenians, they have no national tradition or living language to distinguish them from Iranian Muslims. Except for Semitic-speaking groups in Kurdestan, most Iranian Jews are Persian-speaking. With the inherent conservatism of a dispersed minority, they have preserved Iranian folkways and cultural traditions—in music and food, for example—that have been forgotten by the Muslim majority. Jewish families were also a source of talent for the Iranian ruling class, and by converting to Islam, a number of Jews were able to attain powerful positions in government.

One important source of identity for the Persianized Jews of Iran was not language, but the Hebrew script. Just as the Arabic script connotes Islam for peoples of different languages, the Hebrew script was a means for the Iranian Jews to distinguish themselves from their Muslim neighbors. There is a body of Judeo-Persian literature written in Persian with Hebrew characters, among the most famous of which is a life of Moses, written in imitation of Ferdowsi's eleventh-century *Shahnameh*, by the fourteenth-century poet, Mowla Shahin Shirazi.[3]

The Baha'is of Iran are not a separate ethnic group and have no distinct linguistic or cultural tradition to distinguish them from other Iranians. Baha'is are found among many ethnic groups and are not concentrated in any one area. Even their number is a matter of dispute—estimates vary between 100,000 and 300,000—and their status as a religious group is ambiguous. Without official recognition as a minority, Baha'is lack the right to administer matters such as marriage, divorce, and religious education—the normal prerogatives of other Iranian religious communities.

The Baha'i religion began as a nineteenth-century messianic movement within Shi'a Islam and developed into a new universal religion preaching pacifism, equality for women, and world brotherhood. Since its origins, the Shi'a clergy has strongly opposed the Baha'i religion because it denies Mohammad's status as the last prophet and the Quran's status as the last and perfect divine revelation. The Baha'is enjoyed a measure of personal security under the Pahlavi dynasty of the twentieth century, but the establishment of the Islamic Republic in 1979 has brought a renewal of anti-Baha'i activities and the execution of prominent Baha'is throughout Iran. Although not recognized as an official religion, Baha'ism is still of part of Iranian life and tradition. Perhaps it represents a continuing refusal to accept orthodoxy and a search for religious truth in heterodox beliefs.

PATTERNS OF CULTURE

IS THERE AN IRANIAN NATIONAL CHARACTER?

Beyond following numerous religions and speaking many languages, what sort of people are the Iranians? I approach the subject of national culture with great hesitation because recent events have produced scores of instant, superficial judgments about something called "Iranian culture." Television experts have explained, in thirty-second analyses, that Iran's current political turmoil is the result of some national personality trait. They tell us, for example, that Iranians have a "penchant for martyrdom," that they "dislike all compromise" and "ignore objective truth," and that they are "inherently fanatic."

The authors of such superficial analyses should know better. They have taken some of the characteristics of some Iranians, applied them to a whole people, and made them the explanation for contemporary political conditions.[4] Even worse, such analysts have forgotten that Iranians are, like everyone else, the victims of history and other circumstances that shape political and social systems. To claim that these systems spring from some national character traits (as imperfectly understood by an outsider) ignores all the richness, complexity, and contradictions of the human species. Such facile judgments, in the case of present-day Iran, lead to the exaggeration of some traits (such as religiosity) at the expense of others (such as compassion) that are equally important parts of the Iranian cultural heritage.

Iranians do have a distinct cultural tradition, which is special if not unique among nations, but the relationship of this tradition to whatever political system prevails at a certain time is not certain. Political systems change quickly; cultural traditions change slowly if at all. Some political scientists call those specific cultural patterns that influence political organization a nation's "political culture," a more precise terminology that avoids trying to explain political events by amateurish psychological and sociological analyses of Iranian families and individuals. In the case of Iran, political culture could include, for example, the necessity of having a strong and visible leadership.

CULTURAL TRADITIONS

Although some people do not think so, much of the Iranian cultural heritage is nonpolitical. It has to be, since other societies with similar traditions have developed radically different political systems. These traditions, which are by no means uniquely Iranian, include family solidarity, hospitality, and artistic creativity.

The first, family solidarity, means that everyone in the extended family—siblings, parents, children, uncles, aunts, cousins, and in-laws—supports an individual throughout his or her lifetime. The Iranian family at its best gives its members the combined services of employment agency, welfare office, health insurance agency, family counselor, ward boss, and marriage broker. In return, the individual has his or her obligations. All must pay visible respect to the family elders; males must protect the honor of the family's women; all must defer to family wishes in questions of marriage, career, business, residence, child raising, and education; males must support, economically and politically, other family members; and all must be careful not to bring disgrace on the family by some ill-considered action. In return for deference, family elders are expected to settle disputes, to give final consent to marriages, and to provide for all family members who need support. One is never too busy to help a relative.

Concerning the second tradition, the Persian proverb says that the guest is beloved of God; the Iranian host must provide (and provide generously) for a guest. To visit an Iranian home and not be offered at least tea is a biting insult. Hospitality begrudged or scrimped is as bad as no hospitality at all,[5] and guests, expected or unexpected, are welcomed and cared for in any numbers at all times. The third, artistic creativity, applies to architecture, poetry, music, painting, and dozens of minor arts. Carpet weaving and miniature painting are only the best-known Iranian art forms. Almost every town produces some special handicraft, whether it be pottery, metal, jewelry, calligraphy, cloth, wood, leather, or ivory. The Isfahanis are the leading Iranian craftsmen, fashioning the finest carpets, brass and silver objects, and miniatures. But the Iranians' greatest artistic achievement is their poetry. Poetry, whether the patriotic couplets of Ferdowsi (d. 1020); the mystic, ecstatic songs of Jalal al-Din Rumi (d. 1273); the exquisite rhymes of Sa'adi (d. 1292); or the subtle, mysterious verses of Hafez of Shiraz (d. 1389), permeates the whole fabric of Iranian life.[6]

In their language and art forms, Iranians often favor the ornate and florid. Buildings display brightly colored tiles, mirror work, inlay, and elaborate carving in wood and plaster. On public festivals, such as the birthday of the twelfth Imam, Iranians decorate their cities with lights, carpets, and banners showing fine calligraphy. Even occasions of grief cannot subdue creativity. On the death of a young man, the bereaved create an ornate display of lights and color called *hejleh*, representing the marriage chamber the young man never saw. Public mourning ceremonies for Imam Hosein (the prophet's grandson) and his family may include elaborate banners, costumes, and battle standards. The participants' grief is real; they see no contradiction between sadness and beauty.

IDEALS OF BEHAVIOR

How Iranians describe themselves reveals a great deal about their society and about the personal and social traits they consider important. The Persian language is rich in nouns and adjectives that describe human behavior. *Ta'arof*, for example, is an elusive term that defines behavior in almost all situations outside the immediate family. Ta'arof is the social system that allows individuals to maintain dignity in a crowded and harsh environment. It provides a set of ritualized phrases to use on meeting and departing; a set of euphemisms to describe unpleasant events; and a set of honorifics to substitute for the second- and third-person pronouns. Ta'arof requires that a host describe an enormous meal as "a little bread and cheese," and it requires that the polite guest refuse what is offered (or take very little) until repeatedly urged. When the guest says, "It is time for me to lessen this intrusion," the host must answer, "It is still early." Ta'arof also means that one should not express an idea that will cause pain, even if true, and that criticism, if expressed at all, should be couched in the most delicate of terms.

Although misused ta'arof sometimes creates amusing social situations, it is basically a very serious concept.[7] The origin of the word perhaps best illustrates its meaning: *ta'arof* derives from an Arabic root denoting knowledge and acquaintance. Other words from the same root include *mo'arrefi* ("introduction"), *ta'rif* ("definition," "description"), *ma'ruf* ("famous"), *erfan* ("mystic knowledge"), and *ma'rafat* ("wisdom"). Thus, ta'arof is a means of social knowledge—a way for people to gain an understanding of each other.

Gheirat means pride and honor and the readiness to defend oneself against an insult, especially to the honor of one's family. A man whose wife, sister, or daughter has been insulted must react in some way or be ridiculed as *bi-gheirat*—roughly, "a gutless cuckold." The Persian proverb says, *Mard bud va gheiratash* ("A man exists by his gheirat"). Gheirat is also national, ethnic, and religious pride. During times of civil unrest, pictures of slain compatriots, displays of bloody garments, and photographs of mutilated bodies all appeal to the gheirat of the audience. Skilled orators can rouse a crowd's emotions by questioning its gheirat. In 1964, Khomeini produced such a response to his attack on the U.S.-Iranian bilateral military agreement by challenging the Iranian people to show their pride (when the shah did not have any).[8]

Qahr and *ashti* describe two states of a relationship. The former is a kind of sulk, a cold withdrawal in the face of an insult. Qahr is a way of demonstrating displeasure without making a final break. The offended party has still left the way open to reconciliation, or *ashti*, with the passage of time and with proper mediation. The word *ashti* has strong positive connotations, and few Iranians will reject the role of mediator and peacemaker.[9] They will make great efforts to reconcile quarreling husbands and wives, neighbors, or family members, urging each side to overlook the faults of the other.

In so doing, the mediator will ask both sides to show *gozasht*, that is, tolerance and willingness to forgive. Gozasht is also an understanding of human limitations and imperfections. If a child breaks some valuable object, if someone misses an appointment, if someone does a job poorly or not at all, the injured party should have the generosity of spirit to realize that human beings are weak, misled, fallible creatures who often make unwise choices and take ill-considered actions.

Ta'arof, gheirat, qahr, ashti, and gozasht are just a small part of the Iranians' rich treasury of words describing both desirable and undesirable human behavior. The customs and values these words describe are not uniquely Iranian, Middle Eastern, or Islamic as many of the above statements about Iranians could apply equally to Egyptians, Iraqis, Turks, Greeks, Italians, and other nationalities. Yet these characteristics tell us how Iranians see themselves and their society and how they would like it to work. No society works perfectly, and Iranians may not always obey their own values, but at least these values tell them the best actions and words to use in most situations that occur in daily life.

(*Above*) Hamadan: Main square in winter (courtesy of Michael Jerald); (*below*) central Teheran, looking north toward the Alborz Mountains (USAID)

(*Above*) Tabriz in winter (courtesy of Michael Jerald); (*below*) Fars Province: Landscape (USAID)

Achemaenid ruins at Persepolis (USAID)

(*Above*) Shrine of Hazrat-e-Ma'sumeh at Qom (USAID); (*below*) main square of Isfahan, with Safavid buildings (USAID)

(*Right*) Iranian farmer: Vera-
min, near Teheran (USAID);
(*below*) housewife of Shushtar,
Khuzestan (courtesy of Michael Jerald)

Jute mill worker, Mazanderan (USAID)

(*Right*) Qashqa'i man and child, Fars Province (USAID); (*below*) school for Qashqa'i children, Fars Province (USAID)

3

Myths and Forgotten Kings

More than twenty-five centuries of continuous existence as a nation have given Iran a rich and complex historical inheritance. In the Middle East, only Egypt has a longer history as a unified nation, but Iran retains the stronger ties to an imperial and pre-Islamic past. Iran's heritage has survived devastating foreign invasions that would have obliterated the cultures of less adaptable peoples. Although the invaders destroyed lives and buildings, established new dynasties, and brought new customs, languages, and religions, an underlying Iranian identity always escaped destruction, and the new society that emerged after each conquest remained uniquely Iranian. Unlike other peoples in much of the Middle East and North Africa, for example, Iranians did not become Arabic speakers following the Islamic conquests of the seventh century A.D. Unlike Anatolians, Iranians were not completely Turkified by the medieval Turkish migrations. When the pre-Islamic Sassanian empire collapsed, Iranian language and culture—the symbols of national identity—adapted and flourished within a new Islamic civilization.

In Iran, history is too important to be treated as an academic discipline left to scholars and teachers. The Iranians themselves, who must live with their history, see it as the sum of achievements of saints, prophets, and mythological heroes. The remains of hundreds of buildings, bridges, and rock carvings that cover the Iranian plateau are like history textbooks, teaching Iranians about the past glories of their land. Popular imagination creates its own guides to these monuments, linking them to the heroes of pre-Islamic mythology and Islamic folktales. For example, Iranians associate the Achaemenian palaces at Persepolis, about 50 miles northwest of Shiraz, and the nearby Sassanian rock carvings with the legendary heroes Jamshid and Rostam, respectively. Iran is filled with ruins attributed to the prophet Solomon: The great Zoroastrian sanctuary in southern Azarbaijan is known as Takht-e-Soleiman ("Solomon's throne"), and Cyrus the Great's tomb at Pasargadae, on a remote highland plateau in Fars Province, is called the mosque of Solomon's mother.

Iranians have, however, forgotten some pre-Islamic history and have blended the rest into mythology. Names such as Alexander, Shahpur, and Khosrow survived in legends, but the names of Achaemenian, Seleucid, and almost all the Parthian rulers have vanished from the national memory. Among Iranians, only the few specialists who have studied archaeology and foreign literary sources are familiar with those periods. Popular imagination, faced with the obvious remains of glories from a distant past, has linked them to the familiar Jamshid, Rostam, and Solomon instead of to the unknown Cyrus, Darius, and Xerxes.

HISTORICAL TRADITIONS

The written history and a vast body of legends stretch over twenty-five centuries and record the tenacious survival of certain characteristically Iranian historical traditions. Through centuries of political and social upheaval, four basic historical patterns have endured to preserve the Iranians' sense of national identity: charismatic leadership, a deep religious impulse, concern with justice, and acceptance of foreign ways adapted to Iranian tastes.

Charismatic Leadership

The rock carvings and inscriptions of the pre-Islamic dynasties; the legends of the *Shahnameh*; the grandiose titles of the Safavid, Qajar, and Pahlavi shahs; the popular stories of the heroism of Imam Ali; and the propaganda surrounding Ayatollah Khomeini all emphasize one consistent theme: Iran's kings, emperors, and Imams have ruled by force of individual personality, by their charisma. For all of Iran's historical existence, this royal charisma (modern Persian, *farr;* old Persian, *khwarnah*) has been a prerequisite for Iranian kingship, a sign of divine favor given to those with a legitimate right to rule. Because only rulers with a clear, undisputed line of succession possessed farr, each new dynasty had first to establish its royal legitimacy. Thus, the Sassanians associated themselves with the Achaemenians, the Buyids with pre-Islamic kings, and the Safavids with Imam Musa Kazem, the seventh Imam of the Shi'ites.[1]

The tradition of charismatic leadership has clashed with attempts to limit the ruling power in Iran. When leadership is personal, it has few objective qualifications or standards. Attempts to formally define a leader's power, by means of an effective constitution, for example, have faced strong opposition from people who believe that such attempts violate both divine and popular will. Shi'a Islam provides no formal mechanism for the community as a group to choose its leader; instead, the process is informal and personal. The individual believer selects a source of guidance (*marja'-e-taqlid*), a model to follow in religious matters.[2] In communal prayer, the believer demonstrates his individual choice by praying behind the leader (*pishnamaz, imam*) he considers most virtuous, pious, and learned. Whether the leader derives his charisma from divine favor, community acclamation, or some other source, he is expected to rule personally and decisively. Iranians do not tolerate figureheads for very long and ridicule their ineffective rulers as "Shah Soltan Hosein," the last Safavid monarch (ruled 1694–1722) who was notorious for his weakness and incompetence.[3]

Importance of Religion

Religion has always been central in Iranian history and politics. The Achaemenian kings associated themselves with the Iranian god Ahura Mazda and with the gods of their numerous subject peoples. The Sassanians established Zoroastrianism as a state religion, and the Safavids did the same with Shi'a Islam. Attempts by the Pahlavis to separate religion and politics in the twentieth century met with little success beyond the top levels of society. The current Islamic Republic has drawn its strength from an effective use of the religious vocabulary and symbols familiar to the majority of Iranians, who had successfully resisted the Pahlavis' attempts to transform them into citizens of a secular state.

Even casual visitors to Iran have always noticed the pervasive influence of religion in daily life. Beyond the obvious mixture of religion and politics in the current Islamic Republic, religion also shapes more intimate details, such as speech patterns, personal relations, and family life. Communal prayer has an obvious social side, and pilgrimages to the tombs of holy men and women and visits to the graves of deceased relatives are popular activities. The major shrines at Mashhad, Qom, Rey (a few miles south of Teheran), and Shiraz are tourist centers where pilgrims can shop, sightsee, trade, and meet visitors from other parts of the Shi'a world. Pilgrims can enjoy the sensuous spectacles of monumental buildings, sermons, Quran recitations, and special foods at the major shrines. Many villages have a local saint's tomb (*imamzadeh*), which draws visitors from nearby towns for a day's outing in the country.[4]

This concern with religion shapes the Iranians' special view of their own history—a view that glorifies the achievements of saints, scholars, and poets and ignores the work of kings, ministers, and generals. Judging by the popularity of certain graves as pilgrimage sites, most Iranians revere their mystics, saints, and theologians far more than their political and military leaders, whose graves and monuments usually fall into early obscurity. In the 1970s, for example, the public ignored the new, grandiose Nader Shah Museum in Mashhad and the restored grave of Shah Shoja' Mozaffari (ruled 1358–1384) in Shiraz, but they continued to venerate the saints and poets buried in those same cities. Although the Safavid kings helped bring about the triumph of Shi'ism in Iran, their graves in Ardabil and Qom attract little popular interest. An Iranian visiting the great pre-Islamic sites outside of Shiraz may feel some stirrings of national pride but will experience little of the emotion and joy that come from a visit to Shah-e-Cheragh (brother of the Imam Reza buried at Mashad) or even to a simple village shrine.

If religion is humankind's search for the best way to live in harmony with divine commands, then Iranians have pursued that search with great enthusiasm and in some unexpected directions. They are as prolific in creating and refining religions as they are in creating beautiful objects of cloth, metal, wood, and stone. Iran is not only a land of faith; it is also a land of heresy, heterodoxy, and a continuing rejection of accepted wisdom in the search for divine truth.

The list of Iranian-based heresies is a long one. Manicheanism—whose teachings rejected the physical world as evil, as a manifestation of the devil's work—arose under Persian rule in Mesopotamia in the third century A.D. Originating at the Sassanian court, this doctrine spread far beyond Iran into central Asia and medieval Europe, where it was ferociously attacked by the Catholic church. Mazdakism, which appeared in the late fifth century, advocated radical social reform, including communal possession of property and (according to hostile sources) women. The Sassanian emperor Kavadh (ruled 488–531) accepted this doctrine, which then flourished under royal protection until its bloody suppression in 524 A.D.

Iranians still remained attracted to the unorthodox, even after the coming of Islam in the seventh century. Violent schismatic groups, such as the Assassins in Alamut (a mountain fortress northwest of Teheran) and the Khorram-din in Azarbaijan, mounted serious threats to central authority. Shi'ism itself originated as a schism within Islam and was imposed on a mostly Sunni Iran in the sixteenth century by a dynasty of Turkish origin. Whatever its roots, the revolutionary, activist Islam that overthrew the Pahlavis in 1979 is a radical departure from the religion practiced elsewhere in the Islamic world. Although neither its adherents nor its opponents would agree, the Baha'i faith, which first appeared in Iran in the nineteenth century, is perhaps only the latest manifestation in a series of Iranian dualistic heresies dating to pre-Islamic times.

Importance of Justice

Closely tied to Iranian religion (*din*) is an ancient concern for justice (*dad, adl*). Frequent references to the prophet Solomon in Iranian literature and folklore attest to the importance of justice as a characteristic of a ruler. Both Persian and early Muslim Arabic literature represented the Sassanian emperor Khosrow I Anushiravan (ruled 531–579) as the epitome of the just ruler. The belief in divine justice—that the quality of justice is innate to God's nature—is central to Shi'a Islam. Shi'ism considers belief in *adalat* ("divine justice") a principle of faith as important as belief in *emamat* (Ali's rightful place as leader of the Muslim community).[5]

If one reads only about the brutalities of Iranian history—the towers of skulls, the blindings, and the mutilations—this concern for justice may appear to be a cruel irony, but justice has had a special meaning for Iranians. Instead of a structured guarantee of individual freedom, justice is the preservation of balance and order in society. The just ruler protects his subjects against anarchy and against each other, even by methods that appear harsh and arbitrary. Justice is rapid and visible. By quick sentences publicly executed, a just ruler establishes an obvious relationship between a criminal's act and the ruler's ability to restore public order. The Persian proverb *zolm be'l-saviyeh adl ast* ("oppression equally applied is justice") suggests that the purpose of a ruler's justice is to prevent citizens from gaining an advantage over one another, even if such justice requires applying harsh measures to an entire society.[6]

Adoption of Foreign Ways

Geography has made the Iranian heartland vulnerable to invasion because determined conquerors, who have usually entered Iran from the northeast or the west, have been able to subdue urban centers and control main roads with relative ease once they have penetrated the major mountain barriers to the plateau. Along with this geographic vulnerability there has been a cultural openness, a readiness to adopt foreign ways in religion, politics, and social practice.[7] Iranians have traditionally accepted and then mastered foreign customs by giving them a (refined) Iranian form and making them a part of their own culture. When the Arabs brought Islam to Iran in the seventh century A.D., the Iranians did not so much surrender to the new religion as gradually embrace it and become its enthusiastic adherents and missionaries. Iranians became masters of Arabic poetry and grammar, Islamic history, natural science, mathematics, mysticism, and religious scholarship. Even Shi'ism, today a central element of Iranian national identity, was originally a foreign ideology. The Arabs of Iraq first brought Shi'ism to Iran, and over eight centuries later, a Turkish-speaking dynasty based in northwestern Iran and supported by Turkoman tribesmen from Anatolia made it the state religion. Despite their foreign origins, Islam in general and Shi'a Islam in particular have become inseparable from the Iranian national identity.

In recent times, some Iranians have criticized their compatriots' willingness to adopt foreign mannerisms and ideas because such willingness is seen as a surrender to Western attempts to transform Iran into a "farm" for economic exploitation and a museum for preserving antiquities and exotic folklore.[8] But openness to outside influence was never only the passive imitation of foreign manners. Iranians protected and preserved their identity as Iranians by their adaptability, and Iran has endured because its people have been willing to adapt their great talents to new ways of life and thought. Iranian civilization probably owes its survival and its greatness to the adoption of two "foreign" innovations: the Islamic religion and the Arabic alphabet. The modern Persian language, with Arabic loanwords and written in Arabic script, broke the narrow limits of pre-Islamic Persian to become a language of scholarship, literature, and diplomacy throughout much of the eastern Islamic world. The coming of Islam did not end Iranian civilization but strengthened it and transformed it into a new, universal Islamic-Iranian culture that was no less Iranian than the culture of the Sassanians. Similarly, when the Turks brought their spoken language to northern Iran in the eleventh century, Azarbaijan could become Turkish in speech and remain Iranian in culture. After the Safavids declared Shi'ism the state religion in the sixteenth century, 90 percent of the Iranian population eventually adhered to Shi'ism and made it a vital part of their identity as Iranians.

As Iranians adopted and refined the ways of Greeks, Arabs, and Turks, they also absorbed their conquerors into an enriched Iranian civilization. Iranians borrowed and lent. Their techniques in art, architecture, music, and administration were adopted by Arabs and Turks, whose native traditions in these areas were relatively primitive. Perhaps one explanation for the Iranians' unease in their recent conact with the West was the perception that Westerners, unlike Arabs and Turks, were impervious to Iranian cultural influence and that cultural exchange would proceed in only one direction. Furthermore, it seemed that Western culture was too powerful and too alien for Iranians to absorb without destroying their own identity.

The surivival of these four historical traditions preserved the foundations of national identity through periods when strong outside forces made Iranians change the form of their nation's political and social life. Leaderships, whether from an Achaemenian great king, a Safavid sheikh, or a Shi'ite *imam-e-ommat* ("leader of the community") remained personal and charismatic. Religion in various forms held its central place in Iranian life. Justice remained a constant, living ideal of the society, despite the continuous horrors inflicted on the Iranian people. Finally, Iranian culture owed much of its brilliance to its contact with foreign cultures and the people's ability to shape alien customs into a characteristically Iranian mold.

MYTHOLOGY

Iran has two ancient histories. Alongside the history reconstructed from archaeology and the work of foreign historians is a legendary national history of the epic deeds of both supernatural and historical figures. The latter history, inspiration of both folklore and the greatest works of Persian literature, originated in the ancient oral tradition of the Iranian people. Iranian mythology, first recorded during the Sassanian period, attained its greatest expression in the eleventh century A.D. in the *Shahnameh* of Ferdowsi, a national epic poem of about 50,000 verses. Drawing on pre-Islamic sources, the *Shahnameh* relates the history of the Iranian nation from the creation of the world to the downfall of the Sassanian dynasty in the seventh century A.D. But even this masterpiece did not exhaust the Iranian epic tradition, and the legends of national heroes have been woven into works of Persian art and literature from the eleventh century to the present day.

The mythology of the *Shahnameh* is Iran's view of its pre-Islamic past—a time of gods, evil spirits, superhuman heroes, and wise, just rulers. Of the rulers appearing in Ferdowsi's epic, only Alexander the Great, the Parthians, and the Sassanians are historical. However it happened, other dynasties in Iran's past—Elamites, Achaemenians, Medes, Seleucids—had disappeared from the national memory. Ancient Iran's mythology was not critical history, its purpose was to entertain and to uphold certain ideals of Iranian society. In his discussion of the *Shahnameh*, the scholar Jan Rybka identified three fundamental conceptions of ancient Iranian morality that have remained part of the national faith:

1. The opposition between good and evil and final victory of the former. This opposition appears both in religious dualism and in constant warfare between Iran and Turan (the land east and northeast of Iran-zamin).
2. The necessity for a legitimate ruler with an undisputed line of succession. Only such a ruler will possess that divine gift of royal farr required of kings.
3. The absolute loyalty of the vassal toward his feudal lord, even when that lord acts unwisely.[9]

PREHISTORIC IRAN

Iranians were latecomers to their homeland. When they appeared in history and founded their empires, other Middle Eastern kingdoms, notably Babylonia and Egypt, were already of great antiquity. Information about the prehistory of Iran is scarce, and scholars have had to reconstruct it from archaeological remains and foreign, mostly Assyrian, inscriptions. Invasions and migrations of Indo-European-speaking peoples onto the Iranian plateau are usually dated about the eleventh century B.C., and the Iranian expansion into the Zagros Mountains occurred about a century later.

Both written sources and archaeological remains reveal the existence of indigenous, non-Iranian kingdoms that Iranian immigrants gradually absorbed into their own states. One of these indigenous peoples, the Elamites, had established a rich civilization in Khuzestan, the lowlands between Mesopotamia and the central Zagros. Elam was an important political force during the second millenium B.C., when it warred with the rulers of Mesopotamia. About 1175, the Elamites captured Babylon, taking as booty a diorite stone engraved with Hammurabi's law code. Elam declined after 1150 but reappeared in the seventh century B.C. as an enemy of the neo-Assyrian empire. In 636, the Assyrian emperor Assurbanipal sacked the Elamite capital at Susa (Shush). Elam was then eclipsed first by the Assyrians and later by the growing Iranian power to the east and north.

Elamite influence extended eastward from the Khuzestan plains onto the Iranian plateau. There is an Elamite rock relief at Naqsh-e-Rostam in Fars, and the Elamite language, neither Semitic nor Indo-European, was used for records at the time of Darius I (ruled 522–486 B.C.). Some aspects of Achaemenian art, such as the processional scenes, have been identified as Elamite in origin. One scholar has compared the Elamites' influence on the early Persians with that of the medieval Iranian inhabitants of Azarbaijan on the Turkish invaders.[10] In both regions, the outsiders imposed their language on the original inhabitants while adopting many of their cultural traditions.

Another important pre-Iranian kingdom was Urartu, which ruled the Lake Van region of eastern Turkey, western Azarbaijan, and northern Iraqi Kurdestan. Urartu, which first appeared in Assyrian sources about 850 B.C., was a serious rival of Assyria until the late eighth century. A weakened Urartian kingdom survived until about 600 B.C., when it fell to the Medes and to Scythian invaders from north of the Caucasus. The culture of Urartu dominated the north-western corner of Iran-zamin and the region traditionally called Armenia. It has been suggested that Urartu was the source of much of Achaemenian architecture, art (especially certain animal motifs), and state protocol.[11]

MEDES AND PERSIANS

History records the first appearance of the Medes and the Persians in the ninth century B.C. Assyrian sources relate that King Shalmaneser III (ruled 858–824) invaded the lands of the Parsua, southwest of Lake Urumiyeh, and then moved southeast into the territory of the Mada, the region of modern Hamadan. The region that Assyrians called Mada became the center of the Median kingdom; Parsua became identified with the Persians and with the region of Fars in the southwestern part of the Iranian plateau.[12]

By the eighth and seventh centuries B.C., the Medes and the Persians had settled in their traditional homes. The Median chief Dayyaku, whom Herodotus called Deioces, founded the confederacy of Media, with its capital at Ecbatana (Median, Hangmatana; Persian, Hamadan), in the late eighth century. Median power reached its peak in the late seventh and early sixth centuries under the rule of Cyaxares II and his successor, Astyages. During this period, the Medes defeated the Scythians (625) and, in alliance with the Babylonians, overthrew the Assyrian empire after capturing its capital of Nineveh in 612. In 590, the Medes subdued the Armenians of eastern Anatolia and, following an inconclusive war with Lydia, established their western frontier at the Halys (Kizil Irmak) River.

The dynasty of the Persian Achaemenians gave Iran its first period of glory as a world empire.[13] According to Herodotus, Cyrus II (the Great), founder of the Achaemenian empire, was the son of the Persian Cambyses I and Mandane (Persian, Mandana), daughter of the Median king Astyages. Cyrus, a vassal ruler under his maternal grandfather, rebelled against his lord in 553 and defeated him three years later with the capture of the Median capital Ecbatana. Cyrus did not so much conquer the Medes as stage an armed coup, probably with the help of Median opponents of Astyages. If Herodotus's account is accurate, Cyrus was a member of the Median royal house on his mother's side. His subsequent treatment of the Medes as partners and his transferring the capital from the small and remote Pasargadae to Ecbatana suggest that he saw himself as heir to rather than conqueror of the Median throne. Cyrus's subsequent war against the Lydians was perhaps an effort to confirm the territorial claims and boundaries he had inherited upon gaining his grandfather's throne.

Cyrus's achievements were impressive. By the time of his death in 530 B.C., he had conquered Lydia (546), former rival of the Medes, and much of western Asia Minor. He had extended the northeastern frontier of his empire to the Jaxartes (Syr Darya) River and into present-day Afghanistan. He turned on his former ally, Nabonides of Babylonia, to capture Babylon in 539 and annex Mesopotamia, Syria, Phoenicia, and Palestine. He freed the Jews from their Babylonian exile and ordered the rebuilding of their temple at Jerusalem. Although vast empires were familiar to people in the ancient Middle East, Cyrus's empire was unusual because of its religious toleration and its moderation in dealing with defeated people. Although Persians and Medes clearly dominated the Achaemenian empire, they were willing to learn from their subjects and to respect their protocol, traditions, and beliefs. The early Achaemenians not only ruled their huge empire with skill and flexibility, they also possessed the breadth of vision and tolerance to accept and make use of the best customs of their subject peoples.

Cyrus was killed in 530 while on a campaign against nomads on the eastern frontier. His son and successor, Cambyses II, had ruled as Cyrus's representative in Babylonia and continued his father's work of expanding the empire by his conquest of Egypt in 525. Although Cambyses was blamed for many misdeeds in Egypt, including slaying the sacred Apis bull, the fact is that he continued his father's policies of religious toleration and respect for local customs. While returning from Egypt to Persia, Cambyses died in Syria in 522, by his own hand according to some accounts.

Cambyses's death ended the first line of the Achaemenian dynasty. Before his death, Cambyses had learned that a Median priest (magus) named Gaumata had taken the throne claiming to be Cambyses's (slain) brother Bardiya. The Achaemenians regained power in a counterrevolt led by Darius (Old Persian, Darayavaush), a member of the younger branch of the royal family.[14] By 521 B.C., Darius had gained undisputed control of the empire after suppressing Gaumata's supporters and a series of related revolts in the provinces.

Darius's greatest accomplishment was the reorganization and consolidation of the empire. He introduced those features of administration that the Biblical and Greek writers noted as typically Persian. During his reign, he established a standard gold and silver coinage system, as part of the task of reforming taxation, and divided the empire into provinces, or satrapies. The governor, or satrap, possessed wide civil powers and was responsible for collecting the king's tribute. Military forces were under a separate official responsible directly to the king, and each commander controlled forces in several satrapies. In addition to these officials, there were special royal inspectors, the famous "eyes and ears" of the king. In spite of this system of divided authority, provincial revolts continued to trouble the empire throughout its history.

Under the Achaemenians, scribes were important people, and a bureaucracy was needed to keep records and accounts. Aramaic was the most important written language of the empire; Old Persian appeared only in royal inscriptions and probably not before the time of Darius. During Darius's reign, the former Elamite capital of Susa in Khuzestan became the administrative capital, and Babylon, Sardis, and other cities were important as provincial capitals and commercial centers. Ecbatana, although no longer the administrative center, remained important as a summer resort for the royal court. Darius began construction of the magnificient palaces about fifty miles south of Pasargadae at Persepolis, the ruins of which have fascinated visitors for centuries. Although this site was of great importance to the Achaemenians, its exact purpose is uncertain. The climate of the region and other evidence suggest that the royal court occupied Persepolis in the spring, at the Persian new year, probably for the ceremonies that accompanied their receiving tribute from the provinces and vassal states.

The later Achaemenians were beset by frequent provincial revolts, especially in Egypt, which remained independent under a native dynasty throughout the first half of the fourth century B.C. The able emperor Artaxerxes III reconquered Egypt in 343 and restored the empire to almost its original size. Artaxerxes III was poisoned in 338 B.C.; had he lived longer, he might have been able to resist the Greek forces of Alexander the Great. As it happened, the Achaemenian family was almost exterminated by its generals until the throne came into the hands of Darius IV (Codomannus, ruled 336–330). This last Achaemenian emperor restored Persian authority in Egypt (which had rebelled for the umpteenth time), but his kingdom collapsed before the powerful invaders from the west.

Although the Achaemenian great kings vanished from Iranian popular memory, they left a rich legacy. Their tombs and ruined buildings at Persepolis and Naqsh-e-Rostam are visible reminders of Iran's antiquity, power, and wealth, and the ancient world viewed their empire as a model world state. The Persian empire was *the* empire, and its king was *the* king. The Achaemenian tradition of tolerating diversity in religion and social customs and of adopting the practices of subject peoples provided an example of how to rule a large, multiethnic empire.

SELEUCIDS AND PARTHIANS

The Iranians were aware that Greek soldiers were superior to their own, and the Achaemenian armies contained large numbers of Greek mercenaries. The Persian empire had long exploited the disunity of the Greek city-states by playing factions against each other and by assuming the role of mediator. Thus, when the empire's downfall came, it came less from internal decay than from the unification of the Greeks under Philip II of Macedon. Between 334 and 330 B.C., the small, cohesive, and energetic armies of his son Alexander shattered the large, loosely organized tribal levies of the Achaemenians. Alexander's conquests mark the beginning of the confluence of history and the Iranian national legend, which legitimated Alexander's achievement by giving him an Iranian father and a Macedonian mother. In reality, Alexander saw himself as both messenger of Hellenic culture and successor to the Achaemenian great kings, whose world empire he hoped to revitalize and expand with a mixture of Iranian and Greek ideals. He founded cities in Asia to act as centers of Greek culture, and he encouraged by example the intermarriage of his officers and soldiers with Iranian women to unite the two peoples and create a Greco-Iranian ruling class for his new empire.

Although many of Alexander's men were not happy with their imposed marriages, it seemed for a time that his idea of cultural union would succeed. After the struggles following Alexander's death in 323 B.C., Seleucus, the only one of Alexander's generals who did not repudiate his Iranian bride, became ruler of Babylon in 312. From there he reconquered most of Iran and established the Seleucid dynasty in the eastern portion of Alexander's empire. By the time of his death in 281, Seleucus had established his rule over Iran, northern Syria, and Asia Minor. In 305 he founded Seleucia-on-the-Tigris as his capital. This city and its neighbor Ctesiphon would eventually replace Babylon as the great Mesopotamian urban center and become the administrative capital of the Parthians and Sassanians. In the year

300, following his seizure of northern Syria, Seleucus founded a new capital there at Antioch-on-the-Orontes, which was closer than Seleucia to his dynasty's Macedonian homeland.

We know little about the complex interaction of Greek and Iranian peoples during this period. There were migrations of Greek settlers into former Achaemenian territory and migrations of Iranians into partially Hellenized regions of Asia Minor, such as Cappadocia. Within Iran, the Seleucids controlled the towns and main roads but left village affairs largely untouched. Greek cultural influence was weak outside the Hellenized towns and in areas such as Azarbaijan, which had submitted to Alexander without direct conquest. The Greek alphabet continued to be used for coinage and inscriptions, alongside the traditional Aramaic, for several centuries, but use of the Greek language was probably limited to an elite composed of Greek settlers, the offspring of Greek-Iranian marriages, and those Iranians educated in Greek culture. The great majority of the population must have remained Iranian in language and customs.

Greek cultural influence persisted in Iran under the successors of the Seleucids: an independent Macedonian dynasty in Bactria (modern Afghanistan) and the Parthian, or Arsacid, state. This latter, Iranian, dynasty first appeared in the middle of the third century B.C. Its founder, Arshak (Greek, Arsaces), was a chief of one of the nomadic tribes of northeastern Iran and ruler of the ancient satrapy of Parthava (Parthia), which lay east of the Caspian Sea. Arshak's successors, Tiridates (247–211) and Artabanus (ruled ca. 211–191), held Parthia and the neighboring province of Hyrcania (modern Mazanderan) against attacks by both Bactrian Greeks from the east and Seleucids from the west. The conquests of Mithridates I (ruled ca. 171–138) transformed Parthia from a provincial kingdom into a world empire. His successes in the west included the conquest of Media about 155 and the capture of Seleucia in 141. By the time of Mithridates's death, the Parthians controlled both the Iranian plateau and Mesopotamia. Failing to regain their lost provinces, the weakened Seleucids, under increasing pressure from Rome, Armenia, and Parthia, were reduced to ruling Syria and parts of Asia Minor.

After setbacks on both eastern and western frontiers, Mithridates II (ruled ca. 123–87)—the first Parthian ruler to use the old Achaemenian title "king of kings" on his coinage—restored a flourishing Parthian empire that extended from India to Armenia to the west bank of the Euphrates. In the east, Mithridates made peace with the Saka tribes and restored Parthian rule as far as the Oxus (Amu Darya) River and the frontiers of India.

In the middle of the first century, Parthia came into conflict with Rome, and after that time, classical authors viewed the world as being divided between these two great powers. Pompey's annexation of Syria in 64 B.C. had put an end to the feeble Seleucid monarchy and had brought Rome into direct contact with the Parthians. An expedition by the Roman triumvir Crassus into northern Mesopotamia ended with the famous Parthian victory at Carrhae in 53 B.C., but the Parthians' attack on Syria in 52–51 failed when they were unable to operate effectively against Roman settlements. In 36 B.C., the triumvir Mark Antony led a Roman army onto the Iranian plateau deep into Media Atropatane (Azarbaijan), but the loss of his baggage train and severe cold forced him to retreat with heavy casualties. During this century, the Romans established a defensive base against Parthia at the Euphrates, and contested territory east of the river changed hands according to the varying fortunes of the two powers. The Romans were never able to establish permanent control east of the Tigris, and the territory remained in Parthian hands despite occasional Roman invasions. Armenia was contested by Rome and Iran for centuries. In 63 A.D., the two empires signed a treaty whereby the Arsacid king of Armenia would receive his crown from the emperor Nero at Rome, an arrangement that preserved Armenia as an uneasy buffer between the two empires.

The Parthians had come to power in Iran as nomads and used the existing Seleucid and Achaemenian administrations to control the settled parts of their empire. Local, native dynasties continued to rule in southern Mesopotamia, Fars, Media Atropatane, and Elymais in the Zagros foothills of Khuzestan. Powerful noble families such as the Suren, Karen, and Mehran ruled their lands as independent monarchs and led their own armies. The little we know about the Parthian bureaucracy suggests that it had almost no fixed order of offices, titles, or provincial administration. Apparently the Parthians continued the Achaemenians' policies of social and religious toleration without the latter's centralized administration.

THE SASSANIANS

It was only a matter of time before one of the local revolts against Parthian rule succeeded in overthrowing the dynasty. The successful uprising finally came from the Sassanians of Fars, whose origins are obscured by propaganda, folktales, and heroic legends. The stories of the rise of the Sassanians resemble accounts of the emergence of earlier dynasties (notably the Achaemenian) in which a ruler rose from obscurity to claim a rightful throne. Sasan, namesake of this dynasty, was apparently a local lord of Fars and keeper of the shrine of the goddess Anahita at Istakhr, a religious center near Persepolis. His descendant (or son—the relationship is not specified in the soruces) Babak received the title "King of Fars" from the Parthian ruler Artabanus V (ruled 213–224). Babak and his sons Ardashir Babakan and Shahpur rebelled against their Parthian over-lords, and Ardashir, after the deaths of his father and brother, led a coalition that defeated the Parthians in 224. Although the chronology is uncertain, Ardashir assumed the title "king of kings" about 226 A.D. He and his son Shahpur I (ruled 240–272) established the Sassanian dynasty, which ruled Iran until the Arabs invaded in the seventh century.

The succession of titles in Shahpur's historic inscription from the *Ka'beh-ye-Zardosht*, a major Sassanian monument in Fars, records the expansion of this dynasty's power. This inscription calls Sasan a lord, Babak a king, Ardashir king of kings of Iran, and Shahpur king of kings of Iran and non-Iran. Ardashir and Shahpur reestablished the boundaries of the shattered Parthian state, received the allegiance of provincial rulers, and renewed the war against Rome. Shahpur scored remarkable military successes. He defeated the Roman emperor Gordian in 244 and extracted a heavy tribute from his successor. He captured and devastated the Syrian Antioch in 256 and defeated and captured the emperior Valerian in 260. Shahpur also made certain the world knew of his victories. He founded a new town, which he settled with Roman captives, named Veh Antiok Shahpur ("the better Antioch of Shahpur") in Khuzestan—the present-day Jondishapur. Shahpur commemorated his capture of Valerian in inscriptions and massive rock carvings throughout Fars, at Naqsh-e-Rostam, Bishapur, and Darab.

Although there were elements of continuity between the Par-thians and the early Sassanians—the use of Greek in inscriptions and the continuing role of the great feudal families, for example—the Sassanians introduced at least three important innovations:

1. A centralized administration to replace the Parthian system of independent governors and kings
2. The establishment of Zoroastrianism as a state religion in contrast to the eclectic, tolerant religious policies of earlier dynasties
3. The founding of new cities such as Firuzabad (which was south of modern-day Shiraz), Nishapur, Bishapur, and Jondi-shapur whereas the Parthian court had preserved its nomadic

"heroic" traditions and had been content to rule those cities already founded by the Greeks

These changes did not come easily. During the Sassanian period there was constant tension between official attempts to impose religious uniformity and traditional syncretism and tolerance. Nor could the Sassanians eliminate by decree the traditions of centuries of Parthian rule. Ardashir's court, for example, displayed the same lack of bureaucracy and fixed central authority that had been characteristic of the Parthian system.[15]

During the long reign of Shahpur II (309–379), the Roman emperor Constantine the Great (ruled 306–337) converted to Christianity and the rivalry between Rome and Iran became an ideological and religious struggle—with Armenia and the other borderlands as the battlefields. Shahpur's wars with the emperors Constantius II and Julian ended in 363 with a peace treaty that was advantageous to the Sassanians. On his eastern frontier, Shahpur successfully contained the threat of new nomads, called Chionites.[16] He strengthened the ruler's authority over the nobility and closely associated himself with the ceremonies and doctrines of the state religion. Shahpur's persecutions of Christians, Jews, and Manicheans continued until his death.

The long, turbulent period from the death of Shahpur II in 379 until the empire's recovery during the reign of Kavadh (modern Persian, Qobad, 488–531) saw the weakening of the Sassanian monarchy at the expense of the nobility, an extended famine, and constant warfare in the northeast with the Hephalites, who defeated and killed the emperor Peroz in 484. The Mazdakite movement appeared late in the fifth century and gained strength because of the unstable political climate of the time. Perhaps hoping to use Mazdakite ideology to restore royal supremacy over nobles and priests and to replenish his treasury with their property, the emperor Kavadh supported Mazdak and his movement until 524. In that year Kavadh, with the support of the crown prince Khosrow, executed Mazdak and many of his followers. Kavadh also renewed the war with the Byzantines, waging inconclusive campaigns from 502 to 506 and at the end of his reign against the emperor Justinian's famous general Belisarius.

The reign of Kavadh's son and successor, Khosrow I Anushiravan (ruled 531–579), marked the apogee of Sassanian wealth, power, and prestige. In Iranian national tradition, Khosrow I was *the* pre-Islamic monarch. Islamic writers have called him *al-adil* ("the just") and have portrayed his rule as the model of kingship. For the empire, his reign was a time of financial, administrative, and military reform; of prosperity, building, and the founding of new cities; of a revival of learning; and of territorial conquests. Many of the features Islamic writers portray as typically Sassanian were in reality the work of Khosrow I. His taxation reforms and bureaucratic reorganization survived into the Islamic period, and the latter was perhaps the model for the Abbasid system of *divans*, or ministries. In 540, Khosrow began a new series of wars with the Byzantines, and the Persians won some important victories, including the capture of Antioch in 540 and a large payment from Justinian to Khosrow in 544. Hostilities ended in 561 with a fifty-year peace treaty that reestablished the territorial status quo and granted freedom of trade and religion to Iranians and Byzantines in each other's territory. In the east, Khosrow joined the Turkish tribes of central Asia to finally eliminate the Hephalite federation. The allies divided the conquered territory and fixed the Oxus River as the frontier between Sassanians and Turks.

At Khosrow's death, the Sassanian empire was large, rich, and stagnant, and the reign of Khosrow II Parviz, who came to the throne with Byzantine help in 591, was the beginning of the end for Sassanian Iran. Famous for his wealth, extravagance, and love of luxury and music, his wars with Byzantium brought striking but temporary successes. Iranian forces took Jerusalem and carried off the true cross; they occupied Egypt for the first time in a thousand years; and Khosrow's armies laid siege to Constantinople itself. But these costly wars ended in disaster for the Sassanians. Their armies failed to take Constantinople, and the Byzantine emperor Heraclius led his forces through Armenia and Azarbaijan into the heart of Sassanian territory. Khosrow's generals assassinated him in 628 and made a humiliating peace with the Byzantines. A period of violent anarchy followed until the nobles raised Yazdagerd III (ruled 631–651) to the throne. This last Sassanian king ruled only a few years before he had to face attacks from new and powerful Arab invaders.

4

Islamic Iran

THE ARAB CONQUEST

The Arab conquest marks a crucial turning point in Iranian history: From then on, Iran gradually abandoned the Zoroastrian religion and the stratified social system of its imperial past for the egalitarianism of Islam. At first, the Arab conquest appeared to follow the familiar patterns of Iranian history: the overthrow of an enervated, decadent empire by the smaller, disciplined forces of an energtic conqueror; the collapse of organized resistance followed by the submission of major towns; the payment of tribute to the new rulers; and the establishment of garrison cities for the conquerors. In the past, similar events had brought only a change of rulers and had barely touched the lives of most Iranians, who continued an unchanging existence in the countryside.

In this case, however, the conquest had profound effects. Gradually, unevenly, Iran became part of an Islamic world state as Iranians on all social levels accepted the new religion and its values. By the ninth century A.D., Islam was predominant almost everywhere in Iran. Iranians must have had many reasons for changing their faith: Perhaps the local aristocrats (*dehqans*) accepted Islam to escape taxation as a subject people and to preserve their traditional social privileges; perhaps the common people accepted Islam to escape the rigidities of late Sassanian society—a society that was so stratified most Iranians no longer felt any loyalty to its traditions. The modest lives of early Muslim leaders and their military successes must have attracted many Iranians to the new religion. However it happened, the Islamic conquest altered the shape of Iranian society more deeply and completely than any historical event before or since.

Iran had had contacts with its Arab neighbors to the south and west centuries before the Islamic conquest. In the third century A.D., the Arabs of Palmyra in eastern Syria had defeated the emperor Shahpur I; later, the Sassanians had ruled a number of Arab vassal states, the most important of which was the kingdom of the Lakhmids of Hira, west of the Euphrates. Late in the sixth century, the emperor Khosrow II had brought the Lakhmid kingdom under direct Iranian rule and thus unwisely eliminated a buffer between his empire and its enemies to the west—first the Byzantines and later the Muslims from the Arabian Peninsula.

The Sassanian empire—without its Arab buffer states and demoralized by decades of war with Byzantium—collapsed quickly after the Muslims defeated the Sassanian armies at Qadisiya in Iraq (637) and at Nahavand in Iraq-e-Ajam (641). After these defeats, Sassanian central authority in Iran vanished, and the Arabs met only local resistance. Arab forces based in Bahrain and the Iraqi towns of Basra and Kufa gradually conquered Khuzestan, Fars, Azarbaijan, Kerman, and Khorasan; and many towns in these regions independently negotiated terms of surrender and tribute. Despite these easy conquests, the sources record frequent revolts in areas previously subdued, and serious uprisings against the Arabs occurred in Fars, the homeland of the Sassanian dynasty. Effective resistance continued longest in the remote southeast, the Caspian littoral (Tabarestan), and the Balkh region of eastern Khorasan (Tokharestan)—regions where local Iranian rulers had traditionally governed autonomous kingdoms.

Attracted by fertile land and opportunities for booty, large numbers of Arab tribesmen immigrated to Iran in the first centuries after the Arab invasion. At first, the conquerors controlled only the towns, major agricultural centers, and communications routes. Arabs from Kufa settled at Qom and Kashan, early strongholds of Shi'ism, and Arab warriors from Basra founded Shiraz in the fertile valley in Fars that they had used as a base of operations against Iranian rebels at Istakhr. In Khorasan, a base for plundering expeditions into central Asia, some Arabs settled in garrison towns and others preserved a nomadic way of life on the edge of the great deserts.[1]

Unprepared to govern a large, heterogeneous empire, the Arabs had to adopt the existing administrative and taxation systems in the conquered Sassanian territory. For their part, Iranians began accepting Islam from the first days of the Arab conquest. These early converts remained second-class citizens, however, attaching themselves as *mawali* ("clients") to the Arab tribes. Gradually the distinction between Arab and non-Arab Muslim became unimportant as most Iranians accepted Islam and became integrated into Islamic society.

Yet the Iranians who became Muslims remained Iranian, and the heroic legends and memories of the nation's imperial past survived among the converts to the new faith. When Arabic became the only written language—the language of religion, education, and culture—

it was alien to most Iranians but no more so than the intricate forms of written Sassanian Persian, a language reserved almost exclusively for priests and scribes. It was Persian that remained the vernacular of Islamic Iran (to reemerge as a written language in the tenth century at the independent courts of northeastern Iran—in Khorasan and Transoxiana).

Beginning in the late seventh century, Iran was the scene of anti-Arab and anti-Muslim messianic revolts based on mixtures of local popular beliefs with Manicheanism, Shi'ism, Mazdakism, and para-Zoroastrianism. Some of these revolts originated in the messianic propaganda surrounding the Abbasid rebellion in the mid-eighth century.[2] Although most of these movements originated in eastern Iran, far from the centers of Arab and Islamic rule, one of the most serious—the uprising of Babak Khorram-din—kept Azarbaijan in turmoil for over twenty years (817–838). Since our sources of information about these revolts are usually hostile, we know little about their origins or ideologies. Scholars have variously explained them as Iranian national reactions led by former Sassanian aristocrats, as popular uprisings against an alliance of Arab governors and Iranian feudal lords, and as a reassertion of Zoroastrianism against Islam.[3]

IRANIAN DYNASTIES

The unified Islamic state broke down in the ninth and tenth centuries. Regional ambitions and rivalries began to reassert themselves, first on the periphery and then at the center of the empire. A weakened Abbasid caliphate lost control of its eastern provinces to independent Iranian dynasties. The first of these, the Tahirids (820–872) ruled Khorasan in the name of the Abbasid caliphs. The Saffarids (867–903) arose in Sistan, where they had been warring against rebel schismatics, overthrew the Tahirids and seized Khorasan, Afghanistan, parts of Iraq-e-Ajam, and Kerman. In 876, Saffarid armies advanced to within fifty miles of Baghdad before being defeated by the caliph's forces.

Saffarid power lasted until its overthrow by the Samanids in the early tenth century, a dynasty that claimed descent from a noble Sassanian family. Beginning as governors of Samarkand under the Tahirids, the Samanids occupied Khorasan in 900. The founder of the Samanid state, Isma'il b. Ahmad (d. 907), established his capital at Bukhara and ruled most of northeastern Iran from there.[4]

In the late ninth century, the Saffarids began to encourage a renaissance of New Persian literature; and under the Samanids, New Persian, written in Arabic script, emerged as a mature literary language. The Samanid court patronized Persian poets, the most important being Rudaki (d. 940 or 941) and Daqiqi (d. ca. 975). Ferdowsi composed much of his national epic masterpiece, the *Shahnameh*, during the time the Samanids ruled in Khorasan. It has been suggested that the Samanid bureaucracy was bilingual, using Arabic for most formal matters (such as correspondence with the caliph) and Persian for less formal purposes.[5]

One of the most important Iranian dynasties of this period was the Shi'ite Buyids (Arabic, Buwaihids), mountain people from Deilam, the region between Gilan and the Iranian plateau. The Deilamites were famous as soldiers, and Buyeh, the ancestor of this dynasty, had served as a mercenary with both the Ziyarids—an independent Shi'ite dynasty of Mazarderan—and the Samanids. In the middle of the tenth century, Buyeh's three sons seized central and western Iran from local rulers and Abbasid governors. When the Buyids occupied Baghdad in 945, the caliph gave the three brothers the honorifics Emad al-Dowleh ("arm of the state"), Mu'ezz al-Dowleh ("strength of the state"), and Rokn al-Dowleh ("pillar of the state"). The Buyids reached the height of their power under Fana Khosrow (Azod al-Dowleh ["support of the state"], d. 983), the eldest son of Rokn al-Dowleh. They undertook substantial building projects, especially in Fars where the Ab-e-Rokni canal at Shiraz and the Band-e-Amir dam near Marvdasht still carry their founders' names. In Shiraz, Azod al-Dowleh also founded a library, a hospital (the famous Dar al-Shafa), and a suburb for his troops known as Fana Khosrow Gerd.

The Buyid conquest of Baghdad marked the restoration of an older geographic arrangement in which Mesopotamia, no longer an independent center of power, was again linked to western Iran and ruled as an extension of the Iranian plateau.[6] Within Iran, the Buyids shared power with two other dynasties: the Samanids in the northeast and the Ziyarids in Mazanderan. Each of these dynasties associated itself with the Iranian imperial tradition. The ninth-century Saffarids and Tahirids traced their descent to the epic heroes Jamshid and Rostam, respectively. In the tenth century, the Samanids, Ziyarids, and Buyids all claimed Sassanian royal ancestry. The Buyids went so far as to assume the ancient Iranian titles of "just king" (*al-malik al-adil*) and "king of kings" (*shahanshah*). The renaissance of the New Persian language, however, was limited to the eastern courts, and Arabic continued as the written language of Buyid-ruled western Iran.[7]

TURKISH RULE

Turkish soldiers had gradually entered Iran during the ninth and tenth centuries as caliphs and local rulers, mistrusting Arabs and Iranians, had competed to recruit Turkish *gholams* or *mamluks* (slave troops) into their personal armies and bodyguards. The Samanids, on the northeastern frontier of Iran-zamin, had brought many Turkish soldiers from central Asia, and the dynasties of western Iran, the Buyids and the warlords of Azarbaijan, had added Turkish troops (often cavalry) to their local forces of Kurds and Deilamites. As the power of the Iranian dynasties declined, their Turkish military commanders emerged as independent rulers. In this way, the Turkish Ghaznavids, whose founders Alp-Tegin (d. 963) and Sebuk-Tegin (d. 997) had begun their careers in Samanid military service, replaced their overlords as rulers of Khorasan.

The rise of these Turkish warlords in the late tenth century did not bring a large influx of Turks into the central Islamic world. The Turkish immigration and the accompanying changes in the ethnic map of Iran was an extended process, beginning with the Seljuq conquests in the eleventh century and continuing under later dynasties. These migrations had profound effects on the course of Iranian history: the introduction of new, Turkish-speaking nomadic tribes into the Iranian ethnic mosaic, the Turkification of about one-fourth of the Iranian population, and a thousand years of almost uninterrupted political and military supremacy by Altaic-speaking peoples.

The Seljuq Turks were a tribe of Sunni Muslim Turkomans from central Asia that overthrew the Samanid and Ghaznavid rulers in northeastern Iran in the middle of the eleventh century. Moving west, the Seljuqs ended the rule of the Buyids and of the numerous local warlords that ruled corners of the Iranian plateau. Their leader Toghril Beg captured Baghdad in 1055 and took the title *soltan*. In the West, the Seljuqs' most famous exploit was defeating the Byzantine emperor at Manzikert, in eastern Anatolia, in 1071.

In the wake of the Seljuq conquest came a mass immigration of Turkish tribes. The soltans attempted to minimize their nomadic followers' destruction of Iranian economic life by channeling them through Azarbaijan into Anatolia to fight against the Byzantines. In Iran, the Sunni Muslim Seljuqs adopted the existing administration and urban culture, which, in the east, were heavily Persian. In addition to Turkish immigration and political reunification, this period also brought a further strengthening of the New Persian language at the expense of Arabic and the growth of a rich Persian prose and poetry literature under Seljuq patronage. By overthrowing the Shi'ite Buyids and Ziyarids, the Seljuqs began a period of Sunni control in Iran that would last, with some local exceptions, until the sixteenth century.

Although the Turkish migrations of the eleventh and twelfth centuries disrupted the traditional Iranian economy by converting

farmland into pasture for nomads, these migrations did not destroy
the basic fabric of settled life on the plateau. Already Muslims when
they reached Iran, the Turks became part of an existing Islamic culture
composed of Iranian elements.[8] Most Turkish rulers saw the Iranian
cities and countryside as a source of wealth to be both exploited
and protected, even, if necessary, against other Turks who might turn
agricultural regions into pastureland. In their role as defenders of
(Sunni) Islam, these rulers endowed schools, mosques, and other
religious foundations. They also patronized Persian poets and artists
and supported the union intelligentsia, which administered their
empire and collected their taxes.

THE MONGOL CATACLYSM

A new and much more destructive invasion struck Iran from
the northeast in the early thirteenth century. The first Mongol armies
reached Transoxiana in 1220 A.D. Samarkand and Bukhara both fell
quickly, and the main Mongol forces under Changiz (Genghis) Khan
crossed the Oxus in 1221. The Khorasan cities of Marv, Nishapur,
and Herat were taken that same year and their entire populations
were massacred. Contemporary sources (perhaps exaggerating) estimated that the Mongols killed 700,000 at Marv and 600,000 in a
single quarter of Herat.[9] After Changiz's death in 1227, his successors
continued his conquests until, by 1250, they held all of Iran except
Kerman, Fars, Lorestan, and isolated strongholds of the heretical
Isma'ilis. In 1256, Hulagu Khan (d. 1265) returned to Iran with the
main Mongol armies. During this expedition he destroyed the Isma'ili
fortresses, received the submission of the remaining Turkish warlords,
and, in 1258, sacked Baghdad and murdered the last Abbasid caliph.
Hulagu and his descendants remained in Iran, governing with the
title Il-Khan.

Under the Mongols, a non-Muslim dynasty ruled Iran for the
first time in six centuries. The new rulers were generally indifferent
to religious matters, and both Christians and Jews advanced in the
Il-Khanid service as the Mongols ignored or destroyed the existing
Islamic social system. The Mongols, unlike the Turks, were not Muslims
when they entered Iran, and the Mongol rulers did not convert to
Islam until almost a century after Changiz's first invasion. Their
nomadic aristocracy despised Islamic culture and the traditions of
settled Iranian life, and after the initial destruction and massacres,
most Mongol officials and rulers took only a predatory interest in
their subjects. Their rule destroyed agriculture and trade, the bases
of the Iranian economy, and many regions of Iran have never recovered

from Mongol devastation and rapacity. Cities reverted to villages, villages reverted to desert, and as revenue declined, the Mongols multiplied taxes to squeeze every drop of wealth from their conquered territory.

Ghazan Khan (ruled 1295–1304) was the first Muslim among the Il-Khans, and he and his successors attempted to revive the crippled Iranian economy by checking the uncontrolled looting by Mongol officials. Although trade flourished at the Il-Khanid capitals of Tabriz and Maragheh, the rulers could not repair the widespread economic ruin caused by overtaxation, political anarchy, and the migration of Turkish and Mongol tribes in the wake of conquering armies.

The death of the last Il-Khan, Abu Sa'id Bahador in 1335 was followed by murderous civil strife and the rapid collapse of the Il-Khanid state. By the middle of the fourteenth century, Il-Khanid Iran had disintegrated into five small kingdoms:

1. The Jalayerids (or Ilkanids) in Iraq and Azarbaijan
2. The Inju in Fars and Isfahan
3. The Muzaffarids in Yazd and Kerman
4. The Sarbedarids in the Sabzevar region west of Nishapur in Khorasan
5. The Kurts in Herat

Ironically, this time of political instability and fragmentation was also a brilliant age for Persian culture. Poets, historians, painters, and calligraphers all created superb works of art during the thirteenth and fourteenth centuries. Although economic hardships and the restricted income of the small courts limited royal patronage of large-scale construction, the less costly arts flourished during this period of anarchy and misrule. Hafez of Shiraz (d. 1389) composed the best-known poetic masterpieces of this period, but there were other figures— such as Khwaju Kermani, Salman Savaji, and the satirist Obeid Zakani—who are in the first rank of Persian poets. The reasons for this artistic flowering amid political disaster are unclear. Perhaps the lack of a central authority to enforce religious orthodoxy encouraged literary creativity, and perhaps the existence of numerous, warring princes made it possible for writers and artists who were unsuccessful at one court to find patronage with a rival prince.[10] However it happened, the rulers during this period, such as Abu Eshaq Inju of Shiraz, were able to combine brutality and misrule with patronage of brilliant artistic creations.

THE SAFAVIDS

The history of Iran as a united, independent Shi'a nation begins with the Safavid dynasty. The Safavid kings laid the foundations of modern Iran by making Twelver Shi'ism, until then a minority faith, the state religion and by reuniting Iran-zamin, a territory that for centuries had been either ruled from outside as part of a larger empire (e.g., the Abbasid caliphate centered in Mesopotamia) or divided among warlords such as Buyids, Samanids, and Ziyarids.

Origins

The origin of the Safavids is obscure. Sheikh Safi al-Din (1252–1334) founded the Safaviyyeh sufi order at Ardabil in eastern Azarbaijan. According to official Safavid geneologies, Safi al-Din was a descendant of Musa Kazem, seventh Imam of the Shi'a. Most scholars, however, dismiss this geneology as Safavid propaganda, and recent research suggests that the family's Kurdish ancestors migrated to Azarbaijan in the eleventh century.[11] Whatever his origins, Sheikh Safi al-Din himself was a Turkish-speaking Sunni. His descendant Joneid (ruled 1447–1456) apparently adopted militant Shi'ism from the armed Turkomans of eastern Anatolia, and the Safavid mystic order gradually became a disciplined, religious-military organization ruling the Ardabil region. Under the leadership of Joneid and Heidar (ruled 1456–1488), the Safavids fought the Black Sheep (Qara Qoyunlu) Turkomans of Anatolia and the Shirvanshahs, a local dynasty of the eastern Caucasus. Heidar's followers adopted a distinctive red headgear, which earned them the (originally pejorative) name of qizilbash, ("redheads").

Heidar's son Isma'il was fourteen years old when he assumed leadership of the qizilbash in 1499. In 1501, Isma'il, having defeated the Shirvanshah and the White Sheep (Aq Qoyunlu) Turkoman leader Alvand, occupied southern Azarbaijan and was crowned Shahanshah-e-Iran at Tabriz. There he declared Twelver Shi'ism the state religion and ordered a ritual cursing of the first three caliphs. Between 1502 and 1509, most of western Iran fell to Isma'il, and in 1510, his victory over the Uzbeks extended Safavid rule to Khorasan and the former Timurid state at Herat.

At first, Shah Isma'il must have appeared as just another successful Turkish adventurer motivated by plunder and with a talent for military organization. To these familiar elements, however, the Safavids added religious ideology, the discipline of the qizilbash warriors, and their extreme loyalty to the sheikh and his doctrines. Shah Isma'il's success was the product of centuries of propaganda by a well-organized network of teachers, spiritual advisers, and military leaders. The story of the rise of the Safavids also recalls the ancient traditions of the pre-Islamic Iranian dynasties: the distant ancestor, the royal pedigree, the king who emerges from hiding to defeat his enemies, and the seven allied tribes who form the core of royal support. Beyond their military success, the Safavid rulers laid claim to three important sources of authority: the traditional royal farr of the great Iranian kings; the power of the hidden Imam of the Shi'a; and the prestige of the sufi *morshed-e-kamel*, the perfect spiritual leader of the qizilbash.

Safavids and Shi'ism

The Safavids made Shi'ism part of the Iranian national identity. The relationship between Iran and Shi'ism is complex, and modern ideas of nationalism have sometimes distorted the connection. There was originally no inherent link between being Iranian and being Shi'ite. Shi'ism first came to Iran from Iraq as an Arab movement, and its original Iranian strongholds were the settlements of Arab troops and refugees from the southern Iraqi town of Kufa. Before the arrival of the Safavids, however, the majority of Iranians were Sunni. Shi'ism predominated in Gilan, Mazanderan, and in some of the secondary towns of Iraq-e-Ajam, such as Qom, Kashan, Tafresh, and Nahavand. Sunnism predominated in such major cities as Isfahan, Shiraz, and Tabriz.

We know little about the precise form and extent of Shi'ism in pre-Safavid Iran as the line between moderate Shi'ism and Sunnism was not always clearly drawn. In the ninth century, for example, the Abbasid caliph Ma'mun designated the eighth Shi'a Imam, Reza b. Musa Kazem, as his successor. In the thirteenth century, the Sunni rulers of Fars honored and generously supported the shrine of Imam Reza's brother Ahmad (Shah-e-Cheragh) in Shiraz. There is evidence that popular Shi'ite beliefs existed among peasants and urban workers, groups that receive little attention in the sources. Shi'ite dynasties—such as the Buyids, Sarbedarids, and Black Sheep Turkomans—had ruled parts of Iran before the Safavids, but none had attempted to make Shi'ism the state religion of a Sunni country.

We likewise know little about how most of the Iranian people converted to Shi'ism. Although there was opposition to the compulsory change of religion, especially among the Sunni *ulema*—the religious scholars and officials—by the middle of the eighteenth century most of Iran had apparently accepted Shi'ism, although areas far from central government control—such as Kurdestan, Baluchestan, the garmsirat of Fars, and the Persian Gulf coast—remained predominantly Sunni. In Shah Isma'il's time, Shi'a doctrines were not well-known in Iran, and the Safavids had to bring theological teachers, scholars, and books from Syria and Bahrain. Although the original Shi'ism of the qizilbash was primitive, extremist, and emphasized the semidivine nature of the leader, some aspects of the faith—the discipline and organization of the sufi order and the veneration of Ali and his family—were already familiar to Sunni Iranians. While hiding from enemies in Gilan (1494–1499), the young Isma'il may have learned Twelver Shi'a doctrines from his tutor, the learned Sheikh Shams al-Din Mohammad Lahiji. Whether from faith or politics, Isma'il made his state religion, not the extremist beliefs of the qizilbash, but a moderate form of Shi'ism that was more familiar and acceptable to orthodox believers.

Imposing Shi'ism as the Safavid state religion was not sufficient to create an Iranian nation, but Isma'il's action did create a religious distinction that reinforced the political differences between the Safavids in Iran and their Sunni neighbors, the Ottomans to the west and the Uzbeks to the east. The historian Alessandro Bausani believes that this Arab creed, imposed by Turkish tribesmen, was to be the salvation of the Iranian identity.

> The new doctrine, which had no philosophical connection whatever with the Persians as a people or a nation, nevertheless provided a platform from which they were able to defend themselves from losing their identity in an all-absorbing Islam, and in particular, since the nearest representatives of Muslim Sunnism were the Turks, from being engulfed in the Turkish ocean. What we have in fact is a Persian variation . . . of Islamic culture whose origins date from the Safavid period.[12]

Prosperity and Collapse

Shah Abbas I (the Great, ruled 1587–1628) brought Safavid power to its height. His reign overlapped the reigns of other powerful monarchs in both Asia and Europe: Queen Elizabeth I in England, Philip II in Spain, and Akbar the Great in Moghul India. Abbas defeated the Uzbeks and restored Safavid authority in Herat and Qandahar (now in present-day Afghanistan); in 1603 he ended the Ottomans' occupation of Tabriz and expelled them from Azerbaijan, and he finally curbed the power of the qizilbash praetorian guard by enlisting Christian troops from the Caucasus and by strengthening the urban, Persian bureaucracy. His most enduring achievement, however, was the establishment of his capital at Isfahan. Ottoman pressure had forced his predecessor Tahmasp I (ruled 1524–1576) to move the capital from Tabriz to Qazvin (about 75 miles west of

Teheran), but in 1598 Abbas moved his capital to Isfahan, where he and his successors built superb bridges, markets, palaces, schools, and mosques. Isfahan today is still the finest city in Iran thanks to Safavid town planning.

The Safavid period was a highly creative time for Persian art—especially miniatures, metalwork, ceramics, carpets, and textiles. The "art of the book" reached its peak during the reign of Tahmasp I, with the completion of the magnificent *King's Book of Kings* (*Shahnameh-ye-Tahmaspi*), which contains 250 miniature paintings and over 50,000 verses in superb calligraphy. Shah Abbas made textile and carpet weaving national industries by establishing workshops that produced exquisite pieces for export to Europe, Turkey, and India.

The Safavids' decline, long hidden behind a facade of prosperity, began after the death of Shah Abbas. In the early eighteenth century, the combination of ineffective rulers, a detriorating economy, and religious fanaticism would prove fatal to the Safavids. Their last shah, Soltan Hosein (ruled 1694–1722), was a weak, pleasure-loving religious fanatic, who, under the influence of the theologian M. Baqer Majlesi, persecuted the numerous Sunnis of the empire. Years of neglect and poor morale had so undermined the Safavid military that when Mir Mahmud, leader of the Ghilzai Afghans of Qandahar, revolted in 1709, Shah Soltan Hosein had no reliable forces to oppose him. In 1722, Mir Mahmud, with only 20,000 troops, captured Isfahan after a six-months' siege in which an estimated 80,000 people died of disease or starvation.

The Afghans were able to capture Isfahan and defeat whatever feeble Safavid resistance they met, but they could not control the entire country. Iran became a battlefield for rival looters in a long civil war between the Afghan leader Ashraf (who had murdered Mir Mahmud) and the energetic Nader Khan Afshar, who championed the cause of the nominal Safavid ruler. In 1724, Ottomans and Russians took advantage of Iran's helplessness to sign a treaty that divided the country's northwestern provinces between them. Russian forces landed in Gilan and Baku, but withdrew after the death of Czar Peter the Great in 1725. In 1726, the Ottomans invaded northwestern Iran but were defeated by the Afghans near Hamadan.

Nader Khan gradually extended his control over the entire country. He expelled Afghan and Ottoman invaders, reconquered former Safavid provinces in the Caucasus, and in 1736 finally ended the fiction of Safavid rule and took the title Nader Shah. Continuing his conquests, he took Qandahar in 1738, then invaded northern India and sacked Delhi the next year. Nader's successes were purely military and brought no benefits to the suffering Iranian population.

Instead, the heavy taxes he extracted to support his campaigns depopulated Iranian cities and ruined the countryside. It is estimated that Iran lost over half of its population during this disastrous eighteenth century.

Nader's assassination in 1744 was followed by a three-sided struggle among the Turkish Qajars in Mazanderan, Azad Khan in Azarbaijan, and Karim Khan Zand in Fars. By 1760, Karim Khan had defeated both rivals, and until his death in 1779, he ruled most of present Iran except Khorasan, where the blind Shahrokh, son of Nader, continued to reign. Karim Khan never took the title "shah"; instead he ruled with the old Safavid title *vakil* ("deputy") as the regent of a supposed grandson of Shah Soltan Hosein. In southern Iran, Karim Khan's rule brought a brief respite from the continuing anarchy. He attempted to revive agriculture and crafts there and endowed Shiraz with a fine mosque, bazaar, and caravansary.

During the chaos of the eighteenth century, the position of the religious classes underwent a change that would profoundly affect the course of Iranian history. The early Safavid leaders—both before and after Isma'il's accession—had kept personal control over religious affairs, and because their original movement had combined religious, military, and political elements, the first Safavid officials, often appointed from among the qizilbash, exercised authority in all three areas. Following Isma'il's coronation in 1501, the Safavids began entrusting religious affairs to a distinct class of scholars and jurists, the ulema, first Arab and later Iranian. At first the shah dominated these religious officials, by controlling their appointments and finances, and remained the charismatic, mystic leader of the qizilbash warriors. Gradually, however, the Shi'a ulema achieved a financial and political independence that made them rulers of a virtual state-within-a-state that claimed an authority higher than the shah's and competed with him for the loyalty of the Iranian population.

The ulema built the economic base of their independence through control of religious endowments (*owqaf*) and religious taxes (*khoms* and *zakat*). On the political side, as early as the reign of Shah Abbas I, members of the ulema began to claim that the shah might not be the legitimate trustee of the hidden Imam's powers. In the eighteenth century, some of the ulema made this position more explicit, claiming that they, in the absence of the Imam, had the exclusive right to exercise temporal power in his name—or at least the right to bestow that power on whomever they believed best qualified to execute the Imam's trust. The civil wars of the eighteenth century and Nader Shah's attempts to reconcile Sunni and Shi'a Islam drove many religious leaders out of Iran to settle near the Shi'a shrines (*atabat*) in Iraq. There, free of Iranian government political control, they continued to press their claim to temporal authority in the Imam's name.

The ulema gained further strength by the outcome of a doctrinal dispute between the *akhbari* and *osuli* schools of Shi'a thought. Although details of this technical dispute need not concern us here, the victory of the osulis added a doctrinal basis to the ulema's claim to an authority higher than that of the shah. The osuli position established religious scholars, known as *mojtaheds*, not only as authoritative interpreters of divine law but also as qualified sources of imitation (*maraje'-e-taqlid*) whom every Shi'a believer below the rank of mojtahed was bound to follow. This doctrine meant that on religious matters, and on political matters involving religion, the opinions of a mojtahed carried more weight in the eyes of his followers than the decrees of a king unqualified to interpret the will of the hidden Imam. The doctrine also made the king a virtual usurper by placing his actions outside the framework of religious legitimacy and by making the ulema the trustees of the only legitimate temporal power—that of the hidden Imam.

THE QAJARS

The eunuch Agha Mohammad Khan Qajar had lived in Shiraz as a hostage after Karim Khan had defeated his father. When Karim Khan died in 1779, Agha Mohammad fled Shiraz and returned to his own people in Mazanderan. There he began an energetic political and military campaign against the Zands, which ended at Kerman with the defeat and death of their last prince, Lotf Ali Khan, in 1794. After capturing that city, Agha Mohammad ordered his soldiers to blind 20,000 Kermanis as a vicious revenge for their support of his rival. He established his capital near the Qajar tribal homeland at Teheran, until then an insignificant village near the ancient town of Rey. Having consolidated his power inside Iran, in 1795 Agha Mohammad led a campaign into the Caucasus that ended in the capture and destruction of Tiflis. In 1796, he crowned himself shahanshah of Iran, but he was assassinated the next year while on campaign in Transcaucasia.

Agha Mohammad founded the Qajar dynasty, which lasted until 1925, but the years of this dynasty's rule were not fortunate for Iran. These were years of political weakness, humiliating military and diplomatic defeats, loss of territory, and economic stagnation. European power was growing in Asia, and against that power the Iranians could maintain only a precarious and nominal independence. Internally,

Iran was shaken by the uprisings and violent persecutions of the members of a religious movement, by tobacco concession protests, and, early in the twentieth century, by a constitutional movement. The blatant interference of foreigners in Iranian affairs also turned the country, although officially neutral, into a World War I battlefield for Turks, Russians, British, and Germans. The Qajar period was also a time of reform movements, all seeking some means of placing Iran on an equal footing with the nations of Europe. Some reformers believed Iran's salvation lay in a new political system—such as liberal democracy, constitutionalism, or a rejuvenated Islam. Others emphasized strictly technical improvements—with the help of foreign expertise—in military science, health, education, and transportation.

Early in the nineteenth century, the Russians administered two disastrous military defeats to the Iranians, which supplied clear proof of Qajar weakness. Following the Russian occupation of Georgia in 1801, Iran (called Persia in European sources) went to war to regain its Caucasian possessions, but in the 1813 treaty of Golestan, Iran had to renounce its claims to Georgia, Darband, Ganjeh, and Baku. The provision of this treaty (article 5) by which Russia recognized Abbas Mirza as the rightful heir to the Qajar throne gave Russia the implicit right to intervene in Iran's internal and dynastic affairs. The second Russo-Persian war (1825–1828) ended with the treaty of Turkmanchai, which made Iran officially subordinate to Russia until the Bolshevik revolution. In this treaty, Iran ceded Armenia and northern Azarbaijan (Nakhchevan) to Russia and abandoned its right to maintain a navy on the Caspian Sea. Iran also had to pay a heavy war indemnity, limit duty on Russian goods to 5 percent, and grant Russian merchants extensive and unprecedented extraterritorial privileges or "capitulations."

The Babi Movement

In addition to external difficulties, the Babi religious movement, which first appeared during the reign of Mohammad Shah (ruled 1834–1848), added to Iran's domestic turmoil. Babism originated in the beliefs of the Sheikhi movement within Shi'a Islam, named for its founder Shiekh Ahmad Ahsa'i (1754–1826). Sheikhism preached the existence of a living, human Bab, or gate, who was capable of communicating with the hidden Imam. In 1844, the young Seyyed Ali Mohammad proclaimed himself the Bab in Shiraz. Gathering a following of Sheikhis, bazaar merchants, and some of the lower ulema, he gradually expanded his claims to announce that he was the promised Imam himself and a prophet with a new message (the Bayan) to supersede the Quran. The Bab was attacked as a heretic, but his following grew as he began preaching against both the civil and the religious authorities. In 1847, the government arrested the Bab and imprisoned him in Azarbaijan.

Following the death of Mohammad Shah, Babi uprisings broke out in Yazd, Neiriz (in Fars), Zanjan (in Azarbaijan), and Mazanderan. The Qajars put down these revolts with great difficulty between 1848 and 1851 and, in 1850, executed the Bab himself at Tabriz. After a group of Babis made an unsuccessful attempt to assassinate the young Naser al-Din Shah in 1852, the authorities launched new and bloody persecutions of the group. This pressure finally forced the Babi community into hiding and into exile in Ottoman territory. After the death of the Bab and the subsequent persecutions, most Babis became followers of his disciple Baha'ullah, who, in 1863, declared himself the new prophet whose appearance the Bab had predicted. Baha'ullah lived at Acre in Palestine until his death in 1892, and in his teachings and writings, he transformed the original messianic and radical Babi message into the universal, pacifist doctrines of the modern Baha'i faith.[13]

Iran under the Qajars somehow lost its energy and creativity. The profound technological and social changes in the West during the nineteenth century had opened a vast gap between Iran and Europe, and by the end of the century Iran had become, in relation to Europe, a backward country that was too weak and poor to resist the encroachments of foreign powers, especially czarist Russia. Lacking leadership, military force, or economic strength, Iran tried to use European rivalries—those of Russia and Britain in particular—to maintain at least nominal independence. Internally, the Qajars were unable to create an effective military or a centralized state bureaucracy. The contradiction between secular and religious power that had appeared during Safavid times continued under the Qajars. Although the ruler called himself "the shadow of God," there was no way to accommodate him within the Shi'a system of faith. For many of the ulema, a Shi'a state was a contradiction in terms. The monarch had two choices: He could either become the follower of a mojtahed, effectively surrendering royal authority and becoming merely the executor of clerical power, or he could ignore religious direction and alienate himself from clerical support.[14]

The Qajars' collection of magnificent titles and their elaborate court ceremonies could not hide the country's decay and weakness. The dynasty remained in power thanks to Anglo-Russian rivalry and by manipulating the numerous communal conflicts within Iranian society. The Qajars presented themselves as the sole barrier between their subjects and the country's ever-simmering anarchy. The Qajars set Kurd against Turk, Shi'a against Sunni, and Muslim against Jew, Christian, or Baha'i. When there were no religious or ethnic differences to manipulate, the rulers set tribal faction against tribal faction and town neighborhood against town neighborhood. Having no effective military force, the Qajars had little authority in the provinces, and circumstances forced them to share power with oligarchies of landlords, clergymen, bazaar merchants, and tribal leaders. Although the Qajars did put down the Babi uprisings and could occasionally act against local rebels or bandits, they were almost powerless against determined and united opposition, especially from among the ulema, the *bazaris* ("bazaar merchants") or the volatile urban mobs—the last always ready to riot over increases in basic food prices.

In earlier times, internal or external enemies would have brought down these weak rulers. This time, however, no Ardashir, Changiz, or Mir Mahmud arose to sweep away the Qajars' decrepit structure. The neighboring Ottoman Empire had become the "sick man of Europe," and the Russians controlled most of central Asia, the traditional homeland of Iran's conquerors. The rival British and Russians feared that radical change inside Iran would somehow increase the other's influence, and both powers were willing to keep the Qajars on the throne as nominal rulers of an impotent Iranian state.

Within Iran, popular hostility toward the Qajars intensified toward the end of the nineteenth century. Disturbances previously limited to some local grievance became large-scale national protests, particularly against the sale of economic concessions to foreigners under the guise of "development." These shady schemes produced ready cash for the financially strapped shah and his associates, wealth for European promoters, and unemployment for many Iranians.[15] In 1891–1892, this resentment culminated in effective and well-organized opposition to the fifty-year monopoly of distribution and export of tobacco—a concession the shah had sold to an Englishman. The opposition to this agreement provoked a general strike in the major urban bazaars and a nationwide consumer boycott of tobacco. The united opposition of leading mojtaheds, the secular intelligentsia, and the Russians (who resented such a concession to an Englishman) forced Naser al-Din Shah to cancel the agreement. The cancellation also created Iran's first foreign debt, of £500,000, borrowed from a British-owned bank to pay exorbitant compensation to the concessionaires.

Constitutional Revolution

The united opposition to the tobacco concession foreshadowed the alliance that supported the Iranian constitutional movement of

1906–1911. In 1896, a follower of the famous pan-Islamic agitator Jamal al-Din Afghani (Asadabadi) assassinated Naser al-Din Shah. His successor, Mozaffar al-Din Shah (ruled 1896–1907) was an easy-going and incompetent invalid, unable to control the growing discontent and revolutionary sentiment. In order to pay for his medical trips to Europe and to meet government expenses, the shah borrowed money from European (mostly Russian) banks in return for economic and political concessions such as road building, customs collection, and preferential tariffs. On the eve of the constitutional revolution, foreigners held almost total control of Iran's administration. The British had oil rights in the south; a Belgian, the unpopular M. Naus, was minister of customs and de facto minister of finance; and Russian officers commanded the Persian Cossack Brigade, the only effective armed force in the country.

The troubles of imperial Russia in the early twentieth century also affected Iran. Many Iranians rejoiced at Russia's defeat by Japan in 1904–1905, believing that the defeat would reverse the apparently irresistible tide of Russian imperialism in Asia. In 1905, revolutionary uprisings inside Russia also raised Iranians' hopes for a loosening of czarist political and economic pressures on their country, and revolutionary ideas spilled across the Iranian border from Russia, carried by refugees who had been labor organizers among Azarbaijanis in the Baku oil fields. In 1904, Iranians founded the Social Democratic party of Iran at Baku, and a "secret center" of young radicals in Tabriz circulated the party program.[16]

The heart of the Iranian constitutional movement, however, lay not in the small group of young radicals influenced by European revolutionary thought, but among the middle class of the bazaars and the mosques, people firmly attached to Iranian religious and social traditions. In 1905, an economic crisis threatened this group. A cholera epidemic, revolutionary turmoil inside Russia, and the Russo-Japanese war had all disrupted trade in northern Iran, raised food prices, and lowered government revenues from customs duties. A series of public protests against worsening economic conditions culminated in July 1906 with a general strike and 14,000 bazaris took refuge in the gardens of the British legation in Teheran. In August, the shah capitulated to the strikers' demands and signed a proclamation calling for a Constituent National Assembly.

The first Iranian parliament, the Majles, dominated by the traditional middle classes, met in October 1906 and drew up the constitution, or "fundamental laws." The dying Mozaffar al-Din Shah signed the laws in December of that same year, and in the following year, the new monarch, Mohammad Ali Shah, yielded to pressure

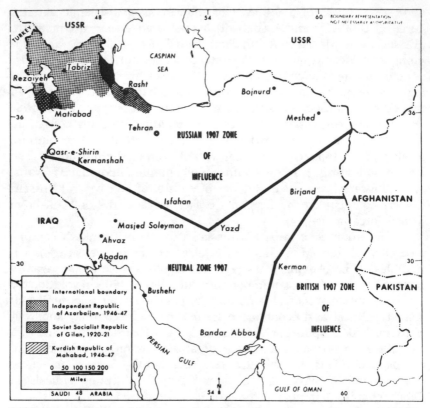

MAP 4.1 Spheres of foreign influence and autonomy movements, 1907–1947. (Reproduced courtesy of Richard F. Nyrop, ed., *Iran: A Country Study* [Washington, D.C.: American University Foreign Area Studies, 1978], p. 50)

and ratified a group of supplementary fundamental laws. These two sets of laws became the Iranian constitution of 1906.

But a constitutional system failed to take hold in Iran. Few ordinary citizens had any appreciation of the meaning of *mashruteh* ("constitution"), and many of the clergy argued that mashruteh should in reality by *mashru'eh* ("religious legislation"). A hostile coalition of Russians, shah, and some clergy—and disunity among the constitutionalists inside and outside parliament—overwhelmed the well-intentioned but precarious new regime.

The Anglo-Russian agreement of 1907 dealt another blow to the hopes of Iranian reformers. Many Iranians saw this agreement, which divided Iran into unequal zones of Russian and British influence (and a neutral zone), as a betrayal of the constitutional movement by its former British supporters. Map 4.1 shows the boundaries established by this agreement. Despite the agreement's commitment to the "independence and integrity of Persia," most Iranians believed that the British, whose representatives had constantly lectured them on public probity, legality, and constitutionalism, had sacrificed Iran for the sake of reaching an understanding with autocratic Russia. Discussing the effect of this agreement on Anglo-Persian friendship, Cecil Spring-Rice, the British minister in Teheran, wrote, in a letter that would again be relevant in a different setting seventy-two years later:

> They have thrown a stone into the windows here and left me to face the policeman. Neither Nicolson [British Ambassador to St. Petersburg] nor the F.O. informed me that the agreement was signed till three days after it had been published here. This was, I suppose, a sign that the Persian public opinion was not to be considered.[17]

The constitutionalists had no more success than the shah in controlling Iran. Russian hostility, British indecision, and internal Iranian divisions made their task impossible. The Russians ignored British representations and treated their zone of influence as occupied territory. In 1911, they forced the Iranians to dismiss Morgan Shuster, an American hired by the constitutional government as treasurer-general. In 1911–1912, belligerent Russian consuls and troop commanders controlled Tabriz, Rasht, Anzali, Mashhad, and other parts of northern Iran. Although British intervention in the south was less overt, British officials there dealt directly with Arab, Baluchi, and Bakhtiyari tribal leaders as though the Iranian government in Teheran did not exist.

Although Iran declared its neutrality at the beginning of World War I, it soon became a battleground of British, Russian, and Turkish armies. The nationalists organized a pro-German Committee of National Resistance, which established itself at Qom. In 1915, when Russian forces occupied that city, the committee fled to Kermanshah, where it operated under Turkish protection until the British arrived in 1916. In the south, the German agent Wassmuss organized tribal resistance to seriously trouble the British in Fars. Major Percy Sykes created a force of 5,000 called the South Persia Rifles to try and bring southern Iran under British control. In 1915, the British and Russians completed their unofficial partition of Iran. In return for agreeing to the future Russian occupation of Constantinople, the British were allowed to extend their influence into the Persian neutral zone, and the British also agreed to grant Russia virtually unlimited freedom of action (short of formal annexation) in northern Iran.

Only the 1917 Bolshevik revolution and subsequent collapse of Russian power in northern Iran halted the course of events leading to permanent partition. The new Bolshevik government renounced czarist privileges and concessions in Iran, and the British tried to maintain what control they could in the chaos that followed the war. In 1919, they signed an agreement with a government headed by Vosuq al-Dowleh that would have made Iran an unofficial British protectorate, much like the Arab states of the Persian Gulf. In the proposed treaty, Britain promised various forms of financial and technical assistance in return for a monopoly of arms supply and military and administrative advisers. Local dissident groups, especially the Democrats in Azarbaijan and the Jangalis in Gilan, vehemently opposed the treaty and threatened rebellion and secession. The Soviet government joined the denunciations and sent military units to Gilan (see Map 4.1) to support local opposition to Vosuq's government in Teheran and to oppose British forces that were assisting anti-Soviet groups in the Caucasus.

Faced with this hostility, the Iranian parliament never ratified the Anglo-Persian treaty. In 1921, the Iranians and Soviets signed a friendship treaty that canceled Iran's czarist debts and annulled almost all imperial concessions. For its part, Iran guaranteed that it would not allow its territory to be used for attacks against the Soviet Union. With this assurance, the Soviets withdrew their forces from Gilan. Left to its fate, the divided Jangali movement finally collapsed in December 1921 before the attacks of central government forces led by Reza Khan, Iran's new military strongman.

5

Pahlavis and Ayatollahs

The history of Iran since 1921 still arouses intense emotions, and both the history and the historians of this period have often fallen victim to violent polemic and fierce political controversy. There has been little spirit of compromise. Competing in a climate of lingering hatred, rivals have waged wars of extermination on each other's persons, works, and values. For example, the Pahlavis, who came to power in 1925, bulldozed streets through the middle of mosques, bazaars, and old quarters to show their contempt for the Islamic components of Iranian tradition. The current Islamic republican regime has retaliated by attacking its predecessors' works with a vicious single-mindedness. In early 1979, for example, the new regime executed an elderly senator for having taken an active role in Reza Khan's treacherous coup d'etat of 1921. The revolutionary government has persecuted its opponents as God's enemies and has condemened the entire Pahlavi system as *taghuti,* i.e., outside the boundaries of humanity and allied with pagan forces in rebellion against divine commands.[1]

Iran has been trying to regain control of its own affairs since the early twentieth century—control it had gradually lost to foreigners over the previous 100 years—and Iran's recent history has been a continuous struggle to make Iranians masters in their own house. The unanswered questions remain: Which masters and what kind of house? This bitter contest has claimed many victims. It has set Iranian against foreigner, foreigner against foreigner, and, tragically, Iranian against Iranian in complex strife among ambitious individuals and factions with irreconcilable visions of their country's future.

Portions of this chapter previously appeared in the *Foreign Service Journal* and are used here with permission.

REZA SHAH TAKES POWER

Fifteen years of civil war and foreign invasion had followed the constitutional revolution of 1906, a movement that failed to establish the rule of law or to unify the country because its supporters were too weak and divided to resist foreign pressure or to control the centrifugal forces within Iranian society. If Iran's history were a guide, this time of weakness and chaos, like earlier periods of turmoil, would lead to one of the following:

1. Invasion and conquest by more-vigorous and well-organized outside forces
2. Disintegration into small, feudal states ruled by warlords
3. Unification under a military leader who, beginning with a tribal or regional following, would subdue his rivals and crown himself king of kings

No foreign invader threatened Iran in 1921: Turkey and Russia were in confusion, and the British attempts to extend their influence were limited to diplomatic means. If Iran were to avoid disintegration, someone had to restore order from within, unify the country, and end the long period of anarchy.

In 1921, there were three important candidates for national leadership: Kuchek Khan, the Jangali leader in Gilan; the popular Col. Mohammad Taqi Khan Pesyan, gendarmerie commander in Khorasan; and Reza Khan, commander of the Persian Cossack Brigade at Qazvin. Of the three, Reza Khan was the strongest and the closest to Teheran. A native of Mazanderan, he had risen through the ranks of the Cossack Brigade, holding his units together during the chaos of World War I. In February 1921, apparently with support from British officers at Qazvin, he joined forces with Seyyed Zia al-Din Tabataba'i—a prominent, pro-British, liberal journalist and politician—to take power by means of a bloodless coup. Appointed commander of the army (*sardar sepah*) after the coup, Reza Khan took the post of minister of war and incorporated the gendarmerie under his control. When Zia al-Din tried to take decisive and independent action against his enemies, he found himself powerless and outmaneuvered by his colleague, who forced him to resign and leave the country after only three months as prime minister. Reza Khan then further consolidated his position by defeating rivals who commanded the gendarmerie at Tabriz (Major Lahuti) and Mashhad (Colonel Pesyan) and by defeating the Jangalis of Gilan, who had already been weakened by internal disputes and the Soviet withdrawal. With his new, combined army of cossacks and gendarmes, Reza Khan organized successful expeditions against rebellious Kurds, Lors, and Turkomans. In 1923, Ahmad Shah Qajar appointed Reza Khan, now de facto ruler of Iran, prime minister and left the country for the last time. Reza Khan's final step to power came in 1925 when a constituent assembly deposed the Qajar dynasty and crowned him Reza Shah Pahlavi.

THE NEW ORDER

A tall, broad-shouldered man with an officer's air of authority, Reza Shah was impatient with the ideologies and debates of politicians and reformers, and his few public speeches were brief and direct. His words at the ceremony laying the cornerstone of the University of Teheran were typical: "The establishment of a university is something that the people of Iran should have done a long time ago. Now that it has been started, all efforts must be made for its speedy completion."[2] Blunt, brutal, and lacking formal education, Reza Shah despised refined Persian society and the "effete" social and religious traditions that, he believed, had undermined Iran's strength and kept it permanently backward and subservient to foreigners.

Reza Shah's goal was simple: to rule a resurrected and unified Iran. This new Iran first needed a modern army that could, if necessary, compel reluctant citizens to pay taxes, obey the orders of a centralized bureaucracy, and exchange their traditional way of life for Western economic and social models. Reza Shah tolerated no opposition to his program. Although keeping the form of the 1906 constitution, his dictatorship effectively buried the few surviving shreds of that document. Opponents of his vision and his methods included liberal nationalists, ethnic separatists, Marxists, and religious leaders, all of whom challenged Pahlavi control from time to time. But only when united around one leader or issue could these disparate opponents become a serious threat to royal power.

During his sixteen-year reign (1925–1941), Reza Shah attempted a radical transformation of Iranian society. His policies emphasized creating an Iranian nationalism that would be distinct from Islam, weakening the power of the clergy, adopting the material achievements of the West, and establishing a highly centralized state and administration backed by a large, modern military. The reforms of Kemal Ataturk in Turkey directly inspired many of Reza Shah's actions, and in imitation of Ataturk, he ordered the wearing of Western dress and outlawed the veiling of women. Old titles were abolished; an Iranian, solar calendar replaced Arabic lunar dates; and the Persian language was purged of many Arabic and Turkish expressions. The regime imposed a system of civil registration and forced citizens to adopt family names. The authorities encouraged families to give their children pure Iranian names (such as Bizhan, Farhad, and Khosrow) instead of names with Arabic or Islamic connotations.

Reza Shah attacked all traditional centers of power that might challenge his authority, and in doing so, he greatly expanded the role of the Iranian state, which traditionally had consisted of little more than an army and a treasury. To build his new army, Reza Shah replaced the old tribal levies with universal conscription, and the ordinary Iranian peasant and townsman found himself with a new burden of military service. The shah created a new economic bureaucracy to run government monopolies and state enterprises and to collect new taxes, such as levies on tea and sugar, and the centralized control of this bureaucracy undermined the power of the largest merchants, whose traditional control of the bazaar had allowed them previously to defy government authority. In southern Iran, new taxes and customs regulations (and perhaps the new social legislation) caused some traders to emigrate to the Arab side of the Persian Gulf in search of a more congenial mercantile environment.

Reza Shah was personally indifferent to religion but bitterly anticlerical. He attacked the privileges of the Shi'ite ulema, whom he considered his regime's most serious opponents, by a series of reforms and abolitions aimed at their social status and the economic base of their political power, and he established secular ministries that broke the clerical hold over endowments, education, and the legal system. A 1932 law deprived the clergy of much of its traditional livelihood, the income from the registration of documents and property, and a 1936 law reorganized the judiciary, replacing members of the clergy with university-trained judges. The new civil and penal codes were basically European (mostly French) documents and limited the role of Islamic law to certain matters of personal status. New laws placed education, which had been mostly the responsibility of clerical teachers in traditional *maktab*s (primary schools) and *madraseh*s (advanced religious schools) under the supervision of a secular government ministry. The new universities and elementary and secondary schools taught a French curriculum. Although foreign (mission) schools were closely controlled, German advisers assisted in the establishment of technical and industrial schools, and foreign professors taught in the new University of Teheran. The government provided scholarships for outstanding students to study abroad (mostly in France or Germany), and many of these students returned to Iran, eventually to become leading figures in education and politics.

Reza Shah's reforms created a new elite of military officers, managers of state industrial enterprises, and senior civilian officials. He rewarded loyal members of the Qajar aristocracy with positions in the cabinet, parliament, and diplomatic service. Those aristocrats he could not co-opt, he eliminated. He imprisoned tribal leaders, disarmed their followers, and forced them to abandon their traditional migrations. He kept leaders of the Kurds, Qashqa'is, Bakhtiyaris, and Khuzestan Arabs under house arrest in the capital, where many died under suspicious circumstances.

Reza Shah's increasing authoritarianism and avarice provoked opposition even among the older generation of the intelligentsia who had originally supported his centralization and secularization policies. He amassed large estates, especially in his rich home province of Mazanderan. Even close associates could not criticize his actions, and some of his early supporters, such as Ali Dashti and Hosein Taqizadeh, were forced out of public life, exiled, or imprisoned. The writer and historian Ahmad Kasravi, who had once served the shah as a provincial judge, described his mixed feelings toward Reza Shah and his achievements. In articles published in 1942, nine months after the shah's abdication, Kasravi praised the former ruler for centralizing the state, pacifying the tribes, limiting the clergy's power, unveiling the women, abolishing aristocratic titles, introducing conscription, and establishing modern cities, industries, and schools. He criticized Reza Shah, however, for ignoring the constitution, favoring the military, accumulating private wealth, stealing others' property, murdering progressive intellectuals, and increasing the gap between rich and poor.[3]

At the end of his reign in 1941, Reza Shah faced opposition from four major centers within Iranian society: the aristocratic politicians of the 1907–1925 period, who had been silenced by the shah's intolerance of criticism and total suppression of public debate; the tribes, who had been left leaderless and vulnerable to the new army and bureaucracy; the clergy and its followers among the traditional middle class of the bazaars; and the younger intellectuals, who criticized the shah as a dictator and a tool of British imperialism. The government's answer to this opposition was repression. New roads and equipment gave the army a clear superiority over tribal opponents. In the summer of 1935, army units violated the sanctuary of the shrine at Mashhad to put down protests against the new secularization policies, particularly the dress laws, and about 300 civilians were killed or injured. A crackdown on intellectuals culminated in the arrest and trial of the famous "fifty-three" in 1937–1938. The government accused this group, many of whom later became the nucleus of the Tudeh (Communist) party, of organizing a secret society, publishing May Day manifestos, organizing strikes, and translating Communist publications.[4]

WAR AND THE NEW POLITICS

In foreign affairs, Reza Shah continued the traditional Iranian policy of seeking the friendship of another world power to offset the predominant influence of Russia (now the Soviet Union) and Britain. To this end, he established close economic and cultural relations with the Germans, who enjoyed a reputation for efficiency, organization, and high-quality merchandise. In the 1930s, Germany supplied Iran with technicians, industrial advisers, heavy machinery, inspiration for most of the new government architecture, and assistance in the building of the trans-Iranian railway. Some Nazi racist propaganda found an audience among extreme Iranian nationalists who were anxious to assert their superiority as "Aryans" over their Semitic and Turkish neighbors.

Although Iran had declared its neutrality in World War II and hoped to maintain normal commercial relations with both sides, the Allies distrusted Reza Shah's pro-German policies and sought to use Iranian territory as a supply route to the USSR. After an ultimatum, Britain and the Soviet Union invaded Iran in August 1941, and Reza Shah's beloved army collapsed after offering token resistance. His expensive facade of military power was ultimately as useless as his son's was to prove thirty-seven years later. In the end, the ordinary soldier, led by unqualified and corrupt officers, was indifferent to the fate of a regime that had offered him little except brutality and taxation. The Allies occupied Iran—the Russians in the north and the British in the south—and Reza Shah, abdicating in favor of his twenty-two-year-old son, Mohammad Reza, left Iran to die in South African exile in 1944.

Although few Iranians welcomed foreign occupation, there was little weeping at Reza Shah's departure. The Allied occupation ended his autocratic rule, and restrictions on political activity vanished almost overnight. The 1941 occupation inaugurated twelve years of lively political activity in which the young shah remained largely a spectator or, at most, a minor player. Despite the inflation and shortages of the war years and the presence of foreign armies until 1946, the period from the Allied invasion until the fall of Prime Minister Mohammad Mossadegh in August 1953 was a time of vigorous, open debate and competition among numerous parties led by strong-willed and ambitious politicians. New voices and new parties appeared to debate their rival views in a boisterous press, and politicians like

Ahmad Qavam, Mossadegh, and even Seyyed Zia al-Din, all veterans of the pre-1925 political arena, emerged from retirement and reentered political life. Qavam, who had led four pre-Pahlavi cabinets (under his aristocratic title Qavam al-Saltaneh), served as prime minister in 1942–1943 and 1946–1947. Mossadegh, who as Mossadegh al-Saltaneh had been minister of justice, finance, and foreign affairs under the last Qajar shah, won election to the Fourteenth Majles in 1943 on a platform of ending foreign concessions and transferring the armed forces from royal to parliamentary control. Seyyed Zia al-Din returned from exile in 1943, organized the National Will (Eradeh-ye-Melli) party, and represented Yazd in the parliament.

Although Mossadegh avoided party affiliation, his stands on the issues of oil concessions, free elections, and enforcing the constitution earned him the support of the Iran party, the most important secular, nationalist party of this period. The party's founders, including Allahyar Saleh and Mahdi Bazargan, were mostly professionals and political moderates advocating a European-style social democracy in an Iranian setting. Strongly nationalistic, they argued for state ownership of basic industries and greater political influence for educated technicians and intellectuals. The Iran party later became one of the most important elements in the National Front (Jebheh-ye-Melli), a coalition of political factions and parties formed under Mossadegh's leadership in 1949.

Reza Shah's abdication also brought the immediate release of thirty-seven members of the famous fifty-three imprisoned in 1937. Meeting in September 1941, soon after their release, these young Marxists announced the formation of the Hezb-e-Tudeh-ye-Iran (Party of the Iranian Masses) under the chairmanship of Soleiman Eskandari, a member of the Qajar family and veteran of the pre-1925 nationalist struggles. Although the founders of the Tudeh supported the policies of the Soviet Union, they avoided the name "communist" for several reasons: to attract a following among reformers and nationalists; to avoid popular and official hostility toward communism, socialism, and the Soviet Union; and to keep themselves independent of the older generation of Iranian communists who had been active in the Caucasus, Azarbaijan, and Gilan. The intellectuals who wrote the Tudeh party program sought mass support through proposals to improve conditions for workers, peasants, and members of the lower middle class.[5]

Religious groups also reentered the political arena. The Mojahedin-e-Eslam (Crusaders of Islam), nominally headed by the preacher Shams Qanatabadi, was in reality a vehicle for the political advancement of the charismatic Ayatollah Abu al-Qasem Kashani who had been active in religious politics since the 1920s. His organization drew its support from the upper levels of the bazaar and advocated a religious-nationalist program, including repeal of Reza Shah's secular legislation and a pan-Islamic alliance against the West. The small terrorist organization called Fedayan-e-Eslam (Devotees of Islam), although associated with Kashani, had an ideology and a constituency that was distinct from the more moderate Mojahedin-e-Eslam. Founded in 1946 by Navab-e-Safavi, a young Teheran theology student, the Fedayan's social base lay among the younger, lower-class elements of the bazaar. It rejected political compromise, assassinated prominent opponents, and insisted on imposing strict Islamic legislation on Iranian society. The more pragmatic Kashani, in contrast, allied himself with Mossadegh's National Front, at least until early 1953.

The weakening of the central government encouraged tribal independence and, in the northwest, important regional movements for autonomy. Tribal leaders, free of Reza Shah's restrictions, returned to their traditional lands and reestablished their authority. In the south, Lor, Qashqa'i, and Boir Ahmad tribesmen took advantage of the military's collapse to escape government "settlements," resume their traditional migrations, and rearm themselves with weapons captured from government arsenals or purchased from deserters.

In the northwest, organized movements for local autonomy, based on ethnic separatism, became serious threats to the central authorities (Map 4.1 shows the extent of these movements). Kurdish nationalists in Mahabad, a town outside the regions of British or Soviet occupation, had formed the Komala-e-Zhian-e-Kurd (Committee of Kurdish Youth) in 1943. In 1945, the Komala became part of the Democratic party of Kurdestan, a party of the small Kurdish urban intelligentsia led by Qazi Mohammad, a respected religious leader from Mahabad. In early 1946, the Democrats, encouraged by the breakdown of the central government's authority in neighboring Azarbaijan, inaugurated the autonomous Kurdish Republic, with Mahabad as its capital and Qazi Mohammad as its president. The tribal leaders in the rural areas, however, were unwilling to forgo their traditional rivalries in the interest of Kurdish nationalism and remained hostile to the new government. Outside of the capital, the new republic controlled only a small territory—including the towns of Bokan, Naqadeh, and Oshnoviyeh—and received armed support from the forces of Molla Mostafa Barzani, leader of the Barzani Kurds in Iraq.

In Azarbaijan, a movement for autonomy fed on local resentment caused by the central government's neglect of one of Iran's richest provinces. For most Azarbaijanis, their economic and political grievances were probably more important than their linguistic or cultural differences with other Iranians. In 1945, the veteran communist Ja'far Pishavari organized the Democrat party of Azarbaijan, calling for both provincial autonomy and greater representation in Teheran.[6] Remaining in the background, the Soviets quietly supported Pishavari and used their military forces to prevent the Iranian government from reasserting its already limited authority in Azarbaijan. In late 1945, the Democrats disarmed army garrisons, took control of the major provincial towns, and declared the formation of the Autonomous Government of Azarbaijan. Their program included the use of Azarbaijani Turkish in schools and offices and administrative and economic reforms to strengthen local control over provincial affairs. Soviet occupation troops, which remained in Iran after U.S. and British units left, kept the Iranian government from sending armed forces into Azarbaijan.

Thus blocked, the astute prime minister, Ahmad Qavam, turned to negotiations and outmaneuvered the Soviets by playing oil concession, Tudeh, Democrat, tribal, United Nations, and foreign cards with great skill. In early 1946, Qavam, after a visit to Moscow, cultivated an image of sympathy toward the Tudeh, friendship with the Soviet Union, and freedom from British influence. These efforts reached fruition in April, when Qavam and the Soviets reached an accord that called for Russian withdrawal by early May, a combined Soviet-Iranian oil venture to be submitted for Majles approval by late October, and negotiations between Teheran and the new regime in Azarbaijan.

Spurred by hopes of an oil agreement and by U.S. and British pressure inside and outside the United Nations, the Soviet Union withdrew its forces from Iran, as it had promised Qavam, in May 1946. Unwilling to give the Soviets a pretext to return and "restore order" in Azarbaijan, Qavam, reached an agreement with Pishavari that granted most of the latter's demands. The Tabriz Democrats, however, had their hands full with economic problems, dissident uprisings, and relations with their Kurdish neighbors. By the middle of 1946, they were busy trying to suppress tribal rebellions in Ardabil, Zanjan, and Miando'ab. The Democrats' heavy-handed methods of dealing with political and economic discontent had made their rule increasingly unpopular, despite the fact that they had initiated some promising reforms and development projects. On December 10, 1946, the Iranian army, under royal command, moved into Azarbaijan. Meeting little resistance, the army entered Tabriz two days later to a tumultuous popular welcome. Pishavari fled to the Soviet Union, and other Democrat leaders were arrested, executed, or killed by mobs.

The collapse of the Democrats in Tabriz also meant the end for the Mahabad Kurdish Republic. The Iranian army entered Mahabad peacefully on December 15, 1946, after the republic's Barzani supporters had evacuated the town. Despite the peaceful reconquest and the genuine popularity of the republic's leaders among the townspeople, the government hanged Qazi Mohammad and two other leaders in the Mahabad public square in March 1947. By summer, the Barzani forces had fought their way out of Iran into the Soviet Union.

Soviet troops were now out of Iran, and the northwest was once again under central government control. All that remained of Qavam's settlement was the Iran-Soviet oil agreement. The prime minister did not submit the agreement for parliamentary ratification until October 1947, following the elections for the Fifteenth Majles. Qavam, however, could not control this new parliament, in which three groups competed for power: royalists, a pro-British National Caucus (Fraksion-e-Melli), and Qavam's Democrat party. Encouraged by the prime minister's refusal to support his own oil agreement and by the U.S. ambassador's strong opposition to its ratification, the Majles rejected it by a wide margin. Qavam himself resigned at the end of 1947, not because of the rejection of the oil agreement, but because of defections from his own party.

MOSSADEGH AND OIL NATIONALIZATION

Although the shah had remained on the periphery of the complex power struggles of this period, Qavam's departure strengthened the monarch's political position by removing a strong-willed, independent prime minister from Iranian politics. Other powerful figures, however, such as Ali Razmara, Mossadegh, Mozaffar Baqa'i, and Kashani, remained on the scene, and they were not going to yield power easily.

The National Front

In 1949, Mossadegh led a group protesting unfair practices in the elections for the Sixteenth Majles. The protesters' twenty-member negotiating council organized the National Front, which demanded honest elections, freedom of the press, and an end to the martial law that had been imposed after an attempt on the shah's life in February 1949. Mossadegh himself preferred to lead a loose coalition rather than head a single party, which, he felt, would represent only limited interests. The National Front drew its organized support from four groups: the Iran party; the Toilers' party (Hezb-e-Zahmat-Keshan) led by Mozaffar Baqa'i and Khalil Maleki; the small, ultranationalist

National party led by Dariush Foruhar; and Ayatollah Kashani's Mojahedin-e-Eslam. The National Front's supporters came from both the traditional middle class of the bazaars—clerics and small merchants—and the modern middle class of students, teachers, civil servants, and other professionals. Although differing in social outlook and ideology, these diverse groups united around three issues; opposition to royal prerogatives, oil nationalization, and the leadership of the charismatic and incorruptible Mossadegh.[7]

The National Front gradually focused its attention on the oil question and a broad power struggle with the shah. In 1950, the government submitted proposals to the Sixteenth Majles for a revision of the 1933 agreement with the Anglo-Iranian Oil Company, but, under Mossadegh's leadership, the small National Front delegation successfully blocked their approval. Frustrated by Prime Minister Ali Mansur's ineffectiveness, the shah replaced him with the strong-minded General Ali Razmara, who was determined to push for political and economic reforms and for approval of the oil legislation. Both conservatives and nationalists disliked the new prime minister's policies, and by late fall, the oil nationalization issue had become a rallying cry uniting his opponents. Razmara's assassination in March 1951 by a member of the Fedayan-e-Eslam brought the crisis to a head. The murder set off a wave of public rejoicing, and a frightened Majles quickly approved an oil nationalization bill. When Hosein Ala, the new prime minister, refused to implement the new law, the Majles nominated, and the shah named, Mossadegh—then chairman of the joint parliamentary oil committee directing the government's negotiations with the British—prime minister on April 29, 1951.

A member of the old Qajar landowning aristocracy with a long, distinguished political record, Mossadegh seemed an unlikely charismatic leader. Although variously portrayed in the West as unstable, xenophobic, erratic, and emotional, he did what few Iranian leaders had ever done: He united the modern and traditional classes under the banner of Iranian national pride. Mossadegh attracted wide support because of his incorruptibility, consistent adherence to nationalist principles, and independence from foreign influence at a time when almost all Iranian leaders were tainted by association with Russians, British, or Americans.

Except for a brief interval in July 1952, Mossadegh served as prime minister until his overthrow in an August 1953 coup. He initially enjoyed the support of both nationalists and royalists, the latter hoping he could solve the oil dispute with Britain and eliminate it as a cause of domestic opposition to the shah and his allies. But inflexibility on both sides kept the crisis at a stalemate and at the center of the political stage throughout Mossadegh's time as prime minister. Despite his prestige and well-known independence, Mossadegh became a captive of his followers' extremism. Any solution he could have achieved—short of complete British capitulation— would have been attacked as surrender to the foreign imperialists. The British referred the dispute to the International Court of Justice at the Hague, but the court ruled that it lacked jurisdiction, by implication favoring the Iranian argument that this question fell under Iranian law. Although the Iranians could operate their nationalized oil fields and related facilities without expatriate employees, they were unable, to sell their production because of a British-inspired international boycott. The United States tried unsuccessfully to mediate the dispute but would not break ranks with Britain over the boycott. A hoped-for U.S. loan failed to materialize, and with few customers for the country's oil, the Iranian government was without revenue and beset by shortages, debt, and inflation.

The Coalition Weakens

In 1952–1953, Mossadegh's coalition began to fall apart as a result of a series of complex power struggles among its leaders. Elections for the Seventeenth Majles in the beginning of 1952 did not go as the National Front had hoped. The front, although victorious in Teheran and some major cities, lost seats in rural areas and in areas under military control. Seeing the unfavorable trend, Mossadegh stopped the elections as soon as a quorum—seventy-nine deputies— had been elected. Beyond the thirty committed National Front deputies, Mossadegh's support in the new parliament was thin. His opponents, fearing his popularity, would support him outwardly only until they could mobilize around a specific issue or a rival leader. Mozaffar Baqa'i's desertion in December 1952 was not a serious blow to the front, since many of his supporters had already left him to join his former ally Khalil Maleki's Third Force (Niru-ye-Sevvom) party. More damaging was Ayatollah Kashani's joining the anti-Mossadegh forces in January 1953, a move that threatened to shatter the religious-secular alliance that constituted the nucleus of the front's political power. Kashani, whose dispute with Mossadegh had been simmering for months, attacked Mossadegh for indifference to the growing power of the Tudeh, hostility to religious legislation, and dictatorial leadership of the front. In February 1953, to demonstrate his strength, Kashani sent a mob to attack the prime minister's residence. Although many of Kashani's followers in parliament and the bazaar remained loyal to Mossadegh, the ayatollah's desertion eventually cost the front much of its support in the Teheran streets, where Mossadegh's fate was ultimately decided.[8]

Beset by political defections and economic problems, Mossadegh tried to consolidate his position by limiting the power of the monarch, the army, and his civilian opponents. He attacked royal prerogatives, including control of the military and certain state funds, and restricted the shah's access to foreign diplomats since the prime minister was often kept uninformed of the content of meetings between the monarch and the British or U.S. ambassadors. He also purged the army and placed officers he trusted in high positions. Following Mossadegh's victory over the shah in the July 1952 crisis over the prime minister's power to nominate the minister of war, parliament granted him power to rule by decree, first for six months and then for another twelve. As a result of parliamentary opposition to his social and political reforms, Mossadegh dissolved the Majles in the summer of 1953 (by ordering the National Front deputies to resign in a bloc) and sought approval of this extralegal move in a general referendum. The result was 99 percent in favor of Mossadegh's action in a blatantly rigged election.

Unable to rule by constitutional means, Mossadegh increasingly resorted to extralegal steps to retain power and advance his programs. It was ironic that a leader with Mossadegh's democratic pretensions and with the fervent support of the Iranian middle class could hold power only with a dictator's tools: rigged elections and plebiscites, rule by decree, and appeals to a "national will" above the fundamental laws. As Ervand Abrahamian notes: "Mossadegh, the constitutional lawyer who had meticulously quoted the fundamental laws against the shah, was now bypassing the same laws and resorting to the theory of the general will. The liberal aristocrat who had in the past appealed predominantly to the middle class was mobilizing the lower classes."[9]

Coup and Countercoup

Although Mossadegh appeared to still be in firm control in August 1953, in reality his strength was waning. Some of his original, liberal supporters objected to his dictatorial methods, and many bazaris had cooled toward his allegedly anticlerical, socialist program. Royalist military officers, led by Gen. Fazlollah Zahedi—a former Mossadegh ally against Razmara—began plotting a coup. Forming a secret Committee to Save the Fatherland (Komiteh-ye-Nejat-e-Vatan), the group made contact with British intelligence, which had created a wide network of agents to report on Iranian conditions.[10] In Washington, the new Eisenhower administration had decided to support Britain and the Iranian officers' efforts to remove Mossadegh, whom Washington saw as a "madman" and an unwitting ally of the Soviet Union.[11] Zahedi's group recruited key officers, including Colonel Ne'matollah Naseri, chief of the imperial guard; General Gilanshah, chief of the air force; and several provincial army commanders. They struck on August 16, 1953. The shah issued an order (*farman*) dismissing Mossadegh as prime minister and replacing him with General Zahedi. When it appeared at first that this coup had failed, the shah and Queen Sorayya left the country, and when the capital learned of the shah's flight, Tudeh demonstrators took to the streets and began pulling down royal statues and demanding that the monarchy be abolished.

In this crisis, the allegiance of the army and the Teheran street mobs ultimately tipped the balance in the shah's favor. Although Mossadegh had earlier used the Tudeh against the Iranian right and to frighten the United States, he now used the army to stop Tudeh excesses in Teheran. By midnight of August 18, the army, at Mossadegh's order, had checked the Tudeh in the streets of the capital. The next day the army and the street mobs, including partisans of the wrestler Sha'ban ("the brainless") Ja'fari, turned against Mossadegh. With army support, pro-shah mobs, reportedly paid with U.S.-supplied "Behbahani dollars" (named for the anti-Mossadegh Ayatollah Mohammad Behbahani), stormed the prime minister's residence in central Teheran. By nightfall, the city was controlled by the anti-Mossadegh crowds and royalist army units.

After the shah's return, Zahedi arrested Mossadegh and his associates and suppressed the Tudeh, the National Front, and other independent political groups. Following almost three years' imprisonment, Mossadegh remained under government "protection" in his village fifty miles west of Teheran until his death in 1967. The regime executed his outspoken foreign minister, Dr. Hosein Fatemi, exiled Baqa'i to Baluchestan, and restricted Kashani's political activities. It dealt harshly with the Tudeh, especially after uncovering a party network within the army in 1954. In the years following Mossadegh's overthrow, many Tudeh members were arrested, tortured, imprisoned, and executed. Others signed letters of recantation, betrayed their comrades, and became vocal supporters of the shah's regime.

CONSOLIDATING ROYAL POWER: 1953–1963

After his victory in 1953, the shah built a system of personal control that characterized his rule until the late 1970s. He put the coup leaders in key positions but skillfully saw to it that none of them became a serious rival. In 1955, determined that he would not be subordinate to powerful, independent politicians, he removed the strong-willed Zahedi and replaced him with the inoffensive Hosein Ala. Most subsequent prime ministers were political nonentities, loyal servants of the crown who would carry out the shah's wishes and not challenge his personal authority. The shah settled the oil dispute by signing a fifty-fifty profit-sharing agreement with a new consortium of European and U.S. oil companies. The stagnant Iranian economy revived, thanks to increased oil revenues and emergency financial aid from the United States, and the shah used the new income to strengthen his armed forces and initiate economic development projects supervised by a rejuvenated Plan and Budget Organization. In 1957, he established a new secret police, which gained international notoriety under its acronym, SAVAK. Silence and strictly controlled political activity replaced the turbulence and open debate of the Mossadegh era. In 1957, the government outlawed the Iran party—keystone of Mossadegh's National Front—and announced the formation of two new parties, both headed by close friends of the shah. The official government National (Melliyun) party and the official opposition People's (Mardom) party were ignored by most Iranians, who derisively named them the "yes" and "yes, sir" parties.

There was a brief and modest liberalization in 1961–1962, when growing debt, political disorders, and U.S. pressure for reforms forced the shah to appoint Ali Amini as prime minister. The shah disliked Amini, who was an ambitious, independent-minded Qajar aristocrat, related to Qavam and Mossadegh, and known for putting his audiences to sleep with long speeches. Realizing that the conservative Twentieth Majles would oppose any economic or social reforms, Amini persuaded the shah to give him a free hand by dissolving parliament. Amini also appointed reformist ministers of justice and education and instituted economic austerity measures requested by the International Monetary Fund. Hasan Arsanjani, Amini's popular and energetic minister of agriculture, began a serious effort at land reform. Ultimately, however, the shah distrusted Amini's political ambitions, which he believed threatened his own prerogatives, and also feared that Arsanjani's vigorous land reform efforts would give the minister of agriculture an independent power base among the peasantry. Amini remained politically isolated when the National Front would not cooperate with him because of his collaboration with the shah and his refusal to hold new elections. Unable to reach agreement with the National Front and unwilling to subordinate himself to the shah, Amini resigned in July 1962 after a clash with the monarch over the military budget.

Having replaced Amini with the obedient Assadollah Alam, the shah no longer had to contend with the political rivalry of an independent prime minister. In January 1963, the shah attempted to preempt the National Front's reformist positions and issues by announcing, with great fanfare, a six-point White Revolution of the Shah and People (enqelab-e-sefid). This program included many of the National Front's social and economic programs: redistribution of land (a modification of Arsanjani's effort); nationalization of public forests; profit sharing for industrial workers; a new electoral law, including the right to vote for women; and creation of a literacy corps using high school and university graduates in national service. A rigged national referendum (boycotted by religious opposition groups and the National Front) approved these measures by a 99.9 percent margin.

By 1962, the major opposition to the shah had split into secular and religious wings, and the White Revolution further divided this opposition. The shah labeled his clerical enemies "black reactionaries" and co-opted those members of the intelligentsia who were willing to accept his social and economic reforms without political liberalization. This secular-religious division simplified the government's work of silencing all opposition. In January 1962, the bazaar remained quiet while paratroopers brutally attacked student protestors at Teheran University; eighteen months later, the situation was reversed when three days of serious rioting broke out in the Teheran bazaars during the mourning month of Moharram (June 1963). In the latter instance, the army held fast and restored order after heavy loss of life among the demonstrators. By conservative estimates hundreds were killed. Although there were some related university disturbances, most of the intelligentsia remained passive while the army slaughtered demonstrators in the bazaar.

A new opposition leader emerged during 1963—the sixty-four-year-old Ayatollah Ruhollah Khomeini. He had originally gone to the holy city of Qom from Arak in 1920 with his teacher, the respected scholar Sheikh Abd al-Karim Ha'eri-Yazdi. Sheikh Ha'eri reorganized religious scholarship at Qom and established there the Howzeh-ye-Elmiyeh, a center of religious learning that would eventually become the spiritual center of Khomeini's revolution. After Sheikh Ha'eri's death in 1935, Khomeini was closely associated with the respected Ayatollah Borujerdi until the latter's death in 1961. Perhaps restrained by the politically inactive Borujerdi, Khomeini had remained largely aloof from the turmoil of the wartime and Mossadegh eras and had gained a reputation at Qom as a gifted teacher of ethics and philosophy.

When he began speaking against the government in 1962–1963, Khomeini's attacks drew popular attention for two reasons. First, he based his opposition on issues that appealed to a larger audience than the clergy and its close supporters in the bazaars. In addition to criticizing the regime's hostility to Islam and the clergy, Khomeini attacked the government's financial and moral corruption, rigged elections, and relations with Israel and the United States. Second, at a time when open, direct criticism of the shah was unheard of, Khomeini refused to keep silent or to moderate his opposition. Although other people might accommodate, yield to official pressure, or express their criticisms in polite allegories, Khomeini remained consistently outspoken and uncompromising in his attacks. Many of the nationalists and liberals in Khomeini's audience, impressed by his daring, glossed over and ignored his attacks on coeducation and the other strains of obscurantism (*akhundbazi*) in his message.

In March 1963, the army reacted to Khomeini's denunciations of the White Revolution by attacking the Feiziyeh Shool in Qom, and after that incident, Khomeini sharpened his criticism of the regime. On June 3, 1963, the tenth of Moharram, he reproached the shah as follows:

> Shah, I don't wish the same to happen to you; I don't want you to become like your father. Listen to my advice, listen to the ulama of Islam. They desire the welfare of the nation, the welfare of the country. Don't listen to Israel; Israel can't do anything for you. You miserable wretch, forty-five years of your life have passed; isn't it time for you to think and reflect a little, to ponder about where all this is leading you, to learn a lesson from the experience of your father?[12]

The government arrested Khomeini the next day, and in Teheran, the news of his arrest turned Moharram processions into the three days of bloody rioting in the bazaars. Released after a few months confinement, Khomeini continued his outspoken opposition and urged his followers to boycott the October 1963 parliamentary elections. In October 1964, following another prison term, he issued a strong public denunciation of the law granting immunity to U.S. military advisers and their families. In response, the government arrested and exiled him, first to Turkey and then to Iraq. He settled in the Shi'a holy city of Najaf, where he continued to speak and write against the shah's regime until the dramatic events of 1978–1979 took him first to Paris and then back to Iran.

IMPERIAL DICTATORSHIP

After the 1963 crisis, the shah began to rule with a new self-confidence. In foreign affairs, encouraged by politial victories over his rivals and steady economic growth based on a continuing demand for Iranian oil, he widened Iran's sphere of contacts and notably improved relations with the Soviet Union. The shah's visit to the USSR in 1965 and the signing of Isfahan steel plant and natural gas agreements in 1966 were signs of this new confidence. Perhaps coincidentally, the next year the United States agreed to sell Iran two squadrons of sophisticated jet aircraft (F-4s), thereby changing a traditional policy of keeping arms sales at least nominally linked to internal reforms. The final demise of this earlier policy came during the Nixon-Kissinger years, when the U.S. administration was confronted with a British decision to withdraw that country's forces from and end its protectorates in the Persian Gulf. In response, the administration devised the so-called two-pillar (or two-pillow) policy to make Saudi Arabia and Iran responsible for regional security. Such a role for Iran, the shah argued, required large amounts of new weaponry. The U.S. administration agreed, and in May 1972, President Richard Nixon visited Teheran and promised the shah he could buy anything he wanted from the United States except nuclear arms.

Without damaging important security and economic ties with Israel, Iran also improved relations with its Arab neighbors. These relations had varied from outright hostility (toward Iraq) to overbearing arrogance (toward the Persian Gulf emirates) to cool dislike and mistrust (toward Saudi Arabia). In December 1971, following the British withdrawal, Iranian forces in the Persian Gulf occupied three small southern islands that were claimed by the new federation of the United Arab Emirates. Although this action was unpopular in the Arab states and provoked sporadic anti-Iranian outbursts, Iran was able to establish generally correct relations with its gulf neighbors.

Iran abandoned its claim to Bahrain and established embassies in Manama, Doha, and Abu Dhabi. Difficulties with Iraq continued until 1975, when the shah and Saddam Hussein, then deputy chairman of Iraq's Revolutionary Council, signed the Algiers agreement, which ended Iranian support for the dissident Iraqi Kurds and adjusted the Shatt al-Arab river frontier in Iran's favor. The Iranian-Saudi coolness had little basis in policy differences and seemed to arise mostly from personal animosity between the shah and King Faisal, who remained suspicious of Iranian intentions in the gulf. The Saudis also had mixed feelings about the presence of Iranian forces in Oman to assist Soltan Qabus against Marxist rebels in Dhofar, a region in the far southwest of the sultanate. Although in principle supporting aid to a monarch against Marxist insurgents, the Saudis resisted accepting the precedent of non-Arab forces on the peninsula. The death of King Faisal in 1975 and softer rhetoric from Iran about its responsibility to maintain security in the Persian Gulf brought significant improvement in the relationship.

The shah's victory in 1963 also encouraged him once again to rule at home with a strong hand and to suppress independent political activity. Throughout the sixties and early seventies, opposition groups remained weak and divided. The 1961–1963 mini-thaw had resulted in the reappearance of the National Front as an alliance between the old, secular pro-Mossadegh parties and the new Iran Liberation movement, a moderate religious group founded in 1961 by the Islamic activist, engineer, and teacher Mahdi Bazargan and the cleric Seyyed Mahmoud Taleghani. But inactivity during the 1963 riots, ambivalence over the shah's reforms, and a continued paralysis of leadership left the front ineffective as a political force. In 1965, the Liberation movement broke with the front over organizational questions and the issue of cooperation with antiregime clergy who had inspired and led the 1963 uprising. The secular parties, remembering Ayatollah Kashani's defection from the National Front in 1953, distrusted the clergy, and the Liberation movement favored an alliance with even those clergymen who opposed the "progressive" parts of the shah's reform program. Bazargan himself, for example, had steadfastly supported the idea of Islam as a force for social change, and he also had long associations with many religious figures, such as Morteza Mottahari and Mohammad Beheshti, who would become close associates of Khomeini.

But all of these opposition groups—secular and religious alike—went into eclipse after the 1962 university clashes, the 1963 bazaar uprisings, and a wave of arrests that followed the assassination of Prime Minister Hasan Ali Mansur in January 1965. On the left, the Tudeh party, after a brief alliance with the National Front, almost completely disappeared within Iran. SAVAK infiltrated the party organization, and its leaders either went into exile or joined the government as apolitical technocrats. During these years—from the mid-sixties to the mid-seventies—the government struck especially hard against its religious opponents. Many people who were later to assume high office in the Islamic Republic, such as Hosein Ali Montazeri, Ali Khamene'i, and Mohammad Reza Mahdavi-Kani, spent much of this period in prison or in internal exile.

After their failures in 1953 and 1962–1963, the traditional political groups—the Iran, National, and Tudeh parties—held little attraction for younger Iranian activists. Like their contemporaries in the West, many of these younger people discovered the works of Mao Tse-tung, Franz Fanon, Ho Chi Minh, and Ché Guevera; turned to revolutionary warfare; and sought inspiration from the radical and violent models of political change in Algeria, China, Cuba, Vietnam, and Palestine. Two new major groups, with distinct origins, advocated armed guerrilla struggle against the regime. One of these, the Iranian People's Crusaders (Mojahedin-e-Khalq-e-Iran), known as the Moja-hedin, began its activities in 1966 as an offshoot of the Liberation movement. Although rejecting Marxist atheism, the Mojahedin ideology owed a great deal to Marxist sociology and economics. Its members emphasized the revolutionary and egalitarian nature of Shi'a Islam, interpreting the martyrdoms of the Shi'ite imams, especially Imam Hosein, the prophet's grandson, as part of the struggle of the dis-possessed against illegitimate rulers and their allies among capitalists and feudal landlords. These usurpers had betrayed the prophet's Nezam-e-Towhid ("monotheistic order"), which, the Majahedin ar-gued, was the true classless society. With a nucleus drawn from the young, middle-class intelligentsia, the Mojahedin began armed activ-ities in 1971 with bombings, assassinations, and bank robberies. The regime, feeling its very existence threatened by such tactics, took very harsh reprisals. Arrested Mojahedin members were tortured into betraying their colleagues; many disappeared, were executed, or were tortured to death. Others committed suicide to avoid capture. Never a large organization, between 1971 and 1977 the Mojahedin lost much of its membership to government executioners and in battles with security forces. In 1975, one wing of the organization abandoned its original Islamic ideology for a purely Marxist orientation. From that time on, there was a Marxist as well as an Islamic Mojahedin.

The other important guerrilla group of this period was the explicitly Marxist People's Sacrificing Guerrillas (Cherikha-ye-Fada'i-ye-Khalq), commonly known as the Fada'i, which originated within the Tudeh party. In the early 1960s, several young Tudeh members, led by the young Teheran University student Bizhan Jazani, broke with the party over its subservience with regard to Soviet policy and its choice of political action over armed struggle. In 1970, Jazani's faction merged with a second revolutionary group to form the Fada'i organization. In February 1971, the Fada'is attacked a gendarmerie post at Siahkal in Gilan, where they had been preparing a base for rural guerrilla warfare against the regime. The government responded quicky and, with the aid of the local population, captured or killed all of the attackers. Although SAVAK arrested or killed most of the Fada'i leadership, through the early and mid-seventies the group managed to undertake occasional assassinations and bombings in the cities.[13]

BAZAAR, BOUTIQUE, AND BONANZA

Ultimately, the shah had more to fear from his own short-sighted policies than from a handful of harassed guerrillas. The 1973 increase in crude-oil prices and the subsequent rise in government revenues raised hopes that Iran's new wealth could improve its citizens' standard of living and create a prosperous economy. The figures were spectacular. Between the beginning of 1971 and the end of 1973, the average posted price for a barrel of crude rose from $1.79 to $11.65, and the government's oil revenues rose from $2.3 billion in 1972 to $18.5 billion in 1974. The fifth development plan (1973–1978) provided for the spending of $69 billion compared to $8.3 billion in the fourth plan (1968–1972).

Economic Failure

But uncontrolled development and spending in all sectors and the government's inability to manage the oil windfall created dangerous economic imbalances and almost destroyed the delicate equilibrium of Iranian society. To some extent, everyone in Iran benefited from the new riches, which paid for roads, schools, electric plants, hospitals, and water supplies. But not everyone in Iran benefited equally. Although the poor were probably better off in absolute terms, their *relative* economic position deteriorated as uneven distribution of the new wealth created increasing and obvious material gaps among classes. Moreover, the growing economic inequalities widened the social distances among classes as westernized "boutique" and tra-ditional "bazaar" cultures came into increasing conflict. Although the new wealth brought the poor job opportunities and consumer goods, these benefits came at the price of living in squalid shantytowns in the shadow of luxury villas and paying higher prices for food, clothing, and other essentials. For the middle class there were new cars, houses, and foreign travel and education, all purchased at the cost of unlivable cities choking on smog, garbage, and traffic. But for the rich there were unprecedented opportunities for conspicuous consumption in the form of villas, palaces, and jewelry—and the chance to get even richer from massive new projects.

The government could not deliver the better life it had promised. For most people daily life, especially in the large cities, became increasingly difficult and unpleasant. Frequent power cuts made people's newly purchased refrigerators, televisions, and coolers useless for long periods of the day. Ships jammed the ports, and goods rotted while waiting to be unloaded or moved, and construction work stopped while waiting for deliveries of imported cement or other construction materials. Failures in agriculture meant price increases, food shortages, and black markets. One day there was no milk or cheese; another day there were no onions. As expected, goods in short supply went to the people who could afford to pay premium prices. Uncontrolled speculation in land and construction created a surplus of luxury apartments in north Teheran and a shortage of affordable housing for middle- and lower-class families. In education, students in the government schools faced overcrowded classrooms and teacher shortages. Families with the means sent their children to the new, booming private schools where students received more foreign language instruction and authorities ignored traditional rules about dress and the separation of the sexes.

The Gold Rush

The shah poured vast sums into military purchases, construction, and operations. Iran's defense budget grew from $1.5 billion in 1973 to $9.4 billion in 1977, and during the same five-year period, Iran signed sales agreements for over $12 billion worth of military goods and services from the United States.[14] Iran purchased advanced destroyers and aircraft from the United States, hovercraft and Chieftain tanks from the United Kingdom, and fast patrol craft from France. Seeking the most modern military technology, Iran built costly new bases for its navy and air force, bought an entire helicopter factory, and installed sophisticated military communications equipment. The U.S. record in this area was a shabby one. Defense contractors such as Northrop, Grummon, and Textron (parent company of Bell Helicopter) all reportedly paid millions in bribes, poorly disguised as agents' fees,[15] and U.S. civilian and military officials previously involved in the arms sale program turned up working for private contractors, such as Philco-Ford and Rockwell International, which dealt with the Iranian military.

The result of this massive spending on arms and development was a bonanza for foreign companies and their Iranian partners. In a twentieth-century gold rush, hordes of foreigners went to Iran to work as technicians, advisers, managers, bankers, sales representatives, mechanics, drivers, cooks, and housemaids. The uncontrolled spending for development in both military and civilian sectors created labor shortages that only foreigners could fill, and the new and sophisticated military technology also took educated Iranians out of the labor force for long periods of training.

By 1976, there were tens of thousands of foreigners working in Iran, including British, French, Germans, Thais, Filipinos, Koreans, and about 40,000 Americans. The employment of so many foreigners created severe social problems and resentment. Bell Helicopter employees in Isfahan were notorious for ridiculing local traditions (writing "Jesus Saves" on mosques) and showing an open contempt for all things Iranian. Foreigners, who almost always earned higher wages than their Iranian counterparts (in the form of incentives Iranians bitterly referred to as "barbarism allowances"—*haqq-e-tavahhosh*), were blamed for many social and economic ills, especially shortages in housing and food. The presence of such a large and conspicuous foreign (especially U.S.) community and the government's obvious failure to keep its unrealistic promises led many Iranians to believe that the regime was squandering their country's wealth for the benefit of foreigners and their Iranian collaborators.

A Time of Self-Deception

Despite some solid achievements in industry, transport, and energy, the new wealth also meant that the shah lost whatever feeble contact he may have had with the religious feelings and emotions of ordinary Iranians. His oil income and his foreign and foreign-trained Iranian advisers encouraged him to plan a fantasy world of skyscrapers, superhighways, and planned communities inhabited by secular "modern" citizens for whom Islam would be of little importance. In reality, however, the majority of Iranians wanted no part of the shah's visions. They remained attached to that Islamic part of Iranian culture that the shah considered backward and threatening, the relic of an unenlightened past.

Because the shah pretended that Islam did not exist as a cultural force, his regime took on the appearance of modernity, stability, and power. With the advantage of hindsight, it is clear that this strength and power were only a facade of pseudowesternization decorated with expensive, imported ornaments. The avant-garde arts festivals, the nightclubs, the restaurants, and the fine hotels of north Teheran were all part of a show staged to mislead the gullible and the foreigner—the visiting U.S. congressional official, the diplomat, and perhaps even the shah himself—into thinking that Iran was something it was not.

The reality of Iran lay elsewhere: in the bazaars and mosques and among people far removed from the royal court and technocrats who thought they were running the country. One center of reality was in the thousands of young men and women who went to the cities and universities from devout, lower-middle-class families in the provincial towns, from strongholds of Shi'ite tradition such as Kazerun, Nishapur, and Yazd. In the large cities, these young people encountered a chaotic, materialistic society that openly ridiculed their religious beliefs, their social customs, and the values of their families and towns. Their response was, not to patronize the hotels and nightclubs (most could not have afforded them), but to meet together and discuss what they had seen, always trying to escape the watchful eyes of the secret police.

In the view of these young people, the shah's regime was foisting three evils on Iran. First, the uncritical imitation of foreign ways in education, society, and culture was debasing traditional Islamic and Iranian values. Students worked from Western texts that had been translated verbatim and with no acknowledgment that the lessons in them perhaps could and should be modified for the Iranian environment. Many young Iranians believed that their country was a dumping ground for toxic influences from the West—its pornography, alcohol, and overpriced luxury goods. They saw their country degraded to the point that an American, who was collecting the infamous "barbarism allowance" for living in Iran, could drive his motorcycle through a mosque. The shah's plans for his "great civilization" would, they feared, exclude those Iranians who followed their national traditions and force them either to withdraw from society or to become imitation Europeans. Iranians were becoming alienated from their roots without gaining any understanding of Western political values, social aspirations, or the scientific bases of technology.

Second, these young people saw pseudodevelopment and a waste of national resources. Money was spent on luxury housing, bowling alleys, well-equipped hospitals for the rich, and factories that produced goods most Iranians could not afford. Iranian universities developed costly affiliations with foreign institutions that granted honorary degrees to royal family members. The gap between the facilities available to rich and poor seemed to increase until the former could shop in Europe and the latter had to stand in line to buy onions.

Third, there was corruption and incompetence among the people in high office, who treated the national wealth as their private property to loot and mismanage. Although everyone in Iran knew about corruption, many outsiders mistook the absence of public protest for acquiescence. Such an attitude assumed that Iranians were so degraded that they would somehow accept being robbed. Since speaking out on such subjects usually meant trouble with the authorities, most Iranians simply concealed their hostility until it became safe to air their grievances. But they did not acquiesce. Instead, the young people found allies among technocrats, military officers, and civil servants who, ironically, had been in the regime's favor and had benefited materially from its policies. But the corruption, venality, and arbitrary misrule of the monarchy eventually made its natural supporters either indifferent or hostile.

REVOLUTION

The events of the Iranian revolution and its tortuous aftermath are still too recent to permit definitive judgment. We know approximately what happened; the *how* and *why* still defy explanation. In late 1977, on the very eve of the revolution, the shah appeared to be firmly in control despite Iran's social and economic problems. He enjoyed the friendship of the world's great powers; he had improved his relations with Iran's Arab neighbors; despite setbacks, his oil income allowed him to undertake ambitious development programs; and his security apparatus kept any opposition weak and divided. Much of the clergy remained indifferent to politics, the urban guerrillas could create only isolated incidents, and the nationalists were preoccupied with endless internal squabbles.

The Revolutionary Coalition

Yet in 1978–1979, the opposition built a coalition of groups that, despite widely varying ideologies and bases of support, brought down the monarchy more quickly and easily than almost anyone—including the revolutionaries themselves—believed possible. These revolutionary forces can be roughly classified into six groups as follows:[16]

1. Radical Clergy. This group included many of Ayatollah Khomeini's close associates inside Iran such as Hosein Ali Montazeri, Mohammad Reza Mahdavi-Kani, Ali Akbar Hashemi-Rafsanjani, and Seyyed Ali Khamene'i. Based in the bazaars and in some mosques and theological schools (especially the Qom Center of Religious Learning), these people were uncompromising in their opposition to the shah and his programs. Fundamentally opposed to the concept of monarchy, they attacked the shah where he was most vulnerable: on the issues of corruption, destruction of Islam, and plundering the country on behalf of the foreigner.

2. Traditional Clergy. These people, such as Ayatollahs S. Mohammad Kazem Shari'at-Madari and Hasan Tabataba'i-Qomi, were uneasy with direct clerical involvement in politics. Although accepting many of the radicals' criticisms of the shah, this group did not reject the institution of monarchy. Instead, it advocated limiting the shah's power by enforcing the 1906 fundamental laws, especially the provision that established a Council of Guardians to ensure that secular legislation conformed to Islamic law. Generally conservative on social and economic issues, this group was politically closer to the moderate nationalists than to the radical clergy.

3. *Religious Nationalists.* This group, which included Ayatollah Mahmoud Taleghani, Mahdi Bazargan, and their associates in the Liberation movement, advocated an Islamic republic that would uphold democratic values. Its members agreed with the radical clergy that Islam should form the basis of the new state, but they disagreed with that group's authoritarian ideology. They opposed doctrinaire anti-Americanism and warned against foreign policies that would isolate Iran from its neighbors and its traditional Western trading partners.

4. *Secular Liberals.* This group was composed of the National Front, the Radical movement of R. Moqaddam-Maraghe'i, and the National Democratic movement of Mossadegh's grandson, H. Matin-Daftari. Basically political moderates with middle-class support, its members considered themselves nationalists and constitutionalists following the Mossadegh tradition. This group, which also attracted considerable support from educated women, distrusted the slogans and themes of the radical clergy because the liberals believed the members of that group would impose their own harsh, obscurantist version of Islam on the entire Iranian population.

5. *Leftist Religious Radicals.* These radicals included the Mojahedin and their allies and advocated radical economic and social changes based on a revolutionary interpretation of Islam. Strongest among young, educated men and women from traditional middle-class families, the members of this group opposed direct clerical rule as they believed such rule would replace pure revolutionary Islam with a reactionary and capitalist version. Despite a common opposition to clerical rule, the Mojahedin's radical social and economic programs created an uneasy relationship with the moderate clergy and the nationalists.

6. *Secular Radicals.* This group was made up of members of the Tudeh, the Fada'i, and small Marxist organizations known as Peikar ("struggle") and Ranjbaran ("toilers"). These people advocated Marxist social and political revolution and considered religion, with or without clergy, to be a reactionary force. They advocated replacing the shah's military with "popular forces," supported the radical clergy's extreme anti-American rhetoric, and, after the shah's downfall, urged the revolutionary courts to order more executions and wider purges of opponents. Members of this group were especially active at the universities and among the national minorities such as the Kurds, Baluchis, and Turkomans.

Among these six groups, the members of the radical clergy held important advantages that enabled them to dominate and control the revolutionary movement. Throughout the period of royal dictatorship, the clergy had preserved its organizational bases—mosques, bazaars, Hoseiniyehs (centers of mourning for Imam Hosein), and religious schools—despite the regime's determined efforts to weaken these institutions. No other opposition group had this degree of organization as the shah's policies had prevented the formation of independent labor unions, political parties, or professional organizations that could have mobilized support for nonreligious groups. Khomeini's immense prestige, incorruptibility, personal magnetism, and record of uncompromising and outspoken hostility to the shah also gave him and his associates an overwhelming advantage over their rivals. These associates included such politically astute and ruthless leaders as Hashemi-Rafsanjani and the former head of the Hamburg Islamic Center, Ayatollah Mohammad Beheshti, who understood mass organization, propaganda, and manipulation of public opinion.

In addition to the leaders of the radical clergy, lower-ranking clerics—former students of Khomeini's disciples at the Qom center and now neighborhood, village, and small-town preachers and prayer leaders—were trained orators who spoke the language of the average citizen, lived close to the ordinary Iranian, and shared many of his or her values. In their preaching, these clerics skillfully emphasized populist themes, mixing appeals to religious and Iranian national feeling. Claiming to speak in the name of the mostaz'afin, the radical clergy built its power in the major cities on the base of a large lower- and lower-middle-class constituency.

By contrast, most of the secular politicians had difficulty working with or speaking to the urban masses. They showed little taste or talent for the street and neighborhood politics that could organize mass demonstrations, elect candidates, and intimidate rivals. Despite long records of opposition activity, many of the secular liberals were personally associated with the traditional social elite and used words and images that were incomprehensible to the ordinary Iranian. They wrote penetrating social and political analyses in small journals and newspapers that were read by only a narrow segment of society.

A Fatal Alliance

Nevertheless, a religious opposition movement by itself might not have toppled the shah. It took the support of the middle-class constituency of the old National Front—professionals, civil servants, students, and teachers—to ensure the success of the revolution. The shah had previously neutralized much of his nationalist opposition by a mixture of economic incentives and police repression, and he had encouraged and exploited the traditional anticlericalism of the intelligentsia by claiming to be their best defense against clerical obscurantism. He posed as a defender of women's rights and social progress against the attacks of "black" (that is, clerical) reaction. The people who could stomach the grosser aspects of Pahlavi rule earned substantial material rewards (especially after the 1973 oil windfall) in the form of large salaries, subsidized loans, and travel and business opportunities. Heedless of popular feeling, the regime allowed the newly wealthy to turn Iran into a private playground of cabarets, fine restaurants, gambling casinos, and coastal resorts.

But when the revolution threatened the monarchy's survival, many people in the modern middle class—hardly members of the mostaz'afin—turned on the shah and joined forces with the clergy to create a united opposition on an unprecedented scale. The hostility (or indifference) of a class that had traditionally supported the shah against his clerical enemies probably contributed as much to the revolutionary cause as did the religious-inspired opposition. To the shah, religious opposition was nothing new. He might have been able to deal with it by making concessions to moderate leaders and, as in 1963, by using force against radicals. But in 1978, simultaneous agitation in mosques and bazaars and strikes in the nation's modern sector—banks, newspapers, power plants, the oil industry, and government offices—meant serious trouble for the government. Strikes by central bank and customs employees paralyzed Iran's import-based economy and created chaos at ports and frontiers. Strikes in the oil industry cut domestic supplies of fuel and heating oil, stopped crude exports, and effectively shut off government income. These strikes did great psychological damage by convincing many Iranians that the regime was losing its grip.

People who had suffered in silence for many years now felt they could safely air their pent-up grievances, real or imagined. Those who had been politically inactive became openly hostile; those who had actively supported the monarchy now became neutrals awaiting the outcome of the crisis. Perhaps this neutrality, this indifference among the shah's former middle- and upper-class supporters threatened his regime even more than the outright hostility of his traditional enemies. In the end, many of the people who had benefited economically from the shah's policies were unwilling to defend him. They either joined the opposition or stood by quietly (sometimes from the safety of Europe or the United States) and watched his collapse.

Wealthy bazaar merchants, disturbed by the government's plans to "rationalize" traditional distribution and commercial patterns and by unpopular measures such as the reconstruction of the Mashhad bazaar near the shrine of Imam Reza, provided important financial and organizational support to the revolution. Because of the merchants' close ties to the clergy, their contributions constructed and maintained the network of independent religious institutions that became revolutionary headquarters. At the height of the struggle, mosques, religious schools, and the homes of religious leaders became print shops, food and fuel depots, information centers, arsenals, clinics, and even mortuaries. Merchants established makeshift shops and sold food from the backs of trucks to the poor at discount prices.

The small guerrilla organizations also contributed to the cause. Augmented by the release of political prisoners in late 1978 and early 1979, Mojahedin and Fada'i units gave the revolutionary coalition vital armed support during the final showdown with the military in February 1979. With arms taken from captured arsenals, the guerrillas organized assaults on army barracks, police stations, and SAVAK offices.

Troubles and Respite

The first signs of discontent gave little warning of the approaching storms. In the summer and fall of 1977, there was an upsurge of dissident activity among the intelligentsia. In open letters to the shah and prime minister, prominent intellectuals, many with National Front connections, began criticizing the regime for censorship, human rights infractions, and violations of the constitution. In August 1977, recurring economic problems led the shah to replace Amir Abbas Hoveida, prime minister since 1964, with Jamshid Amuzegar, who initiated a strict austerity program to cool off the overheated economy. Amuzegar, perhaps with more economic than political wisdom, put a squeeze on credit and drastically cut public spending. The resulting recession, especially in the construction industry, was hardest on casual workers and the small traders and middle-class businessmen who had gone deeply into debt during the boom years. None of these problems, however, suggested that the regime was anywhere near total collapse.

Most authorities date the actual beginning of the revolution from January 1978. An anticlerical diatribe and personal attack on Khomeini published in the January 7 issue of the newspaper Ettela'at provoked a demonstration and strike in Qom, and the clashes that resulted between Khomeini supporters and police left an undetermined number of dead and injured. On the fortieth day after these deaths, Ayatollah Shari'at-Madari called for the nation to observe mourning, in accordance with Shi'a custom. Most of these observances were peaceful, but demonstrators in Tabriz attacked banks and cinemas and briefly seized control of the city from the government. Thus began three forty-day cycles of antiregime demonstrations, each one commemorating victims of the previous event. There was bloodshed in both provincial towns and the capital. The May disturbances were especially serious in Teheran and Qom, where soldiers broke into Shari'at-Madari's home and shot two demonstrators.

Following the May clashes, the government made concessions to the moderate religious opposition while still refusing to negotiate with the National Front. The strategy appeared to work. Observances of the fortieth day of the May victims' deaths passed without incident, and Iran remained quiet through the summer. Significantly, at that time the public obeyed Shari'at-Madari's appeal for peaceful gatherings rather than Khomeini's calls to continue protesting. It appeared that the shah had, as in 1953 and 1963, survived another crisis by applying a mixture of force and diplomacy. Hopes for accommodation, however, began to collapse in the late summer after hundreds burned to death in the southern oil town of Abadan, where arsonists set fire to the Cinema Rex in August. The identity of the arsonists was (and is) unknown, but the opposition used the tragedy to stir up public opinion against the government. In September, larger and more strident demonstrations began echoing Khomeini's call for the end of the monarchy and the establishment of an Islamic republic (instead of a return to the 1906 constitution). Following a declaration of martial law on September 7 in Teheran and eleven provincial cities, clashes between troops and demonstrators in east Teheran's Zhaleh Square left hundreds dead.

"The Shah Must Go"

Khomeini's consistency and firmness were very popular among his unsophisticated constituents, who watched others shift their positions in the hope of accommodating themselves to new political realities. The shah first tried suppressing disturbances by force, but when force had failed, he resorted to seeking compromise from a position of weakness. While veteran politicians, such as former prime minister Ali Amini, tried to negotiate settlements and the government vacillated between concession and repression, Khomeini's attitude remained clear and unchanging: The shah must go and be replaced by an Islamic republic. Khomeini would accept nothing less, and on these points he would compromise with neither monarchists nor secular nationalists. The National Front and Liberation movement leaders, observing Khomeini's growing strength, had to acknowledge his leadership when it became obvious that he, not they, commanded the loyalty of the demonstrators in the streets. These leaders realized that the revolution would proceed, with or without them, under Khomeini's Islamic banners. Marxists, nationalists, and others could either march under these banners or be left behind.[17] Opposition groups temporarily put aside their feuds to achieve what a year earlier had seemed impossible—the overthrow of the shah.

The authorities enforcing martial law could not deal with the spreading disturbances. In Teheran, the once-powerful army stood aside and did nothing to prevent mass marches and rallies on the ninth and tenth days of Moharram (December 11–12). After this symbolic defeat, the army's morale cracked under the strain of continuing street battles, marches, and strikes. Further desertions and mutinies followed every outbreak of violence, as troops turned against their officers rather than continue to fire on unarmed demonstrators. Beginning in the provincial towns, government authority melted away, to be replaced by local neighborhood komitehs ("committees") under clerical leadership. In some areas, the army and revolutionaries tacitly agreed to avoid confrontations while awaiting the final outcome in Teheran. In Mashhad, government soldiers deserted after bloody riots in early January 1979, and Ayatollahs Shirazi and Tabataba'i-Qomi became de facto governors of the city. In Isfahan, Ayatollah Khademi controlled the city through his network of supporters in the mosques and bazaars.

The shah made a last desperate try at political accommodation. In late December 1978, Shahpur Bakhtiyar, a National Front politician, agreed to become prime minister if the shah left the country, and after assuming that position, Bakhtiyar attempted to win popular support by a series of gestures to the opposition: He canceled arms purchases, ended oil sales to Israel and South Africa, released political prisoners, withdrew Iran from the Central Treaty Organization, and began to dismantle SAVAK. Bakhtiyar's measures, inconceivable a year earlier, were now too late. The revolution had gone too far to be satisfied with anything less than the total destruction of the monarchy. Although some moderates supported Bakhtiyar, his former colleagues expelled him from the National Front for collaborating with the shah. Khomeini declared Bakhtiyar's government illegal and called for more strikes and demonstrations.

The shah left Iran for a "short vacation" on January 16, 1979. Almost the entire population celebrated his departure, but Bakhtiyar earned no credit for his part in a step that helped ensure Khomeini's victory. The demonstrations turned against Bakhtiyar, and army discipline deteriorated further. The Americans sent Gen. Robert Huyser to Teheran to try and keep the Iranian military organized as a force supporting Bakhtiyar's reformist government. Huyser's mission stirred up numerous rumors about possible U.S. action. Some people thought he was in Iran to plan a pro-shah coup; others believed he had come to dismantle secret U.S. installations to keep them out of Soviet hands; still others spread rumors that he was trying to get the Iranian air force to send its F-14s to Saudi Arabia.[18]

Bakhtiyar's government stood little chance. The prevailing view was that the Americans had forced him on the shah in a desperate attempt to stop the revolution and keep Khomeini out of power. Many Iranians remembered how the shah had dealt with other reformist prime ministers—Qavam, Mossadegh, and Amini—and felt that Bakhtiyar's program would be abandoned as soon as the shah could regroup his forces and return with military support. For the military, the shah's departure was fatal. Never enthusiastic about Bakhtiyar, they were left without a commander in chief and had to deal with the chaotic situation as best they could. Some military men made deals with the opposition, others packed their bags and fled the country, and others tried to preserve the government's few shreds of authority. On February 1, Khomeini returned to Iran in triumph and set up his headquarters in a Teheran girls' school. Four days later, he asked Mahdi Bazargan to form a provisional government to replace the immobilized and powerless Bakhtiyar cabinet.

The decisive confrontation came soon in the streets of the capital. On February 9, imperial guard units clashed with pro-Khomeini technicians at Doshan-tappeh Air Force Base in east Teheran. The insurgents opened the base arsenal and distributed weapons to crowds that had gathered in their support. The newly armed groups, aided by Mojahedin and Fada'i guerrilla units, stopped the imperial guards and stormed military posts, police stations, prisons, and SAVAK offices, most of which fell easily to the attackers when their occupants fled or surrendered. The leaderless army, demoralized by months of street fighting, declared itself "neutral" and refused to support the Bakhtiyar government against the revolutionaries. Troops were ordered to return to their barracks, although many simply changed clothes and disappeared. By the evening of February 11, the revolutionaries had total control of Teheran and had announced their victory over the state radio. Bakhtiyar went into hiding, and Bazargan became prime minister of the new government.

6

Revolutionary Iran

The twisted course of the Islamic revolution has surprised many of its original supporters and sympathizers, who believed that a change of government would not disturb the basic fabric of Iranian society. The upheavals have gone far beyond just removing the shah, his family, and a few associates. This revolution, although still too recent for anyone to see its final outcome, has shaken the very roots of Iran's political and social structures.

Yet there are limits to the new order's ability to impose change. The revolutionary leaders eventually will have to recognize that Iran's rich cultural heritage will persist despite their attempts to remake an entire society through permanent revolutionary frenzy. If these leaders declare war on Iranian history, they will repeat the mistakes of the shah, who tried to build his version of a modern society that had no place for its inhabitants' religious traditions. In so doing, he challenged his people's ancient social traditions and stirred up contradictions and tensions that eventually overwhelmed him in a wave of revolutionary violence. The current Islamic regime may have equal difficulty altering the basic Iranian political culture in order to force an austere, idiosyncratic, and authoritarian version of Islam on a nation that has long traditions of artistic creativity and of tolerance for cultural and intellectual diversity.

TO WHICH SELF?

Postrevolutionary Iran has become an arena in which competing groups battle over the answer to a question originally posed by the Khorasani teacher and lecturer Ali Shari'ati (d. 1977) in his important work, *Return to the Self: To Which Self?*[1] Shari'ati, a patron saint of the revolution for the Iranian intelligentsia, argued that the only way to political and social freedom for his country lay within Iranian tradition, the Iranian "self." If Iranians were ever to free themselves from oppressive rule, they would first have to find the correct ideology of liberation within their own beliefs and values. Shari'ati rejected foreign ideologies such as capitalism, nationalism, or Marxism. Reliance on such imports would only replace one form of dictatorship and foreign domination with another and would further widen the gulf between the Iranian masses, who were strongly attached to Islamic tradition, and the intelligentsia, who claimed to speak for the masses. Shari'ati saw an Iran in which intellectuals, isolated from their own cultural heritage, spoke a language incomprehensible to most other Iranians.

For its varied groups of supporters, the Iranian revolution was, above all, such a return to the self. It was a massive reassertion of Iranian identity and pride, a rejection of years of real or imagined foreign dominance. For many Iranians, the most obvious manifestation of their cultural and economic subjugation to the West was the shah's elaborate, expensive facade of pseudomodernization—his Iran of sky-scrapers, nightclubs, arts festivals, and planned communities inhabited by citizens loyal to a secular state. Most Iranians, however, wanted no part of this alien vision. The shah's system was not *their* system. Rather, it seemed to be built by and for others, an inhospitable world that debased and ridiculed its inhabitants' traditional culture as *omol* ("backward") and replaced it with nothing except a shoddy imitation of Europe.

In 1962, long before the revolution, the writer and social critic Jalal Al-e-Ahmad (d. 1971) wrote that Iran's relationship with the West had degenerated into blind imitation and complete surrender. Al-e-Ahmad diagnosed his country's rootlessness as a disease, which he called *gharbzadegi* ("infatuation with the West"). He wrote:

> If our politics and economy, to the extent that we've seen, are functions of the West's politics and economy, and if we're so Weststruck, it's because most of our intellectuals—those who've gained a foothold in the country's leadership machinery—in the last analysis, and [supposedly] as the most exalted mission of conscience and perception, are interpreters for Western advisors.[2]

Shari'ati's greatest contribution to the revolution was to answer his own question, To which self must Iranians return? Al-e-Ahmad and others had described their society's illness years before; Shari'ati's strength and originality lay in his idea that all Iranians—masses and intelligentsia—would find their true identity (their "self"), not in some forgotten and ossified pre-Islamic, Aryan past, but in an energetic, purified Shi'a Islam that had rediscovered its origins as an activist, revolutionary, political ideology stripped of rigid formalism and superstition.

> The experts . . . may know a great deal about the Sassanians, the Achaemenians, and even the earlier civilizations, but our people know nothing about such things. Our people do not find their roots in these civilizations. They are left unmoved by the heroes, geniuses, myths, and monuments of these ancient empires. Our people remember nothing from this distant past and do not care to learn about the pre-Islamic civilizations. . . . Consequently, for us to return to our roots means not a rediscovery of pre-Islamic Iran, but a return to our Islamic, especially Shi'i, roots.[3]

This message evoked a response among young and educated Iranians who had previously rejected Shi'ism as reactionary and irrelevant to their society's problems. From 1967 to 1973, Shari'ati lectured at the Hoseiniyeh-ye-Ershad, a progressive Teheran religious center, and to student audiences throughout Iran.[4] Speaking carefully to avoid censorship, Shari'ati asked his listeners to reconsider their indifference to and distaste for Shi'a Islam. The Shi'ism his audience considered hopelessly out of date was a distortion Shari'ati called "Safavid Shi'ism" (Tashayyo'-e-Safavi); true Shi'ism was the Shi'ism of Ali (Tashayyo'-e-Alavi), his family, and followers such as Abu Zarr. Shari'ati's references to Safavid Shi'ism fooled no one. He knew little and cared less about the Safavids; his real target was the establishment's "Pahlavi Shi'ism," the lifeless body of esoteric rules and doctrines that had alienated Iranian intellectuals and driven them into the arms of imperialists or Marxists.

Shari'ati ridiculed the traditional Iranian clergy's obsession with minute regulations and prohibitions. He accused its members of degrading Islam into a set of graveyard rituals and a dessicated religion concerned only with the afterlife, obscure points of doctrine, and trivia such as the legality of marriages among Adam and Eve's children. Shari'ati argued that Ali's religion, unlike the petrified Safavid Shi'ism, was a living ideology of personal responsibility and struggle for social reform and justice. He claimed, for example, that practitioners of Safavid Shi'ism had distorted the principle of entezar (expectation of the promised messiah) into a reactionary caricature of the original—a caricature that rationalized submission, fatalism, and inactivity while waiting for miraculous deliverance. Entezar, Shari'ati argued, actually meant activity and revolution, with the faithful organizing underground resistance in preparation for the messiah's call to rise against oppression.

The members of the traditional clergy responded to Shari'ati's attacks by denouncing him as a Sunni, a Wahhabi, and a Marxist. They criticized him for mixing Islam with ideas from Buddhism, Jean-Paul Sartre, and Fanon and for his view that Marxism was less an enemy of Islam than Western capitalism.[5] Stung by his accusation that their rigidity served the interests of the shah and his Western allies by alienating the young from Islam, the clergy answered that Shari'ati's anticlericalism served the shah by dividing his opposition and turning intellectuals against the ulema. Shari'ati devoted large sections of his works to answering these attacks on him and the Ershad. He urged the members of the clergy to abandon "unproductive" scholarship and to reassume their original role as militant leaders of opposition to an unjust regime.

These outspoken criticisms also earned Shari'ati the enmity of the government. Although he came perilously close to advocating open revolt against the shah's regime, the authorities may have considered him useful for weakening the religious opposition. They tolerated Shari'ati's allegories (perhaps unwilling to admit the authorities themselves were the targets) until late 1973 when his attacks finally provoked the government into closing the Hoseiniyeh-ye-Ershad and imprisoning Shari'ati for eighteen months, much of which time he spent in solitary confinement.

Shari'ati had his greatest success among young people who, like himself, had emerged from the traditional heart of Iranian society—the middle-class families of the provincial towns. The economic expansion of the sixties and seventies had enabled the children of these conservative families to pursue higher education at the new universities and specialized advanced schools. In large cities, however, these young men and women found themselves disoriented in a society that ridiculed their families' traditional values. Like Shari'ati, these young people held numerous grievances against the shah's regime. They believed that regime not only ignored their cultural sensitivities but also betrayed Iranian national interests by allying with Israel and the West against the Arabs and the third world. On the economic level, these young people saw the regime spending the nation's wealth on luxury items and on industries tied to foreign suppliers and technology.

Shari'ati reconciled many of these young and alienated Iranian intellectuals to their Shi'ite heritage—or at least to his revolutionary version of it. In an emotional work, *Father, Mother: We Stand Accused*, he portrayed a young Iranian's view of his parents' religion. The description is merciless. The older generation parrots half-understood rituals and formulas; it confuses the martyrdom of the Shi'ite Imam

Hosein, killed by government forces in Iraq in 680 A.D., with the Christian intercession; it makes Ali, Hosein's father, into an Islamic version of Rostam, the pre-Islamic Iranian hero of superhuman strength; and it prays only for material success and selfish interests. Shari'ati told his audience that true Islam was not their elders' meaningless ceremonies but a living and faith and ideology that would both protect Iranians' cultural identity (their "self") and prepare them to deal effectively with the political and economic realities of the modern world.

BUILDING AN ISLAMIC REPUBLIC

Although opposition to the shah united all revolutionaries, conflicting visions of the self to which Iranians should return were to tear the revolutionary coalition apart. Many of the people who had marched for Khomeini and had shouted "death to the shah" had no goal beyond overthrowing the monarchy. What should follow the Pahlavis was unclear, but it had to be better. At the time of the shah's downfall, however, Khomeini and a small group of close associates already possessed a clear and consistent vision of a revolutionary Islamic republic that would not be just imperial Iran without the emperor.

Khomeini had elaborated his political philosophy in the work *Islamic Government*, originally a series of lectures delivered in early 1971.[6] Without providing a detailed blueprint, Khomeini explained the principles of Islamic rule and the political duties of the ulema. He argued for the resurrection of the pure Mohammadan system (*Nezam-e-Mohammadi*) of seventh-century Medina, which had subordinated political authority to Islamic principles and had united religious, political, and military leadership. He presented a program for establishing such an Islamic government, urging the religious scholars to spread its message. He told them: "We must explain what the form of government is in Islam and how rule was conducted in the earliest days of Islamic history. We must tell them how the center of command and the seat of the judiciary under it were both located in part of the mosque, at a time when the Islamic state embraced the farthest reaches of Iran, Egypt, the Hijaz, and the Yemen."[7]

Khomeini's political vision, although not complete in all its details, was far more coherent than anything offered by his competitors, whether Marxist, nationalist, or traditionalist. Although Khomeini would sometimes change his tactics and methods, he remained firmly committed to his underlying purpose: establishing his version of government by the rules of Islam. Although inspired by the examples of Mohammad, Ali, and their companions in the seventh century, Khomeini's vision was radical for twentieth-century Iran. He and his followers demanded nothing less than complete destruction of the existing order. The shah's system was *taghuti;* that is, all of its parts— its parliament, courts, ministries, and culture—were illegitimate and operated in defiance of divine commands. By definition, such a system was hopelessly corrupt and evil. It could neither do anything right nor have anything worth preserving.[8]

Few of the middle-class professionals who had supported the revolution shared Khomeini's opinions about the need for such a radical transformation of Iranian society. They would have been satisfied with the removal of the shah, his family, and associates while leaving the nation's basic social structure undisturbed. The middle class hoped the revolution would bring a more open political climate, a nonaligned foreign policy, and a more rational economic system. Perhaps unaware of Khomeini's political philosophy, they believed they could help him (or exploit his popularity) to overthrow the monarchy while keeping the economic and social privileges the shah had given them. Whatever regime replaced the monarchy, the professionals believed they could dominate it by virtue of their superior educations and technical skills. The clergy, unable to run the apparatus of a modern state, would have to moderate its most extreme social views in order to placate the technicians, engineers, teachers, doctors, administrators, and others with "indispensable" talents.

But the revolution followed a path that was very different from what its middle-class supporters had anticipated. Following a brief period of postrevolutionary euphoria and free expression, the radical clergy began to isolate its rivals and maneuver its coalition partners out of power. The regime became increasingly strident, authoritarian, and intolerant of opposition. The signs of this narrowing trend included the following:

1. Revolutionary courts were immediately established, independent of Bazargan's moderate provisional government, to mete out swift "Islamic" justice to prominent figures of the old regime. The excesses of these courts, especially the behavior of the flamboyant Sheikh Sadeq Khalkhali, provoked loud protests from both the conservative clergy and the nationalists. The continuing outcry against arbitrary sentences imposed on people convicted for vague offenses such as "making war against God" finally led Khomeini himself to try to impose some standards for capital punishment in March 1979.

2. Bazargan's provisional government was obviously unable either to control domestic turmoil or establish an orderly foreign policy. Extremists on all sides openly defied the moderate nationalists who

held nominal power in the provisional cabinet. Ayatollah Montazeri's son, for example (the notorious "Sheikh Mohammad Ringo"), forced his way in and out of Teheran airport at gunpoint. The passport authorities, part of the national police, were powerless to stop him.

3. Outbreaks of violence occurred between revolutionary guards and ethnic minorities, especially the Kurds. Zealous guards from Shi'ite regions abused Kurdish sensitivities and ignored the settlements and arrangements for local self-management that had been worked out by representatives of the provisional government.

4. A growing intolerance of criticism from the independent press culminated in the announcement of a press law in August 1979. At that time, the authorities shut down the newspaper *Ayandegan* and several journals, notably *Omid-e-Iran* and the popular humor magazine *Ahangar.*

5. There were increasing attempts to govern social and cultural life by religious principles. The authorities banned Iranian classical music from radio and television, encouraged harassment of "improperly dressed" females in public places (including government offices), and closed swimming pools and sports clubs. At girls' schools, uniforms were made "Islamic," and physical education programs were severely limited. At the same time, covered women took a prominent part in marches and demonstrations in support of the radical clergy.

6. There was also increasing harassment of opponents by so-called Islamic associations in offices, schools, and ministries and by street gangs of *hezbollahis* ("partisans of God"). In August 1979, such gangs attacked a demonstration staged by H. Matin-Daftari's National Democratic Front. In late October, speakers at Friday prayers in Teheran denounced opposition intellectuals, threatening to break their pens (or their legs, depending on the translation of *qalam*).

7. The death of Ayatollah Mahmoud Taleghani, first Friday prayer leader of Teheran, in September 1979 eliminated a powerful counterweight to the power of the religious extremists. Very popular among young people and among leftist Islamic groups such as the Mojahedin, Taleghani had been an important link between the dominant clergy and the disaffected National Front and Sunni communities. A long-time ally of Bazargan in the Freedom movement, Taleghani's death was a severe blow to the provisional government and to the chances of preserving the unity of the broad-based coalition that had originally supported the revolution.

LEADERSHIP

One of the most important victories of the extremists was to establish the principle of theocratic rule with Khomeini as chief theocrat. The constitution of the new Islamic Republic, drafted by a Council of Experts in the summer and fall of 1979, recognized the principle of government called *velayat-e-faqih*, the guardianship of the jurist-theologian. This principle made the faqih (i.e., Khomeini) trustee of the hidden Imam's authority until his reappearance. As Khomeini had explained in his works, the faqih was the nation's guardian and had political and judicial authority equal to that of the prophets and the Shi'i Imams.

> With respect to duty and position, there is indeed no difference between the guardian of a nation and the guardian of a minor. It is as if the Imam were to appoint someone to the guardianship of a minor, to the governorship of a province, or to some other post. In cases like these, it is not reasonable that there would be a difference between the Prophet and the Imams, on the one hand, and the just faqih, on the other.[9]

This principle of leadership aroused loud protests among secular nationalists, leftists, the Sunni minority, and some of the Shi'a clergy. The nationalists attacked the Council of Experts for sanctioning theocratic dictatorship and a new monarchy that lacked even the formal limitations of the 1906 constitution. Radical leftists opposed velayat-e-faqih because it undermined popular sovereignty and frustrated their program of total economic reform. Sunni Iranians disliked a ruling principle that made their supreme leader the trustee of a figure (the hidden Imam) whose authority they did not accept. The issue also divided radical and traditional Shi'i clergy. Ayatollah Shari'at-Madari and other senior clergymen, while not openly breaking with Khomeini over the question, were wary of the close association between religion and politics in his theories. In their opinion, political power was essentially corrupt, and inevitable political errors by a religious leader would undermine the prestige of both the clergy and Islam itself.

As the Council of Experts finished its work in November 1979, the issue of the U.S. hostages overshadowed the divisive question of leadership. The partisans of velayat-e-faqih took advantage of the popular excitement generated by the crisis to make endorsement of clerical rule synonymous with supporting the Imam in his struggle against the United States. Despite objections and boycotts, the new constitution was overwhelmingly approved by a referendum in December 1979.

The constitution placed supreme leadership in Khomeini's hands. The leader holds extensive power, including the right to appoint the supreme commanders of the armed forces and the revolutionary guards; the right to declare war and make peace; and the right to appoint half of the twelve-man Council of Guardians, the body responsible for ensuring that parliamentary legislation conforms to Islamic precepts. Beyond the powers specified in the constitution, Khomeini exercises considerable indirect authority by force of personality and through general guidance of his followers. Despite his often-stated desire to imitate the governing style of the early Muslim leaders, Khomeini, unlike the prophet Mohammad or Imam Ali, has left the management of day-to-day affairs to others. When matters go badly—whether food distribution or Teheran traffic—he orders the people "responsible" to remedy conditions (for which he himself may bear ultimate responsibility) and deflects blame away from himself onto ministers and other expendable lower-level officials.

Khomeini, unlike the shah, apparently realizes his power is not absolute. Deliberately leaving his instructions vague and open ended, he is reluctant to issue specific commands that may be ignored lest repeated and open defiance of his orders undermine his leadership and prestige.[10] Khomeini has usually remained aloof from political disputes, urging unity (*vahdat-e-kalameh*) on his subordinates and taking sides only when they are deadlocked. He takes a direct, personal interest in only a few selected policy issues, such as the conduct of the war with Iraq (decisions on the war are exclusively Khomeini's, and there will be no cease-fire, peace, or moderation of Iran's uncompromising position without his explicit approval). But he more often sees himself as a follower, not a leader, of public opinion and does not declare himself before sensing the direction of popular feeling as expressed in demonstrations, marches, and petitions. This "leader-follower" method favors the radical clergy, which has the street organization that is best able to mobilize large, disciplined groups of supporters for impressive demonstrations at marches and Friday prayer meetings.

CONSTITUTIONAL INSTITUTIONS

The Iranian constitution of 1979 created the theoretical skeleton of a political order that combines Islamic and republican principles. The main features of this constitutional system include:

1. A supreme leader
2. A popularly elected president who implements the constitution and regulates relations among the three branches of government

3. A prime minister and cabinet (the Council of Ministers) nominated by the president and approved by the parliament
4. A 270-member unicameral parliament, the Islamic Consultative Council (Majles-e-Shora-ye-Eslami)
5. A 12-member Council of Guardians (Shora-ye-Negahban) with the power to review parliamentary legislation for conformance to Islamic principles

The constitution (articles 113–132) establishes a strong presidency. The Council of Guardians supervises direct popular election of a president for a four-year term; he may be reelected once. If no candidate receives a majority in the first round of elections, the two leading candidates compete in a runoff. Article 115 requires that the president be a man of "political and religious distinction." He must be an Iranian citizen of Iranian origin, a Shi'a Muslim, and a believer in the Islamic Republic. He signs laws and treaties approved by the Majles and the Council of Guardians, receives and dispatches ambassadors, and may return for revision laws proposed by the Council of Ministers.

The constitution does not create a traditional parliamentary system of government but subordinates the prime minister and other ministers to the president and parliament (articles 133–138). Both president and parliament (the latter by a vote of confidence) must approve the prime minister's appointment. The prime minister nominates other ministers, who must also receive both presidential and parliamentary approval. The president also approves the prime minister's dismissal of a minister. The prime minister normally chairs the Council of Ministers, but the president may do so if he finds it necessary. The prime minister remains in office as long as he has a vote of confidence from parliament, which may also question ministers directly, impeach them, or require their resignation individually or as a group through a vote of no confidence.

The 270-member Islamic Consultative Council (articles 62–90) is the legislative body of the republic. Its members serve four-year terms and must have received a majority of the popular vote in their district. Recognized religious minorities—Jews, Zoroastrians, Chaldean (Assyrian) Christians, and northern and southern Armenians—are represented as communities. Each member represents approximately 150,000 constituents, and the constitution provides for the creation of additional seats when a census (taken every ten years) reveals a population increase of 150,000 in a district. Large cities (such as Teheran with 30 seats) elect all of their representatives at large, a method that usually favors candidates for whom the clergy can mobilize lower- and lower-middle-class support. Parliament considers bills proposed by the Council of Ministers or by at least fifteen of its own members. The constitution also gives parliament the power to conduct investigations, approve international agreements, and authorize government lending and borrowing.

Although parliament exercises control over the Council of Ministers and, to some extent, the president, its independence is checked by the powerful Council of Guardians (articles 91–99), which supervises presidential and parliamentary elections and reviews parliamentary acts for their conformity to the principles of religious law. The Council of Guardians has been an assertive body. In May 1984, it invalidated all parliamentary elections in Isfahan, Shiraz, and several smaller cities, and although the parliament approved a bill to nationalize foreign trade in April 1982, two years later the council's objections still had prevented the bill's becoming law.[11] The supreme leader (or leadership council) chooses six of the Council of Guardians' twelve members from "just and religious persons," and the High Council of the Judiciary, with the approval of parliament, chooses six "Islamic jurists." An ingenious provision of the constitution (article 93) ensures the superiority of the Council of Guardians over the parliament, for the latter has no validity until (1) the Council of Guardians has been formed and (2) the parliament has approved the six Islamic jurist members of the council.[12]

Not only does the absence of a Council of Guardians invalidate all actions of parliament, but the council has almost absolute veto power over parliamentary legislation. The Islamic Consultative Council submits its approved bills to the Council of Guardians, which has ten days to review them for conformance to Islamic standards and constitutional law. A majority of the latter council's religious (i.e., Khomeini-appointed) members decide whether a parliamentary law conforms to Islamic standards. If the council finds a law contradicts religious principles, it returns that law for revision. Otherwise the law is ratified and goes to the president for signature. The Council of Guardians is a vital part of the legislative process, and its members may attend parliamentary meetings and express their opinion on bills under discussion.[13]

The constitution (articles 156–174) also creates a five-member High Council of the Judiciary composed of the head of the Supreme Court, the attorney general (both appointed by the supreme leader), and three religious judges (chosen by their colleagues). All members of this council serve for five years. The constitution explicitly places the judiciary council under religious control, requiring that its two leader-appointed members be mojtaheds. This powerful body controls the entire Iranian judiciary by supervising the work of the Ministry of Justice; preparing judicial legislation for parliament; appointing, dismissing, and assigning judges; and suggesting suitable candidates for the minister of justice post to the prime minister. The High Council of the Judiciary has attempted to rebuild completely the Iranian legal system on an Islamic base. Working with revolutionary courts, local religious judges, and the Imam's representatives in the provinces, the council has brought the entire judicial system under the control of the clergy.

In addition to describing the supreme leader's position and establishing the fundamental institutions of government (president, parliament, Council of Ministers, and judiciary), the writers of the constitution were determined that their work reflect the revolutionary origin and character of the new Islamic state. Thus the constitution (article 150) legalizes the Revolutionary Guards' Corps (Sepah-e-Pasdaran), which was informally organized during the first days of the revolution's success, as the "guardians of the revolution and its offshoots." Although the nationalists opposed converting an irregular armed force into an official organ of the Islamic Republic, this constitutional recognition tacitly committed the new regime to continuing revolution and rejecting "order" based on prerevolutionary institutions.[14] The constitution does not define the duties and authority of the corps except to say piously, "the scope of its authority in relation to the duties and scope of the authority of the other armed forces will be determined by law, with emphasis on cooperation and brotherly harmony." Although the constitution provides for a "popular and religiously educated" army, the army's role in the revolution and its association with the shah and the United States made it suspect among the revolutionaries, who believed that a permanent Revolutionary Guards' Corps would prevent counterrevolution and secure the power of the new regime.

In practice, the constitutional system has operated in some unexpected ways. Despite the arrangements for a strong presidency, a tenacious, resourceful, and well-organized political alliance centered in Ayatollah Mohammad Beheshti's Islamic Republican party (IRP) was able to maneuver the new republic's first president, Abu'l-Hasan Bani Sadr, out of power.[15] Although an IRP member had been unable to win the first presidential election in January 1980, the party built a powerful, extended political network that eventually controlled almost the entire state except the presidency—the parliament, cabinet, courts, and provinces. In June–July 1981, this network, having stripped Bani Sadr of most of his powers, drove him from office and captured the presidency for one of its own: first, Prime Minister Ali Raja'i, a former high school mathematics teacher of modest ability, and later, after Raja'i's assassination, the influential cleric and Beheshti's successor as IRP secretary-general, Ali Khamene'i. Khamene'i's election in October 1981 finally made the strong presidency a reality.

For its part, the new parliament turned out to be anything but a rubber stamp. In March 1980, Khomeini increased parliament's power at the expense of the president by making the former (while still unelected) responsible for settling the hostage crisis. The two-stage and at-large election processes favored the IRP candidates and handicapped moderates and leftists, who could have benefited from smaller, more homogeneous urban districts or a system of proportional representation. Some successful non-IRP candidates, such as Khosrow Qashqa'i in Fars and Khosrow Rigi in Baluchestan, faced further obstacles when the parliament refused to accept their credentials. The IRP-controlled parliament and President Bani Sadr remained stale-mated on issues such as the selection of a prime minister and the conduct of the war with Iraq. Although the removal of Bani Sadr helped the radical clergy of the IRP consolidate its control over all branches of government, the parliament has continued to resist sub-servience to the executive. Perhaps because of the presence of strong-willed leaders such as Ali Akbar Hashemi-Rafsanjani and Mohammad Mosavi-Kho'iniha (see Appendixes A and B), the parliament has remained independent, occasionally rejecting ministerial nominations and criticizing government actions with great enthusiasm.

DIFFUSION OF POWER

Despite the constitution's liberal-sounding principles of equality and freedom and its ingenious integration of Islamic principles into a parliamentary-presidential system, this constitution, like its pre-decessor, has not protected the individual Iranian from the authorities' arbitrary exercise of power or given Iranian citizens the benefits of orderly government. Revolutionary turmoil, wartime conditions, and Khomeini's idiosyncratic method of leadership have hindered the establishment of the systematic political process defined in the con-stitution. The supreme leader has continued to preside over an amorphous "nonsystem" in which power is widely diffused among autonomous groups, institutions, and individuals whose authority depends mostly on their connections within the ruling clique and their ability to mobilize followers in the streets of Teheran.

After the shah's downfall, the religious extremists among the revolutionaries—known as *maktabis* ("ideologues")—were determined to prevent the nationalists in Bazargan's provisional government from

operating an "orderly" administration. Permitting such an administration would have required surrendering authority to those "liberal"
and "Westernized" individuals, such as oil minister Hosein Nazih or
foreign minister Ebrahim Yazdi, whom the extremists did not consider
sufficiently revolutionary and with whom they had no intention of
sharing power. Orderly administration would have meant establishing
a normal diplomatic relationship with the United States and allowing
some of the old institutions, such as the shah's army, police, and
foreign ministry, to continue functioning. The maktabis, however, who
shared Khomeini's view of the need for a complete rebuilding of
Iranian political culture, distrusted the political structures and the
personnel inherited from the monarchy. But unable to abolish or
change all of the hated Pahlavi system immediately, they instead
stripped remnants of the ancien régime of the ability to operate and
created their own parallel, "revolutionary" system of government.
The result was a peculiar kind of anarchy in which, simultaneously,
everyone and no one was in charge.[16]

After the collapse of the monarchy, the informal network of
religious leaders, whose long experience in organizing the communal
ceremonies of Shi'a Islam had served them so well during the
revolution, now had the legitimacy of armed force and the Imam's
implicit support. With these power bases, they maintained their
independence and ignored the "official" central government, first
represented by Bazargan's cabinet and later by President Bani Sadr.
In the beginning, this network operated semiclandestinely, through
nonstate organs and the Revolutionary Council, which operated as
a de facto government from February 1979 until its dissolution in
November 1980. Gradually this network assumed overt control in a
two-part campaign. First, the maktabis took over vital government
ministries, companies, and institutions such as the radio and television.
Employees who were unsympathetic to the new order were purged
or retired. Islamic associations (*Anjomanha-ye-Eslami*) appeared in
factories, universities, banks, and offices to ensure conformity with
the new revolutionary ideology and to combat the influence of
monarchists, communists, liberals, unveiled women, and other miscreants. Second, entirely new "revolutionary" organizations took over
functions such as justice and internal security. Neighborhood vigilante
groups supported by groups of armed revolutionary guards took over
the work of the national police, other groups took over the work of
the Customs Office of the Ministry of Finance, and revolutionary
and Islamic courts, controlled by the maktabi clergy, appropriated
the work of the justice and prison systems. In the major provincial
cities, Friday prayer leaders and the Imam's representatives (often the

same person) took over much of the power formerly held by governors-general. These changes reduced to ciphers whole sections of the Ministries of Finance, Defense, Interior, and Justice and replaced them with new power centers whose leaders wielded undefined authority and were apparently answerable to no one but themselves.[17]

Outsiders could hold nominal power in institutions, such as the universities, where the maktabis were relatively weak. The postrevolutionary chancellor of Shiraz University, for example, was a non-maktabi Azarbaijani, whom all parties respected for his independence, integrity, and fair-mindedness. Caught between conflicting ambitions of left and right at the university, however, the new chancellor remained powerless. Similar conditions prevailed at Mashhad University, where, in September 1979 the chancellor needed the permission of his maktabi assistant even to resign. In the words of one professor, "The chancellor resigned, but the vice-chancellor refused to accept his resignation."[18] Eventually the maktabis, unable to gain control of the universities, closed them in 1980. In 1986, only some medical and technical faculties were operating, and the regime still regarded the universities as centers for teaching moral corruption and foreign ideologies.

THE RULING NETWORK

In discussions of the power structure of the Islamic Republic, new terms such as *qeshri* and *maktabi*, for which there are few equivalents in a Western political scientist's lexicon, have replaced the traditional vocabulary of left, right, conservative, liberal, and radical.[19] Yet the maktabis' narrow version of the Iranian self—the version that has triumphed over the more tolerant views of the nationalists and the traditionalists—is truly radical in its insistence on complete social and political change and in its refusal to compromise with ideas it considers heretical, un-Islamic, or inconsistent with Khomeini's *Nezam-e-Mohammadi*. In the five years following the victory of the revolution, the radical clerics of the IRP, who upheld this harsh, maktabi vision, were able to seize exclusive control of the state, consolidate a theocratic system, and exclude their former coalition partners from power. Through the party's control of key state and nonstate institutions, the IRP radicals have driven their opponents—members of the National Front, the Liberation movement, the Kurdish Democratic party, the Mojahedin, the Fada'i, and the Tudeh as well as the religious traditionalists (including some of the most senior and respected clerics in Iran)—into political oblivion.

A powerful network of approximately twenty radical clerics, who rank just below the supreme leader, controls the political life of the

Islamic Republic. These religious leaders (see Appendixes A and B) include the highest officers of the state: the president; the speaker and deputy speaker of the parliament; the Imam's representatives on various high councils; the prayer leaders and the Imam's representatives in the major cities; the prosecutors-general; the head of the Supreme Court; the head of the military revolutionary court; members of the Council of Guardians; and leaders of the IRP. Directly or indirectly, the members of this network also control the various welfare foundations and funds, the revolutionary guards, and the Hezbollah, the street gangs of the IRP. The leading members outrank ministers, commanders, and others with nominal power, even in new institutions like the Revolutionary Guards' Corps.[20]

The influential Ayatollah Hosein Ali Montazeri, chosen in 1985 as Khomeini's successor, remains mostly outside this ruling clerical network of IRP politicians. Although Montazeri held several political offices after the revolution, including speaker of the first Council of Experts and Friday prayer leader of Teheran, since 1981–1982 he has avoided direct involvement in party politics. He has remained in Qom as custodian of the Feiziyeh School (see Chapter 5), where, imitating Khomeini's political style, he receives visitors and makes public declarations. To indicate Montazeri's future leadership role, the state media has raised him to the rank of Grand Ayatollah (*Ayatollah Ozma*) and "exalted jurist" (*faqih-e-ali qadr*).

Although respected for his personal modesty and long and loyal association with Khomeini, Montazeri apparently lacks the Imam's charisma, his single-minded tenacity, and the political skills of the leaders of the IRP network. In September 1979, Montazeri's ineffectiveness as speaker of the first Council of Experts (the constitutional convention) led the deputy speaker, Ayatollah Beheshti, to push him aside gently and chair the council meetings himself with a firm and decisive hand. The evidence suggests that Montazeri will inherit Khomeini's titles but not his power and that the leaders of the IRP clerical network—Hashemi-Rafsanjani, Abd al-Karim Mosavi-Ardabili, and Ali Khamene'i—will exercise real power under Montazeri's figurehead leadership.

Although these powerful clerics do not agree on all questions, their differences on the details of issues such as private property, the export of revolution, the relative evil of the United States and the Soviet Union, and the precise role of the faqih have not weakened their hold on power or prevented them from taking united action— brutal action when necessary—against opponents. The Imam's frequent appeals for unity among his followers have helped suppress their personal rivalries and will probably hold the alliance together, at least during his lifetime.[21] Although each member operates independently, in the style of a bureaucratic-feudal anarchy, the nucleus of shared views is large enough to give this network considerable strength and cohesion. Thanks to its loose organization and the similar views of its members, this network has held power despite losing many of its most important figures by assassination. It was strong enough, for example, to survive the summer of 1981, when bombings of IRP headquarters and the prime minister's office decimated party leadership. With slight variations, all members of this alliance agree on seven basic points.

1. Commitment to political activism for the clergy. They see themselves as political leaders, using ceremonies such as Friday prayers and sermons as "political-religious" occasions. Khomeini himself told delegates at an international congress of Friday imams that their sermons must address the political concerns of Islam.

> Muslims should not allow the sermons to be limited to a few prayers and recitations, as they have been up to now. Change the contents of those sermons. . . . In your own countries and in your Friday sermons, which are designed for this purpose; in your prayers, your pilgrimages, wherever you have an audience, you should raise Islamic issues related to the social problems of the people. Do not discuss private affairs, but raise social problems. Say these things and let them ban the Friday prayers; people will react. If a government bans your Friday prayers because of your sermons, it would be confronted with the reaction of the people, and that is exactly what we want.[22]

2. Commitment to the principle of velayat-e-faqih in which only a righteous jurist, selected by community consensus, can act as trustee of the hidden Imam's power. Some adherents have taken this principle to the extreme of identifying Khomeini with the Mahdi—the promised redeemer of Shi'a Islam—or at least with his predecessor.

3. Distrust of bureaucracy and the traditional manner of conducting a state's international and domestic affairs. For example, the regime has replaced its experienced foreign service personnel with untrained, zealous, maktabi cadres with little knowledge of relations with foreign states.

4. Rejection of Iranian nationalism in favor of pan-Islamic goals. The regime never refers to its war with Iraq in national terms— rather, it is fighting the war of right against wrong, of truth against falsehood. In their attack on nationalism, the clerics have attemped to discredit Mossadegh and rehabilitate his opponent, Ayatollah Kashani.[23]

5. Commitment to imposing, by force if necessary, strict "Islamic" standards of social behavior, including those related to dress, male-female relations, and public entertainment. In one Teheran Friday sermon, the speaker warned that improperly dressed women would "receive corporal punishment decreed by Islamic law."[24]

6. Commitment to a "no East, no West" foreign policy that seeks economic self-sufficiency, rejects close relations with either superpower, and supports third world liberation movements, especially Islamic movements in Lebanon, Afghanistan, Bahrain, and elsewhere.

7. Commitment to a "cultural revolution" in schools, families, and universities that will replace foreign and taghuti values with Islamic principles and methods. In the schools, the regime has purged the staffs and changed programs and textbooks. It has closed the university faculties that it regards as hotbeds of Eastern and Western ideologies hostile to Islam.

The Radical Victory

Five years after the revolution, this clerical alliance had defeated its opponents and consolidated its power. Its first target was the hated group of liberals, nationalists, and intellectuals—heirs of Mossadegh's National Front—who, one by one, were forced into exile or political obscurity. The "second revolution," which began with the capture of the U.S. embassy in November 1979, completed the defeat and humiliation of liberal politicians such as R. Moqaddam-Maraghe'i, Karim Lahiji, and Ahmad Madani, who had voiced outspoken criticism of the increasing authoritarianism and intolerance of the revolutionary authorities.[25] The "third revolution," which began in June 1981, brought the dismissal and flight of President Bani Sadr; the suppression of the Mojahedin; the trial and execution of Sadeq Qotbzadeh, former foreign minister of the republic; and the "demotion" of Ayatollah Shari'at-Madari.

A curious feature of the IRP network's success is that these partisans of Islamic revolution have reached power by discrediting such venerable, respected, and learned practitioners of Shi'a Islam as Ayatollahs Tabataba'i-Qomi, Mahallati, and Shari'at-Madari. In April 1980, Sheikh Khalkhali, for example, violently attacked Qomi for his statement that Islam took no position on the taking of hostages. At the same time, the students occupying the U.S. embassy were publishing documents that indicated Qomi's dissatisfaction with the abuses of the revolutionary courts and with Khomeini's disregard for the opinions of other senior religious scholars. In Shiraz, Ayatollah Seyyed Abd al-Hosein Dastgheib's victory over his rival Mahallati was less dramatic but equally decisive. Of the two ayatollahs, Mahallati had had a longer association with Khomeini (and with Taleghani and the Liberation movement) while Dastgheib and his family had come relatively late to opposition politics. In Eric Hoogland's opinion, Dastgheib's partisans had overwhelmed Mahallati by the end of 1979. According to Hoogland, Dastgheib owed his victory to social factors, specifically the desire of the Shiraz theology students (tollab) for upward mobility. These students saw that the revolution had propelled militant members of the clergy into high political office at a relatively young age. Their colleagues' advancement convinced ambitious tollab to support Dastgheib, because the fact that he favored an active political role for the clergy offered them a way to reach positions previously reserved for persons with secular educations.[26]

The attacks against Ayatollah Shari'at-Madari in April 1982 illustrate how the IRP network could use its control of the media, revolutionary guards, hezbollah goon squads, Friday prayers, the Militant Clerics' Association, and other institutions to arrange a well-organized and effective campaign against a prominent opponent. Shari'at-Madari had opposed Khomeini's militant views since the beginning of the latter's political activities in the 1960s, and in Qom, Shari'at-Madari had sponsored the apolitical Dar al-Tabligh (House of Islamic Propaganda) to oppose the radicalism of Khomeini's followers.[27] Although the two clerics had joined forces against the shah in 1978, Shari'at-Madari had voiced open opposition after the revolution to direct clerical rule and velayat-e-faqih. His Muslim Republican Peoples' party (MRPP), however, was no match for the IRP alliance's ruthless leadership, armed force, and provincial and neighborhood organization, and a December 1979 MRPP uprising in Tabriz found little support even among the Azarbaijanis. The collapse of the Tabriz uprising weakened Shari'at-Madari's position, but he remained a focus of hope for various dissident groups until April 1982, when the regime launched its final attacks against him. Following Qotbzadeh's arrest on April 10 and his public confession that Shari'at-Madari had known of a plot to assassinate the Imam and seize power in a military coup, a carefully organized campaign of public denunciation quickly led to Shari'at-Madari's demotion from the rank of Grand Ayatollah and Source of Guidance (Marja'-e-Taqlid). The campaign, fully reported in the IRP-controlled media, proceeded as follows:

1. April 20. A statement by the Qom Seminary Teachers' Association demanded Shari'at-Madari's demotion from the rank of marja'.
2. April 21. The IRP daily Jomhuri-ye-Islami printed the Qom teachers' action on its front page and reported anti-Shari'at-

Madari demonstrations around the country, especially in his
native Azarbaijan.

3. April 21. The Militant Clerics' Association (MCA) issued the
following statement: "As regards the judicial viewpoint, the
MCA leaves the matters to the judicial authorities to investigate
. . . but the association deems it necessary to announce clearly
the following: Mr. Shari'at-Madari does not enjoy the conditions for holding the status of a source of imitation and is
not eligible for the position." This statement was signed by
some of the most powerful people in the country, including
Mahdavi-Kani (secretary-general of the association), President
Khamene'i, Hashemi-Rafsanjani, Fazlollah Mahallati, Abd al-
Majid Ma'adikhah, and Ali Akbar Nateq-Nuri.

4. April 21. The Friday imams in five cities, including Isfahan,
Tabriz, and Yazd, issued a similar statement.

5. April 23 (Friday). In Teheran, Mahdavi-Kani attacked Shari'at-
Madari in a Friday sermon. Marchers in Tabriz also dem-
onstrated against Shari'at-Madari, and Ayatollah Sheikh Moslem Malakuti, the Imam's representative in that city, denounced him in a Friday sermon.

6. April 24. The Teheran dailies *Ettela'at* and *Keyhan* published
documents from U.S. embassy files showing Shari'at-Madari's
connections to the shah and his contacts with embassy
representatives before and after the revolution.[28]

This campaign effectively eliminated Shari'at-Madari as a factor in
Iranian politics. Citing the orchestrated public outcry as an excuse,
the government closed Dar al-Tabligh and placed Shari'at-Madari
under house arrest in Qom, where he remained until his death in
1986.

Sources of Power

Another crucial factor that aided the members of the IRP network
in their drive for power was their years of close association in the
narrow, intense world of theological schools, opposition politics, and
Pahlavi prisons. Like members of a secret fraternity or an extended
family, these individuals had lived, studied, and worked together for
years, and their ties had been strengthened by pressures from a
hostile government. Khomeini himself had lived continuously in Qom
for over forty years, and during that time he had taught over 10,000
students, many of whom became faithful partisans of his political
ideas and, later, key figures in the IRP network. The heart and brains
of the network—Beheshti, Mohammad Javad Bahonar, Khamene'i, and

Hashemi-Rafsanjani—had all been Khomeini's students. Ayatollah Montazeri and Morteza Mottahari (assassinated, May 1981), one of the leading intellects among the revolutionaries, had also studied with Khomeini. Mottahari himself had taught at Teheran and Qom, and his students had included Beheshti, Bahonar, and Mohammad Mofateh (assassinated, December 1979), dean of the Teheran University divinity faculty. Many of Khomeini's disciples had also shared prison experiences. In 1975, for instance, following a proclamation by Khomeini in which he attacked the shah's new single ("Resurgence") party, the regime had imprisoned many of Khomeini's associates in Iran—including Mahdavi-Kani, Beheshti, Montazeri, Khamene'i, and Jalal al-Din Taheri. Like family members, these people were on a first-name basis, teachers developed paternal relations with their students, and intermarriage further reinforced the ties—Khomeini reportedly has marriage connections with Montazeri, Qodusi (the first revolutionary prosecutor), and Hashemi-Rafsanjani.

So far, the network's harsh, austere, and intolerant vision of the Iranian self has overcome all competitors, and barring an unforeseen catastrophe or outside disaster, the radical clerics of the IRP will probably stay in control as long as they preserve their underlying unity. The clerics' close personal ties, their similarity of views and backgrounds, and their intimacy with the Imam have preserved their network against shocks that would have destroyed weaker groups. Neither economic difficulties—inflation, shortages, and war destruction—nor the heavy losses of young men in the stalemated war with Iraq appear to have weakened the clerics' grip on power. Most important, their network has been able to withstand the assassinations that have occurred. The network's interchangeable membership makes it independent of a single individual's survival (except perhaps Khomeini himself), and the assassinations that have taken place among the IRP leadership have not seriously disrupted the network's operation. There seems to be an almost limitless supply of clerics to replace assassinated presidents, prime ministers, party leaders, and Friday preachers. The network has also made use of loyal, maktabi laymen—such as Prime Minister Mir-Hosein Mosavi and Foreign Minister A. A. Velayati—but such individuals remain outside the extended family of radical clerics that controls the key institutions of the Islamic Republic.

FOREIGN POLICY

The foreign policy of the Islamic Republic has evolved from the original power struggles that took place among the members of the victorious revolutionary coalition. Competing visions within that coalition seemed to drive Iran's foreign policy in conflicting and erratic directions, and in these struggles, foreign policy became, above all, a means of achieving exclusive political control in Teheran. In 1979–1980, an unlikely alliance of extremists of left and right created and manipulated an endless confrontation with the United States in order, in part, to overwhelm Iranian nationalist and democratic forces. Young religious ideologues, some of whom—such as Mohammad Mosavi-Kho'iniha and Hosein Sheikholislam (now the undersecretary for political affairs in the Iranian foreign ministry)—participated in taking and holding the U.S. Embassy in Teheran, were able to seize control of their country's foreign policy.

Although leaders of the Islamic Republic have aggressively advocated a world Islamic revolution, their first goal was to consolidate power and eliminate all political competitors at home. The country's foreign policy took its shape when the people who were seeking to remake Iranian society into Khomeini's harsh version of the *Nezam-e-Mohammadi* had won their victories in the Teheran streets. The resulting absolutist rule at home has created an uncompromising foreign policy that promotes militant Islam, revolution, and confrontation abroad.

Yet in February 1979, Iran's foreign policy, like its domestic politics, could have taken many directions. At that time the victorious revolutionaries had few foreign enemies. The leader of the Palestine Liberation Organization, Yasir Arafat, invited himself to Teheran immediately after the revolution, and many of the Arab countries, even conservative ones, welcomed the Iranians' new anti-Israeli militancy. Iran's non-Arab Islamic neighbors—Turkey, Afghanistan, and Pakistan—sent congratulations and expressed their wish to live in peace with this large and powerful state. The United States, Japan, and the European Economic Community (EEC) countries hoped that the end of revolutionary turmoil would make Iran once again an important oil producer and a trading partner, and the USSR and the Eastern European countries hoped to profit both economically and politically from the new order in Teheran.

A Foreign Policy of Anarchy

But orderly foreign policy required orderly domestic politics. As long as no one was in control at home, Iran could not speak with one voice abroad, and at first, many voices spoke for the new Iran. Some people said the country would continue to live in peace with its neighbors; others called for the overthrow of Iraq's Saddam Hussein and the Persian Gulf emirs. Some said the country would both carry on its own revolution and act as a responsible member of the international community; others denounced the traditions of an international system that, they claimed, worked only for the benefit of the rich and powerful.

The country's foreign policy debate would be ended only when its domestic struggles were settled—when it had been decided to which "self" the nation should return. If the nationalists, who appeared to hold power in the first months after the revolution, were to guide the politics of the new state, they would need to stabilize Iran's relations with the Arab world, Europe, and both the United States and the USSR. But if the revolution were to continue in the direction of a militant Islamic government—toward Khomeini's vision of the Iranian self—then external enemies and scapegoats were needed to fuel the fires of revolutionary militancy.

In the first years after the revolution, extremists of both left and right raised the alarm against foreign conspiracies in order to drive their common enemies—the nationalists, social democrats, and moderates—out of the revolutionary coalition. History, manipulated hysteria, and miscalculations by Iranians and foreigners alike helped evoke a powerful response to the cries of foreign plots. The extremists have had their victory but at an enormous cost: Five years of war with Iraq have left over 100,000 young Iranians dead and ruined much of Khuzestan; Iran trades insults with Saudi Arabia, Pakistan, and the Persian Gulf states; relations with the United States were completely broken in April 1980 during the hostage crisis; and relations with the USSR, Iraq's major supplier of arms, have varied from cool to hostile. Relations with most of the EEC countries and Japan, clouded by Iran's support of terrorist groups and rejection of standards of international behavior, have remained limited mostly to purchases of essential food and industrial goods.

Militant Principles

The Islamic Republic has followed an apparently erratic foreign policy that has confused outsiders and misled foreign experts. Yet the republic, reflecting the philosophy of its leader, has consistently rejected compromise on three important principles. First, although realizing that great-power rivalry—specifically the desire of each superpower to deny the other military access to Iran—represents an important guarantee of Iranian independence, the government holds firmly to the slogan No East, No West and refuses to associate with either great power bloc. Rejection of the West did not mean stopping oil sales or food and machinery purchases, but the antisuperpower campaign, especially that against the United States, became a central

symbol of the overthrow of taghut and of Iran's newly won freedom
from the need to seek superpower protection and goodwill. Eventually,
confounding and confronting the United States and the USSR became
a foreign policy goal in itself, a goal that is more important than
any economic or strategic considerations. Faced with a choice between
confrontation with the United States and, for example, maintenance
of Iran's armed forces, the new regime chose the former. The results
of that choice are a decimated air force, cities that are defenseless
against Iraqi bombers, and a victory on the all-important symbolic
level of Iranian pride and self-respect.

Second, the Islamic Republic rejects Iranian nationalism and
Iranian national interests as bases of foreign policy. The nation is
now the nation of Islam and recognizes no distinction between Iranian
and non-Iranian. As a result, the national interest gives way to
propagating Khomeini's vision of the *Nezam-e-Mohammadi*, in which
loyalty to Islam replaces loyalty to tribe as the cohesive force of the
community. By Islam, the republic means Khomeini's militant and
austere version, an ideology that admits no national boundaries or
sovereignty.

The republic has enthusiastically spread the message of revolution
by the printed word, by cassettes, by powerful radio stations, and
in the case of Lebanon, by direct military action. Although neighboring
countries have not followed the Iranian example, the revolution's
ability both to overthrow a corrupt monarchy and to confront the
superpowers in the name of Islam has impressed many Muslims who
had long associated their religion with political degradation and
military defeats. Few people could remember when Muslims had last
won a victory over non-Muslims, and even the few Muslim successes
that had occurred (the Algerian revolution of 1954–1962, Gemal
Nasser's resistance to Britain and France in 1956) had been achieved
in the name of secular nationalism, not of religion. Turkey, one of
the most militarily powerful of the Islamic countries, had explicitly
rejected religion as a basis of social organization.

Stripped of its peculiarly Shi'ite content, the Iranian revolution's
essential message to the world was simple, appealing, and potentially
very powerful:

1. Most Muslims suffer from misrule and political degradation
   in some form (true).
2. Non-Muslims—Americans, British, Russians, French, and Is-
   raelis—have regularly defeated and ruled Muslim populations
   (true).

3. Foreign ideologies, such as Marxism, secular nationalism, liberalism, and capitalism, have not improved conditions in most Islamic societies (true).
4. A militant and ideological Islam, as represented by Khomeini's Islamic Republic, is the road to freedom, self-respect, and independence (debatable).

Third, the Islamic Republic has appointed itself champion of the world's oppressed (mostaz'afin) against world arrogance (*estekbar-e-jahani*), i.e., the great powers. Thus, Iran now advocates a potpourri of causes—including those of the Palestinians, the Sandinistas, the Filipino Muslims, the Irish Republican Army, and other groups it has decided are victims of world arrogance—and conflicting causes have sometimes led the republic into foreign policy dilemmas. For example, when the Lebanese Shi'ite militias began settling scores with the Palestinians in Beirut in May 1985, the Iranians found themselves caught between two groups of the oppressed, each of which deserved their country's support.

The Islamic Republic will compromise its principles, however, when survival is at stake. Thus, the regime, although ready to send its young people to die on the Khuzestan front in the war with Iraq, is unwilling to commit political and economic suicide by challenging the West in the Strait of Hormuz. Although loudly denouncing followers of Eastern and Western ideologies, Iran carefully maintains relations with Turkey, the USSR, and the European countries that control Iran's overland trade routes and supply needed food and machinery. Although urging the oppressed of the world to reject secular doctrines and to seek salvation in militant Islam, the republic, for the sake of an alliance against Iraq, supports a secular, Ba'ath regime in Syria that slaughters Muslim Brothers—followers of the same militant Islam preached by the revolution.

"War, War, Until Victory"

In addition to militant anti-Americanism, the war with Iraq has had a major influence in shaping the Islamic Republic's foreign policy. There are numerous theories to explain the war: a conflict of ideologies (militant Islam versus secular nationalism); conflict between two authoritarian personalities (Saddam Hussein versus Khomeini); a revival of ancient conflicts between Arab and Iranian; and territorial and boundary disagreements. All of these factors have played a role in the hostilities, but none provides a completely satisfactory explanation. Differences of ideology and culture do not inevitably cause wars; nor do personality conflicts between leaders.

The underlying conflicts would probably never had led to war if there had not been a series of miscalculations on both sides. For the Iranians, their success in challenging the United States in 1979–1980 perhaps clouded their judgment. They began to consider themselves invincible, and they overestimated both their own strength and their ability to deter an attacker. Believing their own revolutionary rhetoric and slogans, they refused to admit that Saddam might react decisively to their provocations, threats, and calls for his overthrow. After all, the slogan of the day in Teheran was America can't do a damn thing. If the United States could do nothing, why should the Iranians fear a collection of despised Arabs ruled by an unpopular military dictator?

The Iraqis made equally serious miscalculations. They foresaw a short war—a quick and easy victory in Khuzestan over demoralized and disorganized Iranian armed forces. More important, Saddam underestimated the Iranians' political will, which enabled them, after the initial shock, to mobilize their large population and to exploit their country's natural advantages. A superficial look at Iran in mid-1980 revealed a prostrate, divided country, an apparently easy victim of a limited Iraqi strike at strategic ports and installations. A military defeat in the south, Saddam thought, would bring down the entire regime in Teheran, just as Reza Shah's expensive house of cards had collapsed in a few days in 1941 after defeats by the Allied armies.

A more careful analysis, however, would have revealed that, despite political unrest and economic problems, the Islamic regime was not on the verge of collapse and it still had enough committed supporters and the means to put armies into the field—not the most modern armies, perhaps, but strong enough to force the Iraqis into a protracted war of attrition. Even most opponents of the regime, members of the traditional armed forces, would defend Iranian territory against Arab invaders. Finally, Saddam underestimated how the regime could exploit the war to rally support at home and to strengthen further its hold on political power.

The Iranians have had to shape their relations with the Arab world according the demands of war. Officially, Iran seeks friendship with states that share its revolutionary credentials, anti-Israeli militancy, and uncompromising anti-Americanism, but the struggle against Iraq has taken precedence over Islamic and revolutionary purity. Iran carefully maintains close links with Hafez al-Asad's Syria despite that country's correct relations with the United States and fundamental ideological differences with the Islamic Republic. The two regimes have little in common beyond enmity for Iraq, but in return for help against the common enemy, the Iranians can overlook the Syrians'

Arab nationalism, secular form of government, and bloody suppression of the Muslim Brothers. Far more important to Iran is Syria's closing of the Iraqi crude-oil pipeline and supplying the Iranians with arms, agricultural goods, and fertilizer in exchange for oil. Similarly, the Libyans' responsibility for the death of the Lebanese Shi'ite Imam Musa Sadr apparently counted for little when weighed against the value of Libya's political and military support of Iran against Iraq.

The Iranians' absolutist view of the war justifies such ideological compromises. The war is not just a conflict between two nation-states called Iran and Iraq; it is a battle between right and wrong, between Islam and heresy. In such a war there can be no compromise. How, the Iranians ask, can right compromise with wrong? How can faith compromise with unbelief? This stance, and the Iranians' insistence that Iraqi President Saddam Hussein must go, have so far frustrated all attempts at mediation by the Nonaligned movement, the Islamic Conference Organization, and the United Nations. Khomeini himself told one mediation delegation that its job was to visit both parties to the war and "if we are wrong, then condemn us. But if they are wrong, then condemn them. Justice demands you do this."[29]

The Great Satans

The Islamic Republic sees its enemies as satanic, as manifestations of absolute evil. In this simplistic view of the world, national interests mean little, and few shadings are admitted. Israel and South Africa are outside humanity; the United States is *Omm al-Fasad*, mother of corruption and leader of world arrogance. Although the regime's anti-American rhetoric sometimes reaches the absurd, the ruling faction, sometimes abetted by the left, has used anti-U.S. demonstrations and slogans to attack domestic opponents (the despised "liberals") for their willingness to compromise with evil and follow an "American" line. Iran's antisatanic foreign policy has led to some unusual policy choices. For example, the regime has established amiable relations with small, distant Marxist states—such as Cuba, North Korea, and South Yemen—that have little interest in a *Nezam-e-Mohammadi* but share Iran's uncompromising anti-U.S. views.

Although Iran will join these states in condemning U.S. imperialism, it does not share their attachment to the USSR. The Iranians have also denounced their northern neighbor as satanic, another representative of (Eastern) world arrogance. Most Iranians distrust the Soviet Union because of its occupation of Afghanistan, its treatment of Islamic minorities, and its historical record of aggression against Iran. Yet proximity and respect for Soviet power have restrained Iranian action, if not rhetoric, against the Soviet Union.

Many Iranian leaders apparently view the Soviet and U.S. threats to Iran as fundamentally different and consider the latter more dangerous. The Soviets threaten to dominate Iran by military force and by the activities of domestic communists, but even though the United States is far away, its threat to Iran is more subtle and more profound. The United States threatens cultural and economic conquest by seducing Iranians away from Islam to follow the materialistic, decadent life of Western movies and television. The USSR makes boring movies that only put an audience to sleep, but the United States makes pornographic ones that keep young people awake and distract them from revolutionary goals. The latter type is more dangerous to a regime that feeds its population a monotonous diet of revolutionary speeches, marches, and sermons. Although Marxism as an ideology rivals Islam, the regime feels seriously threatened by its own citizens' weakness for the material riches and sexual laxity offered by the North American temptress. Marxism, by contrast, has little to offer Iranian hedonists.

Such a consistently uncompromising foreign policy—absolute enmity with Israel and United States, refusal to be drawn into close relations with the USSR, conduct of the war with Iraq as a crusade against evil, and willingness to champion liberation and Islamic causes—bears Khomeini's personal stamp. Iran will continue following such a policy as long as Khomeini remains its leader. After his death, there may be some tacit moderation of those extreme, inflexible positions that have made Iran an international outcast. At that time, the Iranians may be willing to stop attacking their gulf neighbors as ignorant feudalists and traitors to Islam, to discuss seriously a settlement of the destructive war with Iraq, and even to begin exploring ways to establish more normal relations with the United States.

Conclusion: Whither Iran?

Even the most optimistic observer cannot help being discouraged about present-day Iran: a culture denied; a people's religious faith cynically manipulated and exploited; thousands of young people dead, maimed, or in prison; an educational system in chaos; an economy in near ruin; and an educated population shouted down in a political arena that is given over to hate and the mindless chanting of slogans. It sometimes appears that the inmates have taken over the asylum and have tried to turn upside down the ancient Iranian traditions of creativity, tolerance, and compassion. All of the suppressed resentments built up over decades of national humiliation, forced westernization, and unplanned change have been released and manipulated. The regime that came to power in the name of the Iranian self has turned against that very self and declared war on its citizens' most deep-rooted and humane values.

So what is next for this tortured people? Probably not a miraculous rescue from today's darkness by a man on a white horse. Such a pseudosavior could appear only when economic conditions become much worse, when the revolution loses its ideological fire, and when Iranians face the same sort of political and military humiliation they faced in the first decades of this century. Nor is the regime about to collapse by itself, even if its leader were to die, as long as the ruling network and its protectors, the revolutionary guards, retain their cohesion. The ruling network still has enough discipline and devoted followers to answer any challenge to its authority and to keep control of the Teheran streets. There the revolution was fought and won, and only there can the current regime be brought down.

The answer, I feel, lies in the eventual reassertion of a more genuinely Iranian spirit against the prevailing fury and obscurantism. Such a reassertion will take time. It will not happen tomorrow or the next day. But it will happen. For if Iran's long history teaches anything, it teaches that

1. a noble, creative, and humane spirit is no protection against political and social evils. Good people may get bad government.
2. the essential Iranian identity has already endured fearsome invasions, massacres, destruction, and misrule. That identity has survived the horrors of Changiz and Agha Mohammad. Next to those murderers, Khomeini and his followers are small-time miscreants.

In the long run (and Iran's history makes us think in the long term), a nation that has survived so much adversity should have little trouble dealing with the present brutality and eventually restoring a more humane and compassionate system that is in better harmony with Iranian tradition. Such a system will not be perfect—the present Islamic Republic seeks perfection with predictably disastrous results—but at least it will not try to impose by force a harsh, idiosyncratic version of Islam on a people that has always treasured human diversity and creativity.

Six hundred years ago, the poet Hafez lived through a time resembling the present. When the fanatic and brutal warlord Mobarez al-Din Mohammad closed the wineshops and other haunts of the poets in Shiraz, Hafez knew that it was time to endure, to wear the hypocrite's robe until the aberration should pass.

گره ازکار فروبستهٔ ما بگشایند   بود آیا که درِ میکده ها بگشایند

دل قوی دار که این سرِ خدا بگشایند   گر از بهرِ دلِ زاهدِ خودبین بستند

When will they open the doors of the wineshops?
And loosen their hold on our knotted lives?

If shut to satisfy the hypocrite's ego,
Be strong, for they will reopen to satisfy God.

Appendix A

The Ruling IRP-Clerical Network: Political-Religious Leaders, 1979–1986

Bahonar, Hojjat al-Islam (H.I.) Mohammad Javad (assassinated, August 1981). Prime Minister; Minister of Education; Secretary-general, IRP; leading member of first Council of Experts.

Beheshti, Ayatollah Mohammad (assassinated, June 1981). Deputy Speaker, first Council of Experts; Secretary-general, IRP; Chairman, State Supreme Court.

Dastgheib, Ayatollah Seyyed Abd al-Hosein (assassinated, December 1981). Imam's representative and Friday prayer leader of Shiraz.

Do'a'i, H.I. Mahmud. Member of Parliament from Teheran (reelected April 1984); first vice-chairman, Foreign Affairs Committee; Ambassador to Iraq; Chairman, Iranian delegation to Interparliamentary Union.

Emami-Kashani, H.I. Mohammad A. Member, Council of Guardians; temporary Friday prayer leader of Teheran; member of parliament.

Hashemi-Rafsanjani, H.I. Ali Akbar. Speaker of the parliament; Imam's representative on the Supreme Defense Council; Deputy Secretary-general, IRP; temporary Friday prayer leader of Teheran.

Jannati, Ayatollah Ahmad. Member, Council of Guardians; Friday prayer leader of Ahvaz; Friday prayer leader of Qom; Secretary-general, High Council of Islamic Propaganda.

Khalkhali, Sheikh Sadeq. Revolutionary Court judge; parliament deputy from Qom; director of antinarcotics campaign; leader of revived Mojahedin-e-Eslam.

Khamene'i, H.I. Seyyed Ali. President of the Islamic Republic; Friday prayer leader of Teheran; Secretary-general, IRP; Imam's representative on and later chairman of Supreme Defense Council.

Ma'adikhah, H.I. Abd al-Majid. Minister of Islamic Guidance; Deputy Secretary-general, IRP; member of parliament.

Mahallati, H.I. Fazlollah. Imam's representative in the Revolutionary Guards' Corps; member of parliament (Defense Affairs Committee); died 1986 when Iraqis shot down his aircraft.

Mahdavi-Kani, Ayatollah Mohammad Reza. Minister of Interior; member, Council of Guardians; acting Prime Minister; temporary Friday prayer leader of Teheran; Secretary-general, Militant Clerics' Association; Prosecutor-general; member, Cultural Revolution Directorate.

Malakuti, Ayatollah Sheikh Moslem. Friday prayer leader and Imam's representative in Tabriz.

Meshkini, Ayatollah Ali. Friday prayer leader of Qom; Chairman, second Council of Experts.

Mosavi-Ardabili, Ayatollah Abd al-Karim. Chairman, State Supreme Court; member (ex officio) of High Council of the Judiciary; State Prosecutor-general; temporary Friday prayer leader of Teheran.

Mosavi-Kho'iniha, H.I. Mohammad. Deputy speaker of parliament; Imam's representative on the annual pilgrimage to Mecca.

Mosavi-Tabrizi, H.I. Hosein. State Prosecutor-general (until January 1984).

Nateq-Nuri, H.I. Ali Akbar. Minister of Interior; parliament deputy from Teheran; Imam's representative in Reconstruction Crusade; commander in chief for security matters; member, Revolutionary Guards' Council.

Reyshahri, H.I. Mohammad. Chief Judge, Armed Forces Revolutionary Court.

Sane'i, H.I. Yusef. State Prosecutor-general; member (ex officio), High Council of the Judiciary; member, Council of Guardians.

Taheri, Ayatollah Jalal al-Din. Imam's representative and Friday prayer leader of Isfahan.

Va'ez-Tabasi, H.I. Abbas. Imam's representative in Mashhad; custodian of Mashhad shrine; member, IRP central committee.

The honorifics Ayatollah and Hojjat al-Islam refer to first- and second-rank clerics, respectively. The distinction is not always a strict one; individuals such as Meshkini and Mahdavi-Kani are sometimes given one title, sometimes the other. For the most senior second-rank clerics, the media often uses the title Hojjat al-Islam va al-Moslemin.

The first Council of Experts met in 1979 to draft the constitution of the Islamic Republic. The second council, elected in December 1982, was responsible for determining succession to the supreme leadership. This body held a closed session in July–August 1983 and met again in 1985 when it chose Ayatollah Montazeri as successor.

This listing owes a great deal to information provided by G. Rose in "Factional Alignments in the Central Council of the IRP," in Nikki R. Keddie and Eric Hoogland, eds., *The Iranian Revolution and the Islamic Republic* (Washington, D.C.: Middle East Institute and Woodrow Wilson Center, 1982).

Appendix B

The Ruling IRP-Clerical Network: Institutional Structure

Executive
  Bahonar (Prime Minister)
  Khamene'i (President)
  Mahdavi-Kani (Acting Prime Minister)

Military-Security
  Khamene'i (Supreme Defense Council)
  Hashemi-Rafsanjani (Supreme Defense Council)
  Nateq-Nuri (Interior, Revolutionary Guards' Council)
  Mahallati (Revolutionary Guards' Corps)
  Reyshahri (Armed Forces Revolutionary Court)
  Mahdavi-Kani (Interior)

Parliament
  Hashemi-Rafsanjani (Speaker)
  Mosavi-Kho'iniha (Deputy Speaker)
  Do'a'i (Foreign Affairs Committee)
  Mahallati (Defense Affairs Committee)

Judiciary
  Beheshti (Supreme Court)
  Mosavi-Ardabili (Supreme Court)
  Mosavi-Tabrizi (State Prosecutor-general)
  Sane'i (State Prosecutor-general)
  Reyshahri (Armed Forces Revolutionary Court)
  Khalkhali (Revolutionary Court Judge)

Information and Culture
Ma'adikhah (Minister of Islamic Guidance)
Mahdavi-Kani (Cultural Revolution)
Jannati (High Council of Islamic Propaganda)
Bahonar (Minister of Education)

Councils of Experts
Meshkini (Leadership)
Beheshti (Constitution)
Bahonar (Constitution)

Council of Guardians
Emami-Kashani
Mahdavi-Kani
Jannati

Teheran Friday Imams
Khamene'i
Hashemi-Rafsanjani (temporary)
Mahdavi-Kani (temporary)
Emami-Kashani (temporary)
Mosavi-Ardabili (temporary)

Provincial Representatives and Friday Imams
Taheri (Isfahan)
Dastgheib (Shiraz)
Va'ez-Tabasi (Mashhad)
Meshkini (Qom)
Jannati (Ahvaz)
Malakuti (Tabriz)

Other
Khalkhali (Antinarcotics Campaign)
Nateq-Nuri (Reconstruction Crusade)
Mosavi-Kho'iniha (Pilgrimage)

Notes

For most works cited, only the author's name and short title of the work are given in the Notes. For full bibliographic reference, readers should consult the Bibliography.

NOTES TO CHAPTER 1

1. W. B. Fisher, ed., *The Cambridge History of Iran*, vol. 1, pp. 90–101.
2. Paul Ward English, *City and Village in Iran*, pp. 30–39.
3. Donald L. Stilo, "The Tati Language Group," pp. 137–142.
4. W. Madelung, in Richard N. Frye, ed., *The Cambridge History of Iran*, vol. 4, *From the Arab Invasion to the Saljuqs*, pp. 198–206.
5. Homa Katouzian, *The Political Economy of Modern Iran*, pp. 242–273. The author discusses the creation of "petrolic despotism" to replace traditional Iranian despotism based on state control of land.
6. R. Stobaugh, "The Evolution of Iranian Oil Policy, 1925–1975," in George Lenczowski, ed., *Iran Under the Pahlavis*, p. 202.
7. Amin Banani, *The Modernization of Iran*, pp. 113–116. In 1921, customs revenues, collected by foreigners, were the most important source of government income.
8. Islamic Republic of Iran, *Iran Through the Mirror of Statistics*, p. 13.
9. Public statement, September 1979. The writer Ali Shari'ati (see Chapter 6) had noted the disagreement over economics in his famous "Prayer": "Oh Lord, teach our young people that economics is *not* basic. And teach our clergy that economics *is* basic."
10. International Monetary Fund, *Directions of Trade*.
11. In the early 1980s, an estimated 97 percent of Iran's export earnings came from crude-oil sales.
12. *Iran Times* 14:38 (December 7, 1984). In addition, the Iranians have estimated that direct and indirect war damage until March 1983 amounted to about $160 billion—Teheran Iranian Republic News Agency (IRNA), June 24, 1984 (in United States, FBIS, vol. 8, June 27, 1984, p. I.4).

13. The Iraqis might try to shut down Iran's oil production or exports. Until September 1985, sporadic Iraqi air attacks on shipping around the Kharg Island terminal had not had much effect. Although estimates differ, Iran probably has enough reserves to continue fighting, with more austerity measures, for at least a year with no oil income.

NOTES TO CHAPTER 2

1. Donald L. Stilo, "The Tati Language Group," p. 174.

2. For a fictional account of the life of upper-middle-class Azarbaijani merchant families in prerevolutionary Iran, see Donne Raffat, *The Caspian Circle.*

3. Jan Rybka, *History of Iranian Literature,* p. 738.

4. What would a similar analysis tell us about the "American character" as illustrated by the behavior of R. Nixon, H. Kissinger, or the characters on television soap operas?

5. Many Iranians have insisted that the captors of the U.S. hostages were not Iranians but some other nationality. Iranians, they argue, might do many reprehensible things, but they are incapable of mistreating the foreign or the Iranian guest in their home or their country.

6. The subject of Iranian literature deserves its own full and separate treatment. Among the best studies available are Edward G. Browne, *A Literary History of Persia,* 4 vols., and Jan Rybka, *History of Iranian Literature.*

7. There are hundreds of stories about the confusion caused by the misuse of ta'arof. The classic is of the foreigner or Iranian returned from long residence abroad who admires some precious object. When the owner, observing the rules of ta'arof, tells him "it's yours," he pockets the object, to the owner's extreme dismay.

8. For more on this incident, see Chapter 5.

9. As if to disprove this generalization, Khomeini is often described by both supporters and opponents as *ashti na-pazir,* or implacable.

NOTES TO CHAPTER 3

1. On the subject of royal *farr,* see Ehsan Yarshater, ed., *The Cambridge History of Iran,* vol. 3, *The Seleucid, Parthian, and Sassanian Periods,* pp. 345–346.

2. For the history of this "source of guidance" in Iranian Shi'ism, see Chapter 4.

3. For Iranian Shi'ites, the epithet "Shah Soltan Hosein" is even more insulting than "Omar," referring to the second (Sunni) caliph. Although Shi'ites have a special hatred for Omar, whom they hold responsible for usurping Imam Ali's rightful position as leader of the Islamic community, they admit that the second caliph, with all of his faults, at least commanded the obedience of his subjects. The people who argued during the Islamic revolution in 1978–1979 that Ayatollah Khomeini would take a Gandhi-like,

figurehead role and leave government to the technocrats were either ignorant of Iran's history or chose to ignore its lessons.

4. For a fictional account of one such outing, see Terence O'Donnell, "The Pilgrimage," in O'Donnell, *Garden of the Brave in War*, pp. 134–144.

5. Tabataba'i, *Shi'ite Islam*, p. 11.

6. Roy P. Mottahedeh, *Loyalty and Leadership*, pp. 178–179, discusses this ideal of justice in early Islamic Iran.

7. Herodotus (William Beloe, trans., *Herodotus*, 1:135) observed this characteristic of the ancient Persians, noting that the practice of pederasty was unknown among them until their contact with the Greeks.

8. In his famous short story *"Farsi Shekar ast"* [Persian is sweet as sugar], the writer and social critic M. A. Jamalzadeh satirized those Frenchified and Arabized Iranians whose speech was unintelligible to their compatriots. The writer Jalal Al-e-Ahmad's (d. 1971) popular essay "Gharbzadegi" [Infatuation with the West] added a new word to the Persian language. In this work and others, Al-e-Ahmad attacked the Iranian intelligentsia's unreasoning fascination with the West, its blind acceptance of European theories and methods, and its alienation from the Iranian cultural heritage.

9. Jan Rybka, *History of Iranian Literature*, pp. 159–160.

10. Richard N. Frye, *The Heritage of Persia*, p. 59.

11. Ibid., p. 64.

12. The link between Parsua, the Persians, and Fars is unclear. The traditional view is that the early Persians migrated southeast from their original home near Lake Urumiyeh to the area now called Fars. However, according to Frye (*Heritage*, pp. 45–46, 65–66), the evidence does not prove that such a northwest-to-southeast migration ever took place. He argues that some of the original Persians (Parsa or Parsua) migrated directly to Fars, giving that province their ethnic name, at the same time that other Persians migrated farther north where they became the neighbors of the Medes and the Persians. Presumably, Assyrian sources noted only the northern Persians, since the southerners would have been separated from Assyrian territory by the Elamites.

13. The rulers of this dynasty traced their ancestry to Achaemenes (Hakhamanish), of whom little is known except that his son or descendant Theispes (Chishpish) held the kingdom of Anshan under Median suzerainty until his death in 640 B.C. The exact identity of Anshan is uncertain—it seems to have been the mountainous region northwest of the Khuzestan plain. Theispes extended the area under his control toward the southeast, adding to his realm the formerly Elamite region of Persis (Fars). On his death, his territory was divided between his sons, Cyrus I (Korush) and Ariaramnes (Ariyaramna). The former ruled the western area (Anshan), and the latter ruled the eastern territory of Persis. About 600 B.C. Cyrus's son, Cambyses I (Kambujiye), ruling as a vassal of the Medes, reunited the two regions.

14. The facts of Gaumata's revolt and Darius's seizure of power are complex. Herodotus provides a lurid account, and Darius himself had an

official version carved, in three languages, into the mountain at Behistun (Bisitun) overlooking the plains near Kermanshah. Although little is known about these events, one scholar (Alessandro Bausani, *The Persians*, pp. 20–21) has suggested that Gaumata was a religious and social reformer who appealed to the lower classes against the ruling nobility. In such a case, Gaumata would have been the first in a long series of such Iranian reformers, including Mazdak, Babak Khorram-din, and the nineteenth-century Ali Mohammad Shirazi, founder of the Babi/Baha'i region.

15. Frye, *Heritage*, p. 201.

16. The ethnic identity of these people and their successors, the Hephalites, is uncertain. Richard N. Frye (ed., *The Cambridge History of Iran*, vol. 4, *From the Arab Invasion to the Saljuqs*, p. 137, and *Heritage*, pp. 216–217) says they were a mixture of Altaic and Iranian speakers, with the latter predominating.

NOTES TO CHAPTER 4

1. These Khorasani Arabs later became the main supporters of the Abbasid rebellion in the mid-eighth century.

2. In Khorasan, for example, a certain Sindbad the Magian appeared in 756 to claim that Abu Muslim, the murdered leader of the Abbasid revolt, was in fact living in concealment with Mazdak and the Islamic savior (the Mahdi). All three would return to establish justice on earth.

3. Alessandro Bausani, *The Persians*, pp. 76–78.

4. For more on these dynasties, see C. E. Bosworth, "The Tahirids and Saffarids," in Richard N. Frye, ed., *The Cambridge History of Iran*, vol. 4, *From the Arab Invasion to the Saljuqs* (hereafter cited as *CHI* 4), pp. 90–135, and Richard N. Frye, "The Samanids," ibid., pp. 136–161.

5. Frye, "The Samanids," *CHI* 4, p. 145. On the rise of New Persian, see G. Lazard, "The Rise of the New Persian Literature," in *CHI* 4, pp. 595–632. Other minor Iranian dynasties appeared during this period. The Shi'ite Ziyarids ruled Tabarestan and remained independent of both the Samanids to the east and Buyids to the west. In Azarbaijan, dynasties of Sajids, Sallarids, and Rawadids ruled for brief periods during the ninth and tenth centuries. That region was one of the most anarchic in Iran, as Arab, Deilamite, Kurdish, Turkish, and Armenian warlords competed for power. Only the Shadadids of Arran (northern Azarbaijan) survived the eleventh-century Turkish invasions, remaining as vassal rulers of Ani in Armenia until the end of the twelfth century.

6. For discussion of this arrangement, see R. Mottahedeh, "The Abbasid Caliphate in Iran," in *CHI* 4, pp. 85–86.

7. S. M. Stern, "Ya'qub the Coppersmith and Persian National Sentiment," in C. E. Bosworth, ed., *Iran and Islam*, pp. 543–544; Mottahedeh, "Iran Under the Buyids," in *CHI* 4, pp. 273–275.

8. Richard N. Frye, "The New Persian Renaissance in Western Iran," p. 230.

9. J. A. Boyle, "Dynastic and Political History of the Il-Khans," in Boyle, ed., *The Cambridge History of Iran*, vol. 5, *The Saljuq and Mongol Periods*, pp. 313–316.

10. Edward G. Browne, *Literary History of Persia*, vol. 3, pp. 160–161.

11. Roger Savory, *Iran Under the Safavids*, p. 2.

12. Bausani, *The Persians*, p. 141.

13. As noted earlier (Chapter 2), the roots of the Baha'i faith were firmly planted in the traditions of Iranian messianic heresies going back to Mani and Mazdak. Nikki R. Keddie (*Roots of Revolution*, pp. 49–50) suggests there was also an important external stimulus—that the Babi movement was one of many religious-political movements appearing in nineteenth-century Asia and Africa in reaction to the increasing power of the industrial West. She connects the Babi phenomenon to similar movements in India, China, and the Sudan. Certainly the foreign pressures Iran experienced in the first half of the nineteenth century were unprecedented in the country's history. Unable to meet Europeans with political, military, or even cultural equality, many Iranians may have viewed Babism, with its origins in messianic Shi'ism, as the key to their national rejuvenation.

14. Hamid Algar, *Religion and State in Iran*, pp. 21–23.

15. Edward G. Browne, *A Year Amongst the Persians*, p. 90.

16. Ervand Abrahamian, *Iran Between Two Revolutions*, pp. 76–77.

17. Cited by Firuz Kazemzadeh, *Russia and Britain in Persia*, p. 500. The Anglo-Russian agreement gave Russia an exclusive zone in northern Iran, including most of the population, trade, and agricultural centers. In this zone Britain pledged "not to seek for herself, and not to support in favor of British subjects, or in favor of the subjects of a third power, any concession of a political or commercial nature." Britain also promised "not to oppose directly or indirectly, demands for similar concessions in this region which are supported by the Russian Government." Russia made the same promises for a smaller British zone in the southeastern corner of the country. The rest of Iran was left as a "neutral zone."

NOTES TO CHAPTER 5

1. For further explanation of *taghut*, see second section of Chapter 6.

2. Cited in Amin Banani, *The Modernization of Iran*, p. 40.

3. Ahmad Kasravi, "Concerning Reza Shah Pahlavi," *Parcham*, June 23–25, 1942; cited by Ervand Abrahamian, *Iran Between Two Revolutions*, pp. 153–154.

4. Abrahamian, *Iran Between Two Revolutions*, pp. 155–162, provides a detailed account of this incident.

5. The first Tudeh program was published in the party newspaper *Rahbar*, February 12, 1943; cited by Abrahamian, *Iran Between Two Revolutions*, pp. 284–285.

6. According to Richard W. Cottam (*Nationalism in Iran*, pp. 125–126), this party was just a new name for the Azarbaijan branch of the Tudeh. In

Abrahamian's more detailed account, (*Iran Between Two Revolutions*, pp. 398 ff), however, Democrat-Tudeh relations appear to have been severely strained over the issue of regional autonomy.

7. Abrahamian, *Iran Between Two Revolutions*, pp. 253–260, and Cottam, *Nationalism in Iran*, pp. 264–268, discuss the groups and individuals who supported the National Front.

8. Cottam, *Nationalism in Iran*, pp. 278–279.

9. Abrahamian, *Iran Between Two Revolutions*, p. 274.

10. According to Sepehr Zabih (*The Mossadegh Era*, pp. 140–141), one of Britain's most important Iranian agents was appropriately named Shahpour Reporter.

11. Kermit Roosevelt, *Countercoup*, pp. 11, 18. The U.S. role in the events of August 1953 is still controversial. Although most careful examinations of the record indicate internal conditions were more important than the activity of foreign governments in overthrowing Mossadegh, the incident left an important and bitter legacy in Iran. It convinced many Iranians that (1) the Shah was nothing but a U.S. puppet, taking orders directly from Washington and (2) the United States was in complete control of Iranian events. In 1978, as the revolution reached a climax, the U.S. embassy was beseiged by pleas to "do something" to prevent the shah's collapse.

12. Hamid Algar, trans., *Islam and Revolution*, p. 179.

13. On these two organizations, see Abrahamian, *Iran Between Two Revolutions*, pp. 480–495. The Mojahedin's activist interpretation of Islam closely resembled that of the scholar and teacher Ali Shari'ati (see Chapter 6).

14. Rouhollah K. Ramazani, *The United States and Iran*, p. 48.

15. Barry Rubin, *Paved with Good Intentions*, p. 163.

16. This division owes much to Abrahamian's discussion in "Iran's Turbaned Revolution," pp. 89–93.

17. In November 1978, Karim Sanjabi, the elderly leader of the National Front, visited Khomeini in Paris and emerged with a joint declaration to the effect that both Islam and democracy were basic principles. According to Bakhtiyar's account, Sanjabi made this alliance unilaterally. His action surprised the rest of the front, which, unaware of Sanjabi's intention to visit Khomeini, endorsed the agreement after the fact.

18. Fereydoun Hoveyda, *The Fall of the Shah*, pp. 143–144.

NOTES TO CHAPTER 6

1. For more information on Shari'ati's life and works, see Yann Richards, "Contemporary Shi'i Thought," in Nikki R. Keddie, *Roots of Revolution*, pp. 215–225; Ervand Abrahamian, *Iran Between Two Revolutions*, pp. 464–473; and Shahrough Akhavi, *Religion and Politics in Contemporary Iran*, pp. 144–158.

2. Jalal Al-e-Ahmad, *Gharbzadegi*, p. 108.

3. Shari'ati, *Return to the Self*, quoted by Abrahamian, *Iran Between Two Revolutions*, p. 470.

4. On the Hoseiniyeh-ye-Ershad, see Akhavi, *Religion and Politics*, pp. 143–144.

5. In a recorded debate between Shari'ati and the scholar M. Motahhari, the latter critized Shari'ati for calling Marxism the "rival" and capitalism the "enemy" of Islam.

6. Hamid Algar has translated this work, with excellent footnotes, in *Islam and Revolution*, pp. 27–166. Khomeini and his disciples acknowledged their debt to Ayatollah Kashani, the Fedayan-e-Islam movement of the 1950s (see Chapter 5), and Sheikh Fazlollah Nuri (executed 1909), who had attacked the constitutional movement for replacing Islamic principles with Western ideas of parliamentary democracy.

7. Algar, *Islam and Revolution*, p. 129.

8. For further discussion of *taghut*, see ibid., p. 92. Shortly after the revolution, a television reporter asked a young worker in the new *jihad-e-sazandegi* ("construction crusade") the difference between his work and the work of the shah's development corps. The simple answer was: "That one [the corps] was from the taghut; this [the jihad] is not."

9. Algar, *Islam and Revolution*, p. 63.

10. For example, revolutionary guards and neighborhood komitehs have continued to harass citizens in their homes despite repeated admonitions from the imam that such behavior is un-Islamic.

11. Islamic Republican News Agency (IRNA), April 22, 1984; Foreign Broadcast Information Service (hereafter cited as FBIS), vol. 8, April 24, 1984, p. I.4.

12. These provisions were to prevent repeating the experience of the 1906 constitution, which also had called for a Council of Guardians to review parliamentary legislation. From 1906 to 1979, however, no such body was ever established, and the government ignored the constitutional provision calling for its creation.

13. The IRNA report cited above notes, "The council has no legislative powers." Perhaps not, but its judicial review powers give it a strong voice in legislation.

14. In the constitutional assembly (the Council of Experts) debates, R. Moghaddam-Maraghe'i appealed for rejection of this article by citing the historic dangers of creating private armies and paramilitary forces.

15. A former associate of Bani Sadr called him the world's first politician who was simultaneously president and leader of the opposition. Bani Sadr himself (b. 1933) was originally from a distinguished Hamedani clerical family. In the 1960s, he went into exile in France, where he pursued studies in sociology and economics. For more information on his ideas and writings, see Keddie, *Roots of Revolution*, pp. 225–228.

16. To quote W. S. Gilbert (*The Gondoliers*), "When every one is somebody, then no one's anybody."

17. Predictably, actors in this power scramble had mixed motives. Although some had clear political purposes, others, such as the infamous Mashallah Kashani, who guarded the U.S. embassy in the spring and summer

of 1979, had more materialistic goals. In some neighborhoods, the local komitehs did an admirable job of reestablishing security after the collapse of the police during the revolution and protected residents against the excesses of other komitehs. Attempts to bring this confusion under control were mostly unsuccessful. When the Imam forbade searches and arrests without written permission from a komiteh, every local armed group became a komiteh and issued search warrants to its own members.

18. A private conversation, September 1979.

19. There are some excellent studies that attempt to classify and explain the groups and factions in the new power structure. These studies include Sepehr Zabih, *Iran Since the Revolution;* James A. Bill, "Power and Religion"; and articles by S. Akhavi, E. Hoogland, and G. Rose in Nikki R. Keddie and Eric Hoogland, eds., *The Iranian Revolution and the Islamic Republic.*

20. Interview with H.I. Fazlollah Mahallati, the imam's representative in the Revolutionary Guards' Corps, *Keyhan,* February 14, 1984, p. 18 (in U.S., *JPRS,* NEA-84-069 [April 27, 1984]). In his interview, Mahallati notes that the guards' commander is subordinate to the Imam's representative in the corps. He also completely omits the Guards' Corps minister, Mohsen Rafiqdust, from the chain of command. Although both Rafiqdust and the commander, Mohsen Reza'i, sit on the Guards' Corps High Council, Mahallati, as the Imam's representative, has veto power over all council decisions.

21. The authors cited in note 19 have analyzed the groupings within the IRP alliance, noting competing trends and factions called *ulema-ye-mojahedin* ("crusading clergy"), *maktabi* ("ideologue"), *hojjati* (member of the anti-Bahai *Hojjatiyeh* society), etc. Yet its members' rivalries have not yet threatened the ruling network's basic unity or weakened its control of the Islamic Republic.

22. Radio Tehran, May 13, 1984 (in FBIS, vol. 8, May 14, 1984, p. I.3).

23. In April 1979, the IRP preacher H.I. Abu al-Qasem Falsafi, in a speech in Qom, attacked Mossadegh's supporters and eulogized Kashani. His speech provoked an angry response from National Front leader A.A. Haj Seyyed Javadi. The free press of that period was able to carry both sides of the debate (Akhavi, *Religion and Politics,* pp. 175–176; 137–138).

24. H.I. Moqtada'i quoted on Radio Teheran, April 20, 1984 (U.S., FBIS, vol. 8, April 23, 1984, p. I.1). According to Moqtada'i, "the martyr-nurturing nation, particularly the esteemed families of the martyrs, have demanded a decisive campaign regarding this matter."

25. The anti-intellectual campaign of the second revolution featured selective release of U.S. embassy documents, published as *Revelations from the Nest of Espionage.* For further details of this campaign, see John W. Limbert, "Nest of Spies: Pack of Lies."

26. Keddie and Hoogland, *The Iranian Revolution,* p. 40. Hoogland's explanation probably applied throughout Iran and helps explain the militant clergy's ability to mobilize theology students in support of attacks on the more traditional, conservative ayatollahs.

27. On the *Dar al-Tabligh*, see Michael M.J. Fischer, *Iran*, p. 84.

28. Reports from Radio Teheran and IRNA (U.S., FBIS, vol. 8, April 20–26, 1984). Also from *Iran Times*, April 30, 1984.

29. The best, brief treatment of the Iran-Iraq war is Stephen Grummon, *The Iran-Iraq War* (Washington, D.C.: Council on Foreign Relations, 1982).

Glossary

akhund. A general term for an Islamic clergyman. Although originally neutral, the term is often perjorative in popular speech.

akhundbazi. Literally, "clergymen's games." An anticlerical term, meaning religious obscurantism. Refers to the clerics' insistence on enforcing observance of the minutiae of religious practice and to some clergymen's ability to exploit popular gullibility and superstition for political ends.

anjoman. A society or association. Anjomans appeared during the constitutional struggles of the early twentieth century. The ruling network of the Islamic Republic controls ministries, offices, schools, and factories through "Islamic" anjomans that enforce ideological conformity in the workplace.

ayatollah. A title of respect for the highest-ranking Iranian Shi'ite clergymen. No official body grants this title, which one gains by general acknowledgment of learning and sanctity.

bazar. "Bazaar." The traditional commercial center of Iranian towns. The *bazaris* ("bazaar merchants") usually enjoyed close relations with the religious establishment and an uneasy coexistence with the civil authorities.

fada'i. One prepared to sacrifice himself for a cause. Most often refers to the Marxist Cherikha-ye-Fada'i-ye-Khalq ("guerrillas of the people's cause"), a Maoist group organized in 1970.

garmsir (collective, *garmsirat*). Subtropical, lowland regions where dates, citrus, and winter vegetables are grown. Most of Iran's nomads spend their winters in these regions.

159

gharbzadegi. A social sickness; infatuation with the culture and achievements of the West, an infatuation that degenerates into political and economic subservience. The author Jalal Al-e-Ahmad made this term popular in his book of the same title. Persons or groups so infected are called *gharbzadeh.*

haqq-e-tavahhosh. Literally, "an allowance for barbarism." The sarcastic term Iranians used to describe the generous incentive pay foreigners earned for working in Iran.

hezb. "Political party." After the revolution, the pro-IRP street gangs were known as *hezbollahis* ("partisans of God").

Hojjat al-Islam. A title of respect for a learned clergyman who ranks below an ayatollah.

imam. A word of many meanings. In the most general sense, "a leader." In a narrower meaning, a leader of community prayer. In a Shi'ite context, one of the direct descendants of the prophet's daughter Fatemeh and son-in-law Ali. Shi'ites believe that these infallible members of the prophet's family should have been leaders of the Islamic community but lost their position to usurpers. The twelfth Imam (or hidden Imam), in Shi'ite belief, did not die but went into hiding in the ninth century A.D. to return on judgment day.

jebheh. "Front." Often refers to Jebheh-ye-Melli, the National Front.

komiteh. A neighborhood "committee." Part of the parallel administration that arose during the 1978–1979 revolution and expanded its power after the downfall of the monarchy. Responsible for neighborhood security, intelligence, and food and fuel distribution, the komitehs operate with considerable independence despite government attempts to control their activities.

Majles. The parliament established by the constitution of 1906.

maktabi. Religious "ideologues." In revolutionary terminology, a person who follows the most radical and uncompromising form of revolutionary Shi'ism.

marja'-e-taqlid (plural, *maraje'*). Literally, "source of imitation." In Iranian Shi'a practice, a religious figure whose sanctity and learning qualifies him to set an example and make judgments for ordinary believers.

Moharram. First month of the Islamic lunar calendar. In Iran, a month of mourning for the death of Imam Hosein, the prophet's grandson.

mojahed (plural, *mojahedin*). Literally, "one who strives"; a "crusader." A term used by various political groups, the best known being the left-wing religious group, founded in 1966, called Mojahedin-e-Khalq-e-Iran (Iranian People's Crusaders).

mojtahed. Literally, one qualified to practice *ejtehad*, to interpret religious law in accordance with its sources. In Iranian Shi'ism, each believer should accept the judgment and follow the example of a living mojtahed.

mostakber (plural, *mostakberin*). A Quranic term for one who considers himself superior and attempts to dominate and tyrannize others. The related abstract noun *estekbar* ("arrogance") usually refers to the superpowers.

mostaz'af (plural, *mostaz'afin*). The opposite of *mostakber*. A Quranic term meaning one who is considered weak—"the oppressed"; "the poor." Khomeini and his followers have used this term effectively to preempt the Marxists' rhetoric of social justice and to present Islam as the only true ideology of the oppressed. One of Khomeini's titles is "hope of the oppressed of the world."

mo'tadel. Literally, "moderate." Refers to temperate regions where most of Iran's settled population, both urban and rural, lives.

omol. "Backward." Used to describe people, especially women, who continue to follow traditional ways in their personal and family lives. Under the monarchy, omol was often a term of ridicule.

pasdar (plural, *pasdaran*). A "guard," referring to the Revolutionary Guards Corps, the paramilitary force that appeared after the collapse of the army and the police during the revolution. The Revolutionary Guards Corps now has its own ministry and its political and military support is vital to the survival of the revolutionary regime.

qeshri. Literally, "superficial." In revolutionary terminology, the religious radicals use this term to criticize their conservative, clerical rivals as rigid formalists who are obsessed with literal interpretations of Islam at the expense of its revolutionary message.

sardsir. Highland regions of severe winters and mild summers. These regions produce pears, walnuts, plums, apples, and some grain. Nomads use the sardsir as summer quarters.

SAVAK. Acronym for Mohammad Reza Shah's secret police, an organization known for its pervasiveness and brutality.

shora. "Council" or "consultation." The Council of Guardians is Shora-ye-Negahban. The 1906 constitution established a consultative assembly called Majles-e-Shora; the Islamic Republic added an "Islamic" label, renaming the assembly Majles-e-Shora-ye-Eslami.

taghut (adjective, *taghuti*). A Quranic term in commom use after the revolution. Taghut is literally a false god, a pharaoh, but came to refer to the shah. His regime, its supporters, and its values were labeled *taghuti*—that is, false, misled, invalid, and in opposition to divine commands.

tudeh. Literally, "the masses." Name of the Iranian Communist party, founded in 1941. Of the various Marxist groups in Iran, the Tudeh is the most loyal to Soviet policies and interests.

velayat-e-faqih. Literally, "the guardianship of the jurist." Ayatollah Khomeini, in a series of talks during his exile in Iraq, elaborated this theory of Islamic government, which makes the jurist supreme guardian of the authority of the hidden Imam during his absence. The constitution of the Islamic Republic makes this ideology the cornerstone of the new state.

Chronology

PRE-ISLAMIC IRAN

Eleventh–tenth centuries B.C.: Iranian migrations onto Iranian plateau and into Zagros Mountains

Eighth century: Founding of Median confederacy

550–530: Reign of Cyrus II (the Great); founding of Achaemenian empire

521–486: Reign of Darius the Great

334–330: Alexander of Macedon ends the Achaemenian empire

323: Death of Alexander

305: Alexander's general Seleucus founds his capital (Seleucia-on-the-Tigris) in Mesopotamia and rules most of Iran

ca. 171–138: Reign of Mithridates I; establishment of Parthian rule over Iranian plateau and Mesopotamia

First century B.C.: Beginning of three centuries of indecisive conflict between Roman and Parthian states

53 B.C.: Parthians defeat Romans at battle of Carrhae

63 A.D.: Romans and Parthians establish Armenia as a buffer state

Second century A.D.: Parthian empire weakens; Romans capture Seleucia in Mesopotamian campaigns

224: Ardashir Babakan overthrows Parthians and establishes Sassanian dynasty

260: Shahpur I defeats and captures the Roman emperor Valerian

ca. 275: Death of Mani, founder of Manichean heresy

363: Peace treaty with Rome settles frontier for over a century

488–531: Reign of Kavadh (Qobad); recovery of Sassanian power; growth of Mazdakite movement

524: Execution of Mazdak

531–579: Reign of Khosrow I Anushiravan; apogee of Sassanian power

632–651: Reign of Yazdagerd III, last Sassanian ruler

ISLAMIC PERIOD

570: Birth of the prophet Mohammad

610: Mohammad begins his mission at Mecca

622: Mohammad establishes his Islamic state at Medina

632: Death of Mohammad

637: Arabs defeat Sassanians at Qadisiya and occupy Mesopotamia

641: Arabs defeat Sassanians at Nahavand; end of organized Iranian resistance

Seventh–eighth centuries: Arab domination of Iran

Ninth–tenth centuries: Breakdown of unified Islamic state and rise of independent Iranian dynasties

867–903: Saffarids rule much of Iranian plateau

945: Buyids occupy Baghdad

1011: Ferdowsi completes the *Shahnameh*

1055: Seljuqs occupy Baghdad; Toghril Beg becomes Soltan

Twelfth century: Iran dominated by local Turkish dynasties

1221: Mongol armies under Changiz Khan cross the Oxus; Marv, Nishapur, and Herat captured and destroyed

1258: Mongols sack Baghdad and establish Il-Khan dynasty

1335: Death of last Il-Khanid ruler; Iran ruled by minor dynasties

1501: Shah Isma'il Safavi crowned Shahanshah at Tabriz; Twelver Shi'ism declared the state religion

1587–1628: Reign of Shah Abbas I (the Great); high point of Safavid power

1722: Afghans capture Isfahan; end of Safavid rule

1796: The eunuch Agha Mohammad Khan Qajar crowns himself Shahanshah and establishes Qajar dynasty

1813: Treaty of Golestan ends Russo-Persian war; Iran renounces its claims to Caucasian territories

1828: Treaty of Turkmanchai ends second Russo-Persian war; Iran pays war indemnity, cedes territory, and grants Russia commercial privileges

1852: Group of Babis attempts to assassinate Naser al-Din Shah; wave of anti-Babi persecutions follows

1891–1892: Boycott forces government to cancel British tobacco concession

1906–1911: Constitutional movement

1907: Anglo-Russian agreement divides Iran into spheres of influence

1921: Reza Khan takes power in bloodless coup

THE PAHLAVIS

1925: Reza Khan becomes Reza Shah Pahlavi

1925–1941: Reign of Reza Shah; program of centralization and modernization

1941: Allies invade Iran; Reza Shah abdicates in favor of his son Mohammad Reza

December 1946: Iranian army ends separatist movements in Azarbaijan and Kurdestan

1949: Formation of the National Front under Mossadegh's leadership

1950–1953: Oil crisis with Great Britain

April 1951: Mossadegh becomes prime minister; oil crisis with Great Britain

August 1953: Mossadegh overthrown in royalist coup with U.S. support

1961–1962: Prime Minister Ali Amini attempts to introduce economic reform measures and resigns after struggle with both shah and National Front

January 1963: Shah announces program of economic and social reform known as White Revolution

June 1963: Khomeini attacks the shah and his program; hundreds die in rioting in Teheran bazaar

October 1964: Government exiles Khomeini

1966: Founding of Iranian People's Crusaders (Mojahedin-e-Khalq-e-Iran)

1971: Maoist Fada'is attack gendarmerie post in the north

1973: Oil price increase; beginning of economic boom

1977: Jamshid Amuzegar replaces Amir Abbas Hoveida as prime minister and institutes austerity program; economic boom cools off

January 1978: Editorial attack on Khomeini provokes violent clashes in Qom, where police kill a number of demonstrators; forty-day mourning cycle of demonstrations begins

February 1978: Violent demonstrations in Tabriz; government briefly loses control of city

May 1978: Serious demonstrations in Teheran and Qom

August 1978: Hundreds die in theater fire in Abadan

September 1978: Government declares martial law; troops kill several hundred demonstrators in east Teheran's Zhaleh Square

January 1979: Shah leaves Iran; Shahpur Bakhtiyar becomes prime minister

February 1979: Khomeini returns; monarchy is overthrown; Mahdi Bazargan becomes prime minister of provisional government

THE ISLAMIC REPUBLIC

March 1979: Referendum approves establishment of Islamic Republic

August 1979: First Council of Experts meets to write constitution of new state

November 1979: U.S. embassy seized and diplomats held hostage for return of shah; Bazargan's government falls

December 1979: Referendum approves new constitution; disorders in Tabriz

January 1980: Abu'l-Hasan Bani Sadr elected first president of Islamic Republic

September 1980: War with Iraq begins

June 1981: Bani Sadr removed from office; explosion at party headquarters decimates IRP leadership; bloody clashes between revolutionary guards and Mojahedin

August 1981: President Rajavi and Prime Minister Bahonar assassinated

October 1981: Ali Khamene'i elected president; radical religious groups consolidate their control of Iranian state

April 1982: Former Khomeini supporter Qotbzadeh arrested and later executed; government campaign discredits and "defrocks" Ayatollah Shari'at-Madari

January 1983: Government jails Tudeh leaders

Bibliography

Readers who would like to know more about the topics covered in the text should find this listing helpful. It is not comprehensive, and some of the most recent works may not be included. Most of the items listed are in English and are available in any good university library.

Abrahamian, Ervand. *Iran Between Two Revolution.* Princeton, N.J.: Princeton University Press, 1982.
———. "Iran's Turbaned Revolution." *The Middle East Annual,* ed. D. Partington, pp. 82–103. Boston: Hall, 1982.
Adamec, Ludwig W. *Historical Gazeteer of Iran.* Vol. 1, *Tehran and Northwestern Iran.* Graz, Austria: Akademische Druck- und Verlagsanstalt, 1976.
Aghajanian, Akbar. "Ethnic Inequality in Iran: An Overview." *International Journal of Middle East Studies* 15:2 (May 1983), pp. 211–224.
Ajami, Fouad. *The Arab Predicament.* Cambridge: Cambridge University Press, 1981.
Akhavi, Shahrough. *Religion and Politics in Contemporary Iran.* Albany, N.Y.: State University of New York Press, 1980.
Al-e-Ahmad, Jalal. *Gharbzadegi* ("Weststruckness"). Translated by John Green and Ahmad Alizadeh. Lexington, Ky.: Mazda, 1982.
———. *Iranian Society.* An anthology compiled and edited by Michael C. Hillman. Lexington, Ky.: Mazda, 1982.
Alexander, Yonah, and Allen Nanes, eds. *The United States and Iran: A Documentary History.* Frederick, Md.: University Publications of America, 1980.
Algar, Hamid. *The Islamic Revolution in Iran.* Edited by Kalim Siddiqui. Transcript of a four-lecture course given at the Muslim Institute, London. London: Open Press, 1980.
———. *Religion and State in Iran, 1785–1906.* Berkeley and Los Angeles: University of California Press, 1969.
Algar, Hamid, trans. *Islam and Revolution: Writings and Declarations of Imam Khomeini.* Berkeley, Calif.: Mizan Press, 1981.

Arberry, A. J., trans. *Muslim Saints and Mystics.* Persian Heritage Series no. 1. London: Routledge and Kegan Paul, 1966.

Avery, Peter. *Modern Iran.* London: Peter Benn, 1965.

Bakhash, Shaul. *The Reign of the Ayatollahs: Iran and the Islamic Revolution.* New York: Basic Books, 1984.

Banani, Amin. *The Modernization of Iran: 1921–1941.* Stanford, Calif.: Stanford University Press, 1961.

Banisadr, Abolhassan. *Islamic Government.* Translated by M. R. Ghanoonparvar. Lexington, Ky.: Mazda, 1981.

Baraheni, Reza. *The Crowned Cannibals: Writings on Repression in Iran.* New York: Vintage Books, 1977.

Barth, Fredrik. *Nomads of South Persia: The Basseri Tribe of the Khamseh Confederacy.* Boston: Little, Brown and Company, 1961.

Barthold, W. *Turkestan Down to the Mongol Invasion.* Edited by C. E. Bosworth. E.J.W. Gibb Memorial Series, vol. 5. London: Luzac and Company, 1968.

Bashiriyeh, Hossein. *The State and Revolution in Iran.* New York: St. Martin's Press, 1984.

Bausani, Alessandro. "Muhammad or Darius? The Elements and Basis of Iranian Culture." In *Islam and Cultural Change in the Middle Ages,* edited by Speros Vryonis, Jr., pp. 43–57. Wiesbaden, W. Ger.: Otto Harrassowitz, 1975.

————. *The Persians: From the Earliest Days to the Twentieth Century.* Translated by J. B. Donne. London: Elek Books, 1971.

Bayat, Mangol. "The Iranian Revolution of 1978–79: Fundamentalist or Modern?" *Middle East Journal* 37:1 (Winter 1983), pp. 30–42.

————. *Mysticism and Dissent: Socioreligious Thought in Qajar Iran.* Syracuse, N.Y.: Syracuse University Press, 1982.

Bazin, Marcel, and Christian Bromberger. *Gilan et Azarbayjan Oriental: Cartes et Documents Ethnographiques.* Paris: Editions Recherche sur les Civilisations, 1982.

Beloe, William, trans. *Herodotus.* 3 vols. New York: Harper and Brothers, 1844.

Benard, Cheryl, and Zalmay Khalilzad. *"The Government of God": Iran's Islamic Republic.* New York: Columbia University Press, 1984.

Bengtson, Hermann, ed. *The Greeks and the Persians.* Delacorte World History, vol. 5. Translated by John Conway, New York: Delacorte Press, 1968.

Bevan, Robert E. *The House of Seleucus.* 2 vols. London: Routledge and Kegan Paul, 1966. First published 1902.

Bill, James A. "Power and Religion in Revolutionary Iran." *Middle East Journal* 36:1 (Winter 1982), pp. 22–46.

Bosworth, C. E. *The Ghaznavids, 994–1040.* Edinburgh: Edinburgh University Press, 1963.

————. *The Islamic Dynasties.* Edinburgh: Edinburgh University Press, 1967.

Bosworth, C. E., ed. *Iran and Islam.* Edinburgh: Edinburgh University Press, 1971.

Boyle, J. A., ed. *The Saljuq and Mongol Periods. The Cambridge History of Iran,* vol. 5. Cambridge: Cambridge University Press, 1968.

British Naval Intelligence Division. *Persia.* Geographical Handbook Series. London: September 1945.

Browne, Edward G. *A Literary History of Persia.* 4 vols. Cambridge: Cambridge University Press, 1956.

———. *The Persian Revolution of 1905–1909.* London: Frank Cass and Company, 1966. Reprint of 1910 edition.

———. *The Press and Poetry of Modern Persia.* Los Angeles, Calif.: Kalimat Press, 1983. Reprint of 1914 edition.

———. *A Year Amongst the Persians.* London: Adam and Charles Black, 1893.

Bulliet, Richard W. *Conversion to Islam in the Medieval Period.* Cambridge: Harvard University Press, 1979.

———. *The Patricians of Nishapur.* Harvard Middle Eastern Studies, 16. Cambridge: Harvard University Press, 1972.

Chaliand, Gerard, ed. *People Without a Country: The Kurds and Kurdistan.* London: Zed Press, 1980.

Coon, Charleton S. *Caravan: The Story of the Middle East.* Huntington, N.Y.: Robert E. Krieger, 1976.

Cottam, Richard W. *Nationalism in Iran.* Pittsburgh, Pa.: Pittsburgh University Press, 1964.

Eagleton, William. *The Kurdish Republic of 1946.* London: Oxford University Press, 1963.

Economist Intelligence Unit, Ltd. *Quarterly Economic Review of Iran.* London: Spencer House. Published quarterly.

Enayat, Hamid. *Modern Islamic Political Thought.* Austin: University of Texas Press, 1982.

English, Paul Ward. *City and Village in Iran: Settlement and Economy in the Kirman Basin.* Madison: University of Wisconsin Press, 1966.

Eshraghi, F. "Anglo-Soviet Occupation of Iran in August 1941." *Middle Eastern Studies* 20:1 (January 1984), pp. 27–52.

Europa Publications. *The Middle East and North Africa: 1982–3.* 29th edition. London: Europa Publications.

Fatemi, Faramarz S. *The USSR in Iran.* South Brunswick and New York: A. S. Barnes and Company, 1980.

Fischer, Michael M.J. *Iran: From Religious Dispute to Revolution.* Cambridge: Harvard University Press, 1980.

Fisher, W. B., ed. *The Cambridge History of Iran.* Vol. 1, *The Land of Iran.* Cambridge: Cambridge University Press, 1968.

Frye, Richard N. *The Heritage of Persia.* Cleveland and New York: World Publishing, 1963.

———. "The New Persian Renaissance in Western Iran." In *Arabic and Islamic Studies in Honor of Hamilton A.E. Gibb,* edited by George Makdisi, pp. 225–231. Cambridge: Harvard University Press, 1965.

Frye, Richard N., ed. *The Cambridge History of Iran.* Vol. 4, *From the Arab Invasion to the Saljuqs.* Cambridge: Cambridge University Press, 1975.

Garthwaite, Gene R. *Khans and Shah: A Documentary Analysis of the Bakhtiyaris in Iran.* Cambridge: Cambridge University Press, 1983.

Girshman, R. *Iran from the Earliest Times to the Islamic Conquest.* New York: Penguin Books, 1954.

Graham, Robert. *Iran: The Illusion of Power.* London: Croom Helm, 1978.

Grumman, Stephen. *The Iran-Iraq War.* Washington, D.C.: Council on Foreign Relations, 1982.

Halliday, Fred. *Iran: Dictatorship and Development.* New York: Penguin Books, 1979.

Higgins, Patricia J. "Minority-State Relations in Contemporary Iran." *Iranian Studies* 17:1 (Winter 1984), pp. 37–71.

Holod, Renata, ed. *Studies on Isfahan.* Proceedings of the Isfahan Colloquium sponsored by the Fogg Museum of Art, Harvard University, January 21–24, 1974. *Iranian Studies* 7:1–4 (1974).

Holt, P. M.; Ann K.S. Lambton; and Bernard Lewis, eds. *The Cambridge History of Islam.* Vol. 1, *The Central Islamic Lands.* Cambridge: Cambridge University Press, 1970.

Hoogland, Eric J. *Land and Revolution in Iran, 1960–1980.* Austin: University of Texas Press, 1982.

Hoveyda, Fereydoun. *The Fall of the Shah.* Translated by Roger Liddell. London: Weidenfeld and Nicolson, 1980.

Huart, Clement. *Ancient Persia and Iranian Civilization.* Translated by M. R. Dobie. New York: Barnes and Noble, 1972. Reprint of 1927 edition.

Irving, Clive. *Crossroads of Civilization.* London: Weidenfeld and Nicolson, 1979.

Islamic Republic of Iran. *Bulletin of the Central Bank of Iran.* Vol. 20, nos. 187–188 (3rd and 4th quarters of 1359 [1980–1981]).

———. "Constitution of the Islamic Republic of Iran." With an introductory note by Rouhollah K. Ramazani. *Middle East Journal* 34:2 (Spring 1980), pp. 181–204.

———. *Iran: Guide to the Islamic Consultative Assembly.* Compiled by the Public Relations Office, Islamic Consultative Assembly, Teheran, 1982–1983. Translated by U.S. Joint Publications Research Service. JPRS-NEA 84-020. Washington, D.C., February 1, 1984.

———. *Iran Through the Mirror of Statistics.* Statistics published by the Iranian Center for Statistics, Plan and Budget Organization. Translated by U.S. Joint Publications Research Service. JPRS-NEA 84890. Washington, D.C., December 6, 1983.

Islamic Student Followers of the Imam's Policy. *Revelations from the Nest of Espionage.* Aprpoximately 35 volumes to date. N.p., n.d. In English and Persian.

Issawi, Charles Philip. *The Economic History of Iran, 1800–1914.* Chicago: University of Chicago Press, 1971.

———. "The Iranian Economy 1925–1975: Fifty Years of Economic Development." In *Iran Under the Pahlavis,* edited by George Lenczowski, pp. 141–166. Stanford, Calif.: Hoover Institution, 1978.

Jacqz, Jane W., ed. *Iran: Past, Present, and Future*. Aspen Institute/Persepolis Symposium. New York: Aspen Institute for Humanistic Studies, 1976.

Katouzian, Homa. *The Political Economy of Modern Iran: Despotism and Pseudo-Modernism, 1926–1979*. New York and London: New York University Press, 1981.

Kazemi, Farhad. *Poverty and Revolution in Iran*. New York and London: New York University Press, 1980.

―――― . "Some Preliminary Observations on the Early Development of Babism." *Muslim World* 63:3 (1973), pp. 119–131.

Kazemzadeh, Firuz. *Russia and Britain in Persia, 1864–1914: A Study in Imperialism*. New Haven and London: Yale University Press, 1968.

Keddie, Nikki R. *Iran: Religion, Politics, and Society*. London: Frank Cass and Company, 1980.

―――― . *Roots of Revolution: An Interpretive History of Modern Iran*. With a section by Yann Richards. New Haven and London: Yale University Press, 1981.

Keddie, Nikki R., and Eric Hoogland, eds. *The Iranian Revolution and the Islamic Republic*. Conference proceedings of the Woodrow Wilson International Center for Scholars, May 21–22, 1982. Washington, D.C.: Middle East Institute and Woodrow Wilson Center, 1982.

Khalilzad, Zalmay. "Islamic Iran: Soviet Dilemma." *Problems of Communism* 33:1 (January-February 1984), pp. 1–20.

Kuniholm, Bruce R. *The Origins of the Cold War in the Near East*. Princeton, N.J.: Princeton University Press, 1980.

Lambton, Ann K.S. *Landlord and Peasant in Persia*. London: Oxford University Press, 1953. Reprinted 1969.

Lenczowski, George. *Russia and the West in Iran, 1918–1948*. Ithaca, N.Y.: Cornell University Press, 1949.

Lenczowski, George, ed. *Iran Under the Pahlavis*. Stanford, Calif.: Hoover Institution, 1978.

LeStrange, G. *The Lands of the Eastern Caliphate*. Lahore: Al-Biruni, 1977. Reprint of the 1905 Cambridge University Press edition.

Levy, Reuben, trans. *The Epic of Kings*. Chicago: Chicago University Press, 1967.

Limbert, John W. "Indigenous Revolution." *Foreign Service Journal* 60:9 (October 1983), pp. 17–19.

―――― . "Nest of Spies: Pack of Lies." *Washington Quarterly* 5:2 (Spring 1982), pp. 75–83.

Lockhart, Laurence. *Nader Shah*. London: Luzac and Company, 1938. Reprinted 1973.

Looney, Robert E. *Economic Origins of the Iranian Revolution*. New York and Oxford: Pergamon Press, 1982.

McDaniel, Robert S. *The Shuster Mission and the Persian Constitutional Revolution*. Minneapolis: Bibliotheca Islamica, 1974.

MacEoin, Dennis. "Early Shaykhi Reactions to the Bab and His Claims." In *Studies in Babi and Baha'i History*, vol. 1, edited by Moojan Momen. Los Angeles: Kalimat Press, 1982.

Mokri, M. "Pre-Islamic Mythology" section of article on "Iran." In *Encyclopedia of Islam*, vol. 4, pp. 11–13.

Momen, Moojan. "The Social Basis of the Babi Upheavals in Iran (1848-53): A Preliminary Analysis." *International Journal of Middle East Studies* 15:2 (May 1983), pp. 157–183.

Momen, Moojan, ed. *The Bahi and Baha'i Religions, 1844–1944: Some Contemporary Western Accounts.* Oxford: George Ronald, 1981.

Mottahedeh, Roy P. "Iran's Foreign Devils." *Foreign Policy* 38 (Spring 1980), pp. 19–34.

———. *Loyalty and Leadership in an Early Islamic Society.* Princeton, N.J.: Princeton University Press, 1980.

———. "The Shu'ubiyah Controversy and the Social History of Early Islamic Iran." *International Journal of Middle East Studies* 7:2 (April 1976), pp. 161–182.

Naby, Eden. "The Iranian Frontier Nationalities: The Kurds, the Assyrians, the Baluchis, and the Turkmens." In William O. McCagg, Jr., and Brian Silver, eds., *Soviet Asian Ethnic Frontiers*, pp. 83–114. New York: Pergamon Press, 1979.

Nashat, Guity. *The Origins of Modern Reform in Iran, 1870–80.* Urbana: University of Illinois Press, 1982.

National UNESCO Commission. *Iranshahr.* 2 vols. Teheran: University Press, 1963.

Nyrop, Richard F., ed. *Iran: A Country Study.* Washington, D.C.: American University Foreign Area Studies, 1978.

O'Donnell, Terence. *Garden of the Brave in War: Recollections of Iran.* New Haven and New York: Ticknor and Fields, 1980.

Perry, John R. *Karim Khan Zand.* Chicago: University of Chicago Press, 1979.

Peterson, J. E., ed. *The Politics of Middle Eastern Oil.* Washington, D.C.: Middle East Institute, 1983.

Pipes, Daniel. *In the Path of God: Islam and Political Power.* New York: Basic Books, 1983.

Radji, Parviz C. *In the Service of the Peacock Throne.* London: Hamish Hamilton, 1983.

Raffat, Donne. *The Caspian Circle.* Boston: Houghton Mifflin, 1978.

Ramazani, Rouhollah K. *Iran's Foreign Policy, 1941–1973.* Charlottesville: University Press of Virginia, 1975.

———. *The United States and Iran.* New York: Praeger Publishers, 1982.

Roosevelt, Kermit. *Countercoup: The Struggle for the Control of Iran.* New York: McGraw-Hill, 1979.

Rouleau, Eric. "Khomeini's Iran." *Foreign Affairs* 59:1 (Fall 1980), pp. 1–20.

Rubin, Barry. *Paved with Good Intentions: The American Experience in Iran.* New York: Penguin Books, 1981.

Rubinstein, Alvin Z. *Soviet Policy Toward Turkey, Iran, and Afghanistan.* New York: Praeger, 1982.

Rybka, Jan. *History of Iranian Literature.* Edited by Karl Jahn. Dordrecht, Holland: D. Reidel, 1968.

Savory, Roger. *Iran Under the Safavids*. Cambridge: Cambridge University Press, 1980.

Shari'ati, Ali. *Marxism and Other Western Fallacies*. Translated by R. Campbell. Berkeley, Calif.: Mizan Press, 1980.

Stempel, John D. *Inside the Iranian Revolution*. Bloomington: Indiana University Press, 1981.

Stilo, Donald L. "The Tati Language Groups in the Sociolinguistic Context of Northwestern Iran and Transcaucasia." *Iranian Studies* 14:3–4 (Summer-Autumn 1981), pp. 137–187.

Sullivan, William H. *Mission to Iran*. New York: W. W. Norton, 1981.

Tabataba'i, Allameh Sayyid Muhammad Husayn. *Shi'ite Islam*. Translated and edited by Seyyed Hossein Nasr. Albany, N.Y.: State University of New York Press, 1975.

Taleqani, Mahmood. *Islam and Ownership*. Translated from the Persian by Ahmad Jabbari and Farhang Rajaee. Lexington, Ky.: Mazda, 1983.

Tapper, Richard. *Pasture and Politics: Economics, Conflict, and Ritual Among the Shahsevan Nomads of Northwestern Iran*. London and New York: Academic Press, 1979.

United Nations Economic and Social Commission for Asia and the Pacific. *Statistical Yearbook for Asia and the Pacific 1979*. Bangkok: United Nations Publications, 1980.

United States. Foreign Broadcast Information Service (FBIS). *South Asia Daily Report*, vol. 8. Springfield, Va.: National Technical Information Service.

United States. Joint Publications Research Service (JPRS). *Near East/South Asia Report*. Springfield, Va.: National Technical Information Service.

United States, Senate, Committee on Foreign Relations. *U.S. Military Sales to Iran*. A staff report to the Subcommittee on Foreign Assistance. Washington, D.C.: Government Printing Office, 1976.

Yarshater, Ehsan, ed. *The Cambridge History of Iran*. Vol. 3, *The Seleucid, Parthian, and Sassanian Periods*. 2 parts. Cambridge: Cambridge University Press, 1983.

————. *Encyclopedia Iranica*. Center for Iranian Studies, Columbia University. Vol. 1–. London and Boston: Routledge and Kegan Paul, 1983–.

Zabih, Sepehr. *Iran Since the Revolution*. Baltimore, Md.: Johns Hopkins University Press, 1982.

————. *The Mossadegh Era: Roots of the Iranian Revolution*. Chicago: Lake View Press, 1982.

Index